Hildegard of Bingen

CISTERCIAN STUDIES SERIES NUMBER TWO HUNDRED FORTY-ONE

Hildegard of Bingen

Homilies on the Gospels

Translated with Introduction and Notes by

Beverly Mayne Kienzle

α

Cistercian Publications
www.cistercianpublications.org

LITURGICAL PRESS
Collegeville, Minnesota
www.litpress.org

A Cistercian Publications title published by Liturgical Press

Cistercian Publications
Editorial Offices
Abbey of Gethsemani
3642 Monks Road
Trappist, Kentucky 40051
www.cistercianpublications.org

1   2   3   4   5   6   7   8   9

Library of Congress Cataloging-in-Publication Data

Hildegard, Saint, 1098-1179.
      [Expositiones Euangeliorum. English]
      Homilies on the Gospels / Hildegard of Bingen ; translated by Beverly Mayne Kienzle.
            p.   cm. — (Cistercian studies series ; no. 241)
      Includes bibliographical references (p.   ) and indexes.
      ISBN 978-0-87907-241-4 — ISBN 978-0-87907-203-2 (e-book)
      1. Bible. N.T. Gospels—Sermons.   2. Sermons, Latin—Translations into English.   3. Sermons, Medieval.   4. Catholic Church—Sermons. I. Kienzle, Beverly Mayne.   II. Title.

BS2555.54.H5513   2011
226'.0609021—dc23   2011019850

For all who have aided this work:
students, staff, colleagues,
and especially for Edward, Kathleen, and the cats,
"when at home we sit and find, entertainment to our
mind." (*Pangur Ban*, ninth-century poem)

Contents

Abbreviations

CCCM	Corpus Christianorum, Continuatio Mediaeualis (Turnhout: Brepols, 1966–)
CCSL	Corpus Christianorum, Series Latina (Turnhout: Brepols, 1954–)
CSEL	Corpus scriptorum ecclesiasticorum latinorum (Vienna, 1866–)
PL	*Patrologiae cursus completus, series latina*, ed. J.-P. Migne, 221 volumes (Paris: Garnier, 1844–64)
SCh	Sources chrétiennes
Vulg.	*Biblia Sacra iuxta Vulgatam versionem*, 3rd ed. (Stuttgart: Deutsche Bibelgesellschaft, 1983).

Hildegard of Bingen's Works

Cause	*Cause et cure*, ed. Laurence Moulinier and Rainer Berndt, Rarissima mediaevalia Opera latina 1 (Berlin: Akademie Verlag, 2003).
De reg. Bened.	*De regula Sancti Benedicti*, ed. Hugh Feiss, in *Opera minora*, 67–97.
V. Disib.	*Vita sancti Disibodi episcopi*, PL 197:1095–1116 (Paris: Garnier, 1855).
Diu. operum	*Hildegardis Bingensis Liber diuinorum operum*, ed. Albert Derolez and Peter Dronke, CCCM 92 (Turnhout: Brepols, 1996).
Epistolarium, 1	*Hildegardis Bingensis Epistolarium. Pars prima*: I–XC, ed. L. Van Acker, CCCM 91 (Turnhout: Brepols, 1991).

Epistolarium, 2   *Hildegardis Bingensis Epistolarium. Pars secunda*
                     XCI–CCLR, ed. L. Van Acker, CCCM 91A (Turn-
                     hout: Brepols, 1993).

Epistolarium, 3   *Hildegardis Bingensis Epistolarium. Pars tertia*
                     CCLI–CCXC, ed. Monika Klaes, CCCM 91B
                     (Turnhout: Brepols, 2001).

Expl. Atha.   *An Explanation of the Athanasian Creed*, trans.
                     with intro. and commentary by Thomas M. Iz-
                     bicki (Toronto: Peregrina, 2001).

Expl. Symb.   *Explanatio Symboli Sancti Athanasii*, ed. Christo-
                     pher P. Evans, in *Opera minora*, 109–33.

Expl. Rule   *Explanation of the Rule of Benedict by Hildegard of
                     Bingen*, trans. with intro. and commentary by
                     Hugh Feiss (Toronto: Peregrina, 1990).

Expo. Euang.   *Expositiones euangeliorum*, ed. Beverly M. Kien-
                     zle and Carolyn A. Muessig, in *Opera minora*,
                     185–333.

Letters   Hildegard of Bingen, *Letters*, trans. Joseph L.
                     Baird and Radd K. Ehrman, 3 vols. (Oxford and
                     New York: Oxford University Press, 1994, 1998,
                     2004).

Life of Hildegard *The Life of the Saintly Hildegard by Gottfried of
                     Disibodenberg and Theodoric of Echternach*, trans.
                     with notes by Hugh Feiss (Toronto: Peregrina,
                     1996).

Opera minora   *Hildegardis Bingensis Opera minora*, ed. Peter
                     Dronke, Christopher P. Evans, Hugh Feiss,
                     Beverly Mayne Kienzle, Carolyn A. Muessig,
                     and Barbara J. Newman, CCCM 226 (Turnhout:
                     Brepols, 2007).

Ordo   *Ordo uirtutum*, ed. Peter Dronke, in *Opera minora*,
                     503–21.

V. Rup.   *Vita sancti Ruperti ducis, confessoris Bingensis*, PL
                     197:1083–92 (Paris: Garnier, 1855).

Sciuias   *Hildegardis Sciuias*, ed. Adelgundis Führkötter
                     and Angela Carlevaris, CCCM 43, 43A (Turn-
                     hout: Brepols, 1978).

Scivias (Eng.)	*Scivias*, trans. Columba Hart and Jane Bishop; intro. Barbara J. Newman; preface by Carolyn Walker Bynum (New York and Mahwah, NJ: Paulist Press, 1990).
Solut.	*Solutiones triginta octo quaestionum*, PL 197:1037–54 (Paris: Garnier, 1855).
Symph.	*Symphonia armonie celestium reuelationum*, ed. Barbara Newman, in *Opera minora*, 371–477.
V. Hild.	*Vita Sanctae Hildegardis*, ed. Monika Klaes, CCCM 126 (Turnhout: Brepols, 1993)
Vite mer.	*Hildegardis Liber uite meritorum*, ed. Angela Carlevaris, CCCM 90 (Turnhout: Brepols, 1995).

Preface

The English translation of Hildegard of Bingen's *Expositiones euangeliorum* follows my coediting of the text, with Carolyn A. Muessig and George Ferzoco, published in *Corpus Christianorum Continuatio Mediaevalis* (*Hildegardis Bingensis Opera minora*, 2007), and my book, *Hildegard of Bingen and Her Gospel Homilies* (Turnhout: Brepols, 2009). My comprehension of Hildegard's method and theology of exegesis and her use and interpretation of sources has grown during the process of editing the texts and reflecting and commenting on them and their historical and monastic context. Still, the *Expositiones*, described by the fifteenth-century monastic scholar Johannes Trithemius (1462–1516) as "quite obscure" and "intelligible only to the learned and devout," pose a formidable challenge to the translator.

I wish to acknowledge first my mentors in monastic spirituality, the scholars in Cistercian studies who first welcomed and encouraged me and guided my work in the sessions at the International Congress on Medieval Studies in Kalamazoo beginning in the 1980s. My research on Hélinand of Froidmont and especially on Bernard of Clairvaux paved the way for my study of Hildegard and Benedictine monasticism. It seems most appropriate to have the translation published jointly by Cistercian Publications and Liturgical Press. I am grateful to Fr. Mark Scott and the editors at Liturgical Press for their thoughtful and capable editing.

Barbara Newman first made me aware of the need for work on the *Expositiones euangeliorum* over a decade ago, when I was searching for evidence that medieval religious women preached to their sisters. Carolyn A. Muessig, my coeditor of the *Expositiones*,

and George Ferzoco provided important insights on the Riesenkodex that bear on the analysis of the *Expositiones* and thus on
the translation. Discussions with Carolyn over the meaning and
appropriate punctuation of the Latin edition, and the interweav-
ing of patristic sources, helped elucidate the possible ways of
interpreting the Latin text and translating it. The editor of the
Opera minora for Brepols, Luc Jocqué, raised important questions
that shed light on the reading of the homilies. Stephen D'Evelyn, a
scholar working primarily on Hildegard's *Symphonia*, was a teaching assistant in my 2005 course on "Hildegard and the Gospels"
and a valuable discussion partner for the translations we looked
at in class. I am grateful also to my colleagues François Bovon and
Kevin Madigan, who invited me to their courses on exegesis for
fruitful discussions of the *Expositiones*. Bovon, a New Testament
scholar, guided my first efforts at analyzing Hildegard's exegesis.
Bernard McGinn shared his insights on Hildegard's visionary
exegesis.

My students have been eager participants in the ongoing
intellectual exchange about the *Expositiones*. Deserving of spe-
cial mention are Fay Martineau, Annelies Wouters, and Regina
Christianson, all of whom worked on the translation itself. Fay
Martineau undertook the translation of all the *Expositiones*; she
worked from the transcription that predated the examination of
the manuscript in order to produce a rough draft that we discussed and corrected. Annelies Wouters checked both the transcription from photocopies of the microfilm and an early draft
of the translation. The early draft underwent many changes after
examination of the manuscript and preparation of the critical
edition. Debates in my classes provoked a periodic reexamina-
tion of the translation and a method for breaking Hildegard's
lengthy sentences into comprehensible English. In class discussions Norman Sheidlower and Justin Stover made noteworthy
suggestions on the translation of problematic passages. Kyle
Highful reviewed the translation, added additional scriptural
allusions, and checked the biblical references for the entire text.
Jenny Bledsoe and Katherine Wrisley assisted with checking
the proofs and with the indexing. Finally, the Reverend Regina

Christianson translated many of the *Expositiones* as preparation for her Doctor of Ministry thesis at Episcopal Divinity School, and my correction of her translations provided a further opportunity to check my translation and examine the questions she raised as well as to add several more allusions to Scripture she identified.

I am grateful for the institutional assistance that has supported this work. Harvard Divinity School allowed me research leave during which I completed the revision of the manuscript. I also owe thanks to the staff at Harvard Divinity School, the Information Technology Department, the Andover-Harvard Library, the Operations Department, and my faculty assistants, especially Kathleen Shanahan, Katherine Lou, Cole Gustafson, and Kimberly Richards O'Hagan, who have helped with organizing various phases of the project. Cole Gustafson made helpful suggestions on methods for punctuating the homilies.

Finally, I express thanks to friends and family who have followed the progress of the book over the years. Christopher Jarvinen has been a generous supporter of my research. Six cats—Walter, Basile, Athena, Tecla, Cecilia, and Stella—joined the household after the project began and graced its many drafts, notebooks, and boxes with the warmth of their presence. My family has supported the course of this project, as of others, for many years: my daughter, Kathleen Cary Kienzle, debated translations with me and assisted with typing and preparing the manuscript, and my husband Edward read, indexed, typed, listened, commented, helped sort out the complex theology of some Hildegardian sentences, and provided unfailing encouragement. His love and support sustain all that I do.

Introduction

Hildegard of Bingen and her *Homilies on the Gospels* (*Expositiones euangeliorum*)

The virtues hastened to Fortitude, in order that they would be taught
by her, and that they would be edified in those things, because she
remained in the fire of the Holy Spirit.

Hildegard of Bingen (1098–1179) thus describes the virtue of
Fortitude and its instruction of the virtues.[1] Like Fortitude, Hildegard was enkindled by the fire of the Spirit and edified many
with her teaching. As the *magistra*, teacher and superior, to her
sisters she probably spoke to them in the chapter house, with the
scriptural text either before her or recited from memory, section
by section, according to Benedictine liturgical practice and as
described in her own commentary on the Rule of Benedict.[2] The
sisters recorded and preserved that informal preaching in a collection of homilies on the gospels, the *Expositiones euangeliorum*.

The learned abbot Johannes Trithemius (1462–1516) observed
that Hildegard of Bingen composed a book of fifty-eight homilies
(*homelias*) on gospel readings and that they were "quite obscure"
and "intelligible only to the learned and devout."[3] Those homilies,

---

[1] Hom. 45 on Luke 5:1-11; p. 174.

[2] *De reg. Bened.* 67–97; *Expl. Rule* 24–25.

[3] Johannes Trithemius, *Catalogus illustrium uirorum, Johannes Trithemii Opera Historica*, ed. Marquand Freher (Frankfurt, 1601; repr. Frankfurt am Main:

1

the *Homilies on the Gospels* (*Expositiones euangeliorum*), recently
edited and now translated for the first time into English, expound
twenty-seven gospel pericopes—selections used for the liturgy
on Sundays and feast days. They establish Hildegard as the only
known female systematic exegete of the Middle Ages. The homilies are preserved in Wiesbaden, Hessische Landesbibliothek 2,
the so-called Riesenkodex, which includes all Hildegard's writings considered as "inspired," and in two later manuscripts.[4]
The *Homilies on the Gospels* prove essential for comprehending
the coherent theological vision Hildegard constructs throughout
her works, including the themes of salvation history, the drama
of the individual soul, the struggle of virtues against vices, and
the life-giving and animating force of greenness (*uiriditas*). Before
further exploration of these important texts it will be useful to
survey briefly Hildegard's life and works.

Life and Works

Hildegard was born in 1098 at Bermersheim (near Mainz) to
Mechthild and Hildebert, who ranked in the lower free nobility. At
around eight years of age she was devoted to a religious life and
placed in the care of the holy woman Jutta, daughter of the count of
Sponheim, who had ties to Hildegard's father. Jutta and Hildegard
entered the Benedictine monastery of Disibodenberg on All Saints'
Day, 1 November 1112.[5] A small community of women developed in

---

Minerva, 1966), 138: *Liber super Euangelios Dominicalibus [sic] homelias LVIII
composuit ualde obscuras et nisi deuotis eruditis intelligibles.*

[4] *Expo. Euang.*; discussion of the manuscripts on 144–69. The earlier edition
was *Expositiones quorumdam evangeliorum quas divina inspirante gratia Hildegardi
exposuit*, in *Analecta Sanctae Hildegardis opera Spicilegio Solesmensi parata*, ed.
Joannes Baptista Cardinal Pitra, *Analecta Sacra* 8 (Paris, 1882). The first full
study of the *Expositiones* is Beverly Mayne Kienzle, *Hildegard of Bingen and
Her Gospel Homilies: Speaking New Mysteries*, Medieval Women: Texts and
Contexts 12 (Turnhout: Brepols, 2009).

[5] See Anna Silvas, trans. and annot., *Jutta and Hildegard: The Biographical
Sources* (University Park: Pennsylvania State University Press, 1999), 54. See
also John Van Engen, "Abbess: 'Mother and Teacher,'" in *Voice of the Living*

dependence on the abbot of Disibodenberg with Jutta as superior.[6] Hildegard remained under Jutta's tutelage for around thirty years. When Jutta died in 1136, Hildegard became the *magistra*.[7] Hildegard obtained permission to found Rupertsberg, where she and her nuns settled around 1150; then in 1165 Eibingen was founded across the Rhine from Bingen. From the Rupertsberg Hildegard journeyed to other audiences, primarily monastic communities whom she admonished about monastic and clerical reform.[8]

The *magistra* received exegetical mandates in three decisive visions of 1141, 1163, and 1167. In 1141 Hildegard experienced a forceful vision that instructed her to "speak and write" what she heard and saw.[9] About that 1141 vision she states: "And suddenly I knew the meaning of the exposition [*intellectum expositionis*] of the Psalter, the Gospels, and other catholic books from the volumes of the Old as well as the New Testaments."[10] Hildegard specifies that she did not possess a command of "the interpretation of the

---

Light: Hildegard of Bingen and Her World, ed. Barbara Newman (Berkeley and Los Angeles: University of California Press, 1998), 30–51 (at 32). The foundational study on Jutta is Franz Staab, ed., *Vita domnae Juttae inclusae*, in "Reform und Reformgruppen in Erzbistum Mainz. Vom *Libellus de Willigisi consuetudinibus* zur *Vita domnae Juttae inclusae*," in *Reformidee und Reformpolitik im Spätsalisch-Frühstaufischen Reich. Vorträge der Tagung der Gesellschaft für Mittelrheinische Kirchengeschichte vom 11. bis 13. September 1991 in Trier*, ed. Stefan Weinfurter, Quellen und Abhandlungen zur Mittelrheinische Geschichte 68 (Mainz: Selbstverlag der Gesellschaft für Mittelrheinische Kirchengeschichte, 1992), Appendix II, 172–87 of 119–87. Subsequent references will be made to the Silvas translation.

[6] See the letter of Guibert of Gembloux to Bovo in Silvas, *Jutta and Hildegard*, 99–117, at 109–11. Guibert of Gembloux, *Epistolae quae in codice B.R. Brux. 5527–5534 inueniuntur*, ed. Albert Derolez, Eligius Dekkers, and Roland Demeulenaere, CCCM 66, 66A (Turnhout: Brepols, 1988–89), II, 38, 367–79.

[7] Guibert of Gembloux to Bovo, Silvas, *Jutta and Hildegard*, 111. Guibert of Gembloux, *Epistolae* II, 38, 375, ll. 297-99.

[8] Kienzle, *Speaking New Mysteries*, 47–57.

[9] *Sciuias* 3–4, ll. 24-33; *Scivias* (Eng.), 59.

[10] *Sciuias* 3–4, ll. 24-33: *Et repente intellectum expositionis librorum, uidelicet psalterii, euangelii et aliorum catholicorum tam ueteris quam noui Testamenti uoluminum sapiebam.*

words in the text, the division of syllables, the cases and tenses."[11]
She seems to have distinguished between the exegetical training acquired in the schools ("the interpretation of the words in
the text"), including syntactic analysis, and the spiritual understanding of Scripture that came from her instant enkindling.[12]
After that divine command she began to produce her first
work, *Sciuias*, which was followed by two more visionary treatises. Hildegard discloses in the second work of her trilogy, the
Liber uite meritorum, that she "sweated over" the "true visions"
of her first book for ten years.[13] The commentary and images of
that first book, *Sciuias*, create a vast didactic edifice, a primary text
of visions upon which ensue further explanations in a different
mode. In *Sciuias*, Hildegard in God's voice criticized contemporary exegetes for their neglect of patristic commentary and
identified herself as the one to revive and continue the teaching
of the doctors.[14] Hildegard toiled over the *Liber uite meritorum*
for five years, approximately 1158–1163. Inspired by a vision she
received at age sixty, the *magistra* began to write it down at sixty-
one. Through the work's six visions the figure of a man, super-
imposed on the universe, looks in four directions and describes
what he sees. The *magistra* explains that the man, the *uir preliator*
in Isaiah 42:13, represents God and Christ. Following a description
of the visions Hildegard highlights vices, specifying the remedial
virtues along with the corresponding punishment and penance.
Hildegard recounted two additional visions that furthered her
understanding of Scripture. A powerful vision in 1163 opened her
first understanding of Genesis 1 and John 1 and shook her pro-
foundly. A gentler vision in 1167, in which she received knowledge
from the Spirit of God in the form of "soft raindrops," compelled

[11] *Sciuias* 4, ll. 33-35: . . . *non autem interpretationem uerborum textus eorum
nec diuisionem syllabarum nec cognitionem casuum aut temporum habebam.*
[12] See also *Epistolarium* 1, 4: *Scio enim in textu interiorem intelligentiam expositionis librorum, uidelicet psalterii, euangelii et aliorum uoluminum, que monstrantur
mihi de hac uisione.*
[13] *Vite mer.* 1, 8, ll. 4-5.
[14] *Sciuias* III, 11, 586, ll. 379-91; *Scivias* (Eng.), 499.

her to "explore every statement and word of this Gospel regarding the beginning of the work of God."[15] The 1167 vision heightened her comprehension of those texts to such a degree that she could no longer refrain from writing her third visionary treatise, the *Liber diuinorum operum*. She states that she had barely completed the work after seven years.[16] The *Liber diuinorum operum* adopts the quasi-homiletic style of vision followed by commentary as it explains the spiritual significance of creation: the interrelationship of the human microcosm, body and soul, with the macrocosm of the universe.[17] Ten visions, comprised in three books, advance from the creation through the history of salvation. The percentage of the text devoted to exegesis increases significantly as compared to *Sciuias*.[18] Final changes to the work were finished probably in 1174 and incorporated into its earliest manuscript.[19]

In addition to the visionary treatises, Hildegard composed the *Ordo uirtutum*, the first extant morality play; the lives of Saints Disibod and Rupert; the *Cause et cure* (*Causes and cures*), a medical work on the humors; the liturgical songs of the *Symphonia*;

[15] *V. Hild.* 2.16, 43–44; *Life of Hildegard*, 66–67. For Hildegard's self-comparisons see *V. Hild.* 2, 28–29, 32, 34, 38; *Life of Hildegard*, 50, 54, 56, 60.

[16] Hildegard states in the Prologue that she was sixty-five years old (hence in the year 1167) when she felt compelled to write down these visions, the first of which occurred in 1163, when she had just completed the *Vite mer.* See *Diu. operum* 45, ll. 5-14; *V. Hild.* 2.16, 43, ll. 1-10; *Life of Hildegard*, 66–67.

[17] The Lucca manuscript (Biblioteca Governatina MS 1942), which probably was made as part of an effort to canonize Hildegard in the 1220s, contains remarkable illustrations. See Madeline Caviness, "Artist: 'To See, Hear, and Know All at Once,'" in *Voice of the Living Light*, 110–24, at 112; and Caviness, "Hildegard as Designer of the Illustrations to Her Works," in *Hildegard of Bingen: The Context of Her Thought and Art*, ed. Charles Burnett and Peter Dronke (London: Warburg Institute, 1998), 29–62. On the canonization effort, see Sabina Flanagan, *Hildegard of Bingen, 1098–1179. A Visionary Life*, 2d ed. (London and New York: Routledge, 1998), 11–12.

[18] See Bernard McGinn, "Hildegard of Bingen as Visionary and Exegete," in *Hildegard von Bingen in ihrem historischen Umfeld*, ed. Alfred Haverkamp (Mainz: von Zabern, 2000), 321–50, at 343.

[19] See Peter Dronke and Albert Derolez, "Introduction," *Liber diuinorum operum*, xii.

commentaries on the Rule of Saint Benedict and the Athanasian Creed; the *Solutiones triginta octo quaestionum* (*Solutions for Thirty-Eight Questions*); over three hundred letters, including several that preserve sermons she delivered; a coded language for her nuns; and the *Expositiones euangeliorum*.[20] During the 1170s Hildegard began organizing the writing of her *Vita* as she completed other works.[21] A well-known letter (23) deals with the interdict imposed on Hildegard's monastery in 1178–1179, because she allowed the burial of a man she thought to be wrongly excommunicated. The interdict was finally lifted six months before her death.[22]

The *Expositiones euangeliorum*

When did Hildegard compose the "quite obscure" texts of the *Expositiones euangeliorum*? Some of the *Expositiones* had been written at least in part by the time Hildegard wrote the prologue to the *Liber uite meritorum*, for there she refers to "*certain expositions.*"[23] Four *Expositiones* (1–4) may have been delivered to the religious at Disibodenberg around 1170.[24] Two *Expositiones* contain intratex-

---

[20] Hildegard's published works are found in the list of abbreviations for this volume.

[21] On the dating, see Silvas, *Jutta and Hildegard*, 122.

[22] *Epistolarium* 1, 23, 24, 24r, 61–69; *Letters*, 1, 23, 24, 24r, 76–83. See the detailed study of Wolfgang Felix Schmitt, "Charisma gegen Recht? Der Konflikt der Hildegard von Bingen mit dem Mainzer Domkapitel 1178/79 in kirchenrechtsgeschichtlicher Perspektive," *Hildegard von Bingen 1098–1998, Binger Geschichtsblätter* 20 (1998), 124–59. On Hildegard and the archbishops of Mainz, see also Van Engen, "Letters and the Public Persona of Hildegard," in *Hildegard von Bingen in ihrem historischen Umfeld*, 379–418, at 379–89; Flanagan, *A Visionary Life*, 17–18, 22–26.

[23] *Vite mer.* I, 8, 6–13: *postquam eadem uisio subtilitates diuersarum naturarum creaturarum, ac responsa et admonitiones tam minorum quam maiorum plurimarum personarum, et symphoniam harmonie celestium reuelationum, ignotamque linguam et litteras cum quibusdam aliis expositionibus, in quibus post predictas uisiones multa infirmitate multoque labore corporis grauata per octo anos duraueram, mihi ad explanandum ostenderat.*

[24] *Epistolarium* 1, 77, 77R, 174, ll. 226–27: *hec uerba in magnis egritudinibus uidi et audiui, ut ea in loco uestro uiua uoce proferrem iussa sum; Vita sancti Disibodi episcopi,* PL 197:1095–1116 (Paris: Garnier, 1855).

tual references that allow for tentative dating of the texts. One of these alludes to heretics and the other to schism, which may place them respectively to 1163, when heretics suspected of Catharism were burned in Cologne, and somewhere between 1159 and 1177, a period of schism.[25] The *Vita Hildegardis* sets a chronology of her works that would indicate that Hildegard wrote the collection of *Expositiones* after the *Symphonia* and extended her *oeuvre* of liturgically-linked compositions with gospel commentaries and explanations of the Rule of Saint Benedict and the Athanasian Creed.[26] Furthermore, if Hildegard gave the *Expositiones* their final form after she composed the *Symphonia*, it is plausible to assume that the content of the *Expositiones* took shape as Hildegard composed her other works.[27] The *magistra* would have added to them and filled out her coverage of the liturgical year.

While the *Expositiones euangeliorum* show the fruit of Hildegard's exegetical visions, no vision opens any of the *Expositiones*. The collection presupposes the *magistra*'s visionary authority, but Hildegard does not claim it therein. Nonetheless, the dominant themes present in Hildegard's other compositions permeate the collection. One may locate a unifying thread in the frequent elaboration of the theology of history, or in the drama of the individual soul, or in the struggle of virtues against vices within the soul and throughout the universe, or in a number of key words and motifs such as the life-giving and animating force of greenness (*uiriditas*).

A taste of this richness can be savored in a brief summary of how the *Homilies on the Gospels* portray the Holy Spirit. The Spirit's circular motion guides all of salvation history with its life-giving

---

[25] See *Expo. Euang.* 54 and 55, 323–27; Homs. 54–55, pp. 192–96. In *Expo. Euang.* 54 Hildegard attacks the Cathars' docetic tendencies: 323–24, ll. 1-12 and 21-29; in *Expo. Euang.* 55 she refers to schism: 326, ll. 28-29 and 46-48.

[26] *V. Hild.* 2.1, 20, ll. 16-17; *Life of Hildegard*, 41. See Kienzle, *Speaking New Mysteries*, 43–44.

[27] Beverly M. Kienzle, *The Sermon*, Typologie des sources du moyen âge occidental, fasc. 81–83, (Turnhout: Brepols, 2000), 172–73, 974–78. See Barbara Newman, "Introduction," *Symphonia armonie celestium reuelationum*, ed. eadem, in *Opera minora*, 371–477, at 350, on the composition of the *Symphonia*.

power (Hom. 35).[28] It directs the creation, moving with God across the waters (Hom. 34), tracing circles like the flight patterns of birds (Hom. 1), moving into the fastenings of the human body (Hom. 23) and whirling in the tempests of the soul within (Hom. 56), and, in several homilies, sending the virtues to rescue the sinful soul.[29] The Spirit's light works miracles (Hom. 9), the small as well as the major events of salvation history.[30] It animates the power of greenness in the universe, touching and kissing the sinful soul in need of healing (Hom. 19).[31] Hence the Spirit participates in the work of creation and redemption. It also directs the transformation of history, which Hildegard saw as the transformation of the Scriptures from the Old Law to the New, accompanied by their interpretation according to spiritual understanding (Hom. 47).[32]

Theology of Exegesis and the Senses of Scripture

Monastic exegesis tended to interpret the Scriptures according to the spiritual meaning, a term that designates the senses of Scripture that are not literal or historical, namely, the allegorical, the tropological—that is, moral—and the anagogical, which regards the soul's union with God in heaven. The concept of the spiritual meaning, inspired by Origen, Augustine, and others, underlies all of Hildegard's exegesis. It comprises a hermeneutic that is tropological in its aims but typological in its concept and method, that is, it finds "types" in the Old Testament that point to the New.[33] For Hildegard, spiritual interpretation illumined what was previously hidden, and it ushered in truth, humility, purity, and spirituality. Not one word (*nec iota unum*) of the old remained

[28] Hom. 35, pp. 143–46.
[29] Homs. 1, p. 31; 23, p. 104; 34, p. 141; 56, p. 197.
[30] Hom. 9, pp. 58–60.
[31] Hom. 19, p. 92.
[32] Hom. 47, pp. 178–79.
[33] The best-known explanation of the four senses comes from John Cassian (ca. 360–435), who defined *spiritualis scientia* as having three genres of interpretation: tropology, allegory, and anagogy, which contrast with the historical. See Kienzle, *Speaking New Mysteries*, 93–94, and the sources cited there.

unchanged by the new interpretation, an indication that every word of Scripture must be interpreted spiritually.[34] Homilies like Hildegard's were part of both the written culture and the oral practice of monasticism. Until the eleventh century and the growth of cathedral schools, medieval biblical interpretation circulated primarily in monasteries. Monastic commentators heard, read, echoed, responded to, and extended patristic works as they developed the hermeneutical methods that grounded the scholastic exegesis of subsequent centuries. The *magistra* gained access to patristic and medieval authors by listening to them in the Office and by reading them. In the Benedictine milieu, sermons, informal and formal, were part of the monastic liturgy and routine. The community listened to patristic works that were read aloud during the nocturns of Matins; public reading occurred in the refectory; devotional reading was integral to monastic discipline. Benedictine life holds at its center the Scriptures and their interpretation through the spoken and written word as well as the "lived exegesis" of the Rule and the Divine Office—the *opus Dei*.[35] Hildegard herself wrote a commentary on the Rule in which she paraphrases its directives for reading the gospel after the nocturns on Sunday and other feast days, and she emphasizes the importance of committing the Scriptures to memory.[36] In accordance with the Rule, Hildegard's community would have heard patristic readings in the nocturns, followed by the gospel text itself.[37] The foundation for the *magistra*'s familiarity with the history of

---

[34] *Expo. Euang.* 47, 312–13, ll. 18-21: "carnales institutiones in spiritali intellectu ad humilitatem ducent. *Et non relinquent lapidem*, id est nullam litteram, nec iota unum, nec ullam culturam tuam, super lapidem, nisi mutetur." See Hom. 47, pp. 178–79 and Kienzle, *Speaking New Mysteries*, 80–84.

[35] See Adalbert de Vogüé, *The Rule of Saint Benedict: A Doctrinal and Spiritual Commentary*, Cistercian Studies 54 (Kalamazoo, MI: Cistercian Publications, 1983), esp. 133–36.

[36] *De reg. Bened.* 67–97, at 73–74; *Expl. Rule*, 24–25.

[37] Angela Carlevaris calls attention to the importance of those readings in "Ildegarda e la patristica," in *Hildegard of Bingen: The Context of Her Thought and Art*, ed. Charles Burnett and Peter Dronke (London: Warburg Institute, 1998), 65–80.

biblical interpretation, as for others in the religious life, remains the liturgy, with the patristic readings for the night office.[38] What scholars have observed about other twelfth-century monastic sermons may extend to Hildegard's as well. Chrysogonus Waddell noted the patristic influence on language in Cistercian sermons, notably those of Bernard of Clairvaux. As often as not the biblical texts used by the Cistercians in their sermons were drawn not directly from the Scriptures but from ecclesiastical writers and from glossed Bibles. Consequently, the Scripture texts as they appear in so many sermons by Cistercian authors were surrounded with resonances of the patristic exegesis at large.[39]

Hildegard never identifies her sources directly, but she names Gregory the Great, Ambrose, Augustine, and Jerome, whom she calls interpreters of Scripture, as well as Origen, whom she cites as an example of pride. She praises the first four commentators together for changing the Old Law and Testament into the new spiritual understanding (*spiritalis intellectus*) through spiritual interpretation (*spiritalis interpretatio*). This concept was inspired

---

[38] According to Guibert of Gembloux the cells of Hildegard and Jutta at Disibodenberg were situated so that they could hear the Divine Office. Guibert of Gembloux, *Epistolae* II, 38, 373: *Tres . . . incluse . . . et preter fenestram admodum paruam, per quam aduentantibus certis horis colloquerentur et uictui necessaria inferrentur . . . in orationibus sacrisque meditationibus sedule Deo intendentes.* See Flanagan, *Hildegard of Bingen*, 26–32. Textual claims are being examined against the archaeological evidence from Disibodenberg. See Eberhard J. Nikitsch, "Wo lebte die heilige Hildegard wirklich? Neue Überlegungen zum ehemaligen Standort der Frauenklause auf dem Disibodenberg," *"Im Angesicht Gottes suche der Mensch sich selbst": Hildegard von Bingen 1098–1179*, ed. Rainer Berndt (Berlin: Akademie Verlag, 2001), 147–56; and Falko Daim and Antje Kluge-Pinsker, eds., *Als Hildegard noch nicht in Bingen war: Der Disibodenberg—Archäologie und Geschichte* (Regensburg: Schell and Steiner; Mainz: Verlag des Römisch-Germanischen Zentralmuseums, 2009). I am grateful to Professor Franz J. Felten for providing me with a copy of this book.

[39] Chrysogonus Waddell, "The Liturgical Dimensions of Twelfth-Century Cistercian Preaching," in *Medieval Monastic Preaching*, ed. Carolyn A. Muessig (Leiden: Brill, 1998), 335–49, at 348. Waddell notes that readings in Bernard's sermons that Jean Leclercq identified as coming from a pre-Vulgate Bible actually derive from patristic sources.

by Origen, whose works Hildegard could have consulted; she also could have become acquainted with Origen's terms and ideas through any number of patristic and medieval Latin exegetes. Ambrose followed Origen's exegesis of Luke; Augustine drew from him for *De doctrina Christiana*, probably the most influential guide to hermeneutics for Western exegetes, which includes the theory of signification.[40] Nearly one-half of the *Expositiones* deal with some aspect of the soul's inner struggle, a consistent theme in monastic literature that draws on Origen's use of Platonism. Most of the other homilies interpret the text according to an allegory of salvation history. At most six offer a literal interpretation, while elements of anagogy are evident in several homilies but do not constitute the primary mode of exegesis. Hildegard often blends the senses of Scripture within one homily, reading a passage in the context of salvation history, for example, but including a moral interpretation of some verses. She does not label the senses of Scripture in the *Expositiones*, but the rubrics added to the manuscript at a later time identify a few of the texts as either literal, allegorical, or moral.[41]

When Hildegard focuses on the inner struggle of the soul, particularly in the monastic life, she expounds the gospel texts in such a way as to create dramatic readings that engage the virtues and

[40] The exegete prepares himself to interpret signs, natural and conventional, knowing that "things are perceived more readily through similitudes." Augustine of Hippo, *De doctrina Christiana*, ed. Josef Martin, CCSL 32 (Turnhout: Brepols, 1962), 2.6.6, 37, ll. 15-23: *Nunc tamen nemo ambigit et per similitudines libentius quaeque cognosci et cum aliqua difficultate quaesita multo gratius inueniri.* See Bernard McGinn, "The Originality of Eriugena's Spiritual Exegesis," in *Iohannes Scottus Eriugena: The Bible and Hermeneutics, Proceedings of the Ninth International Colloquium of the Society for the Promotion of Eriugenian Studies,* Leuven and Louvain-la-Neuve, June 7–10, 1995, ed. Gerd Van Riel, Carlos Steel, and James McEvoy (Leuven: University Press, 1996), 55–80, at 75 n. 21; and on Augustine's interpretation of Scripture, see Pamela Bright, ed. and trans., *Augustine and the Bible* (Notre Dame, IN: University of Notre Dame Press, 1999).

[41] See "Introduction," *Expo. Euang.* 144–50, where George Ferzoco describes the Riesenkodex.

vices in conflict and dialogue. The tropological readings of Scripture instruct her audience on how to live according to the ideals of the Benedictine Rule. The *magistra* stresses the key virtues of humility, charity, and obedience. Several homilies, such as those on Luke 16:1-9 and Matthew 20:1-16, emphasize the importance of obedience to a superior, whether Adam to the Creator or the other creatures to Adam. The obedience the nuns owed to Hildegard as their superior underlies the message rather forcefully, given that she was the speaker, teacher, and preacher.

In some instances Hildegard simplifies thorny exegetical questions for her sisters, speaking from the perspective of a commentator who knows the stumbling blocks and theological controversies around a particular verse of Scripture. In both homilies on the parable of the Prodigal Son, for example, Hildegard digresses briefly to explain an apparent discrepancy in the biblical story: the son mentions the hired servants when he rehearses his repentance speech (Luke 15:19) but omits them when he actually addresses his father (Luke 15:21).[42] Hildegard's awareness of controversy is apparent in the exegesis of John 1:3-4. For John 1:3, *sine ipso factum est nihil* ("without him nothing was made"), Hildegard introduces two interpretations.[43] When she turns to verse 4: *quod factum est*

[42] *Expo. Euang.* 26 and 27, 260–69; Homs. 26–27, pp. 117–26.
[43] *Expo. Euang.* 9, 210, ll. 14-22: "*Et sine ipso,* scilicet sine racionalitate, id est sine filio, *factum est nichil* quod est contradictio. Deus angelum racionalem fecit; sed quod racionalitas Deum in angelo contradixit, ipse non fecit sed fieri permisit. Quamuis etiam alio modo intelligatur, ita quod sine filio nichil factum sit. Deus deleri non potest. Sed quod ipsum deleri uoluit, nichil erat, quia hoc fieri non potuit. Angelus enim id quod est nichil inuenit, quem homo postea subsecutus, idem per inobedientiam fecit." Augustine, *In Iohannis euangelium tractatus* CXXIV, ed. Radbodus Willems, CCSL 36 (Turnhout: Brepols, 1954), I, 13, 7, ll. 3-11; Haymo of Auxerre, *Homiliae de tempore* I, 5, PL 118:57; Heiric of Auxerre, *Homiliae per circulum anni,* ed. Richard Quadri, CCCM 116, 116A, 116B (Turnhout: Brepols, 1992–1994), I, 11, 95, ll. 148-56; 95, ll. 149-53 (*negationem*). The interlinear gloss reads: *nulla res subsistens sine ipso est facta*; the marginal gloss has entries from Origen, Augustine, John Chrysostom, and Hilary. *Biblia Latina cum Glossa Ordinaria*: facsimile reprint of the *Editio Princeps,* Adolph Rusch of Strassburg 1480/81, introduction

in ipso ("what was made in him"), she again offers two readings and states which she prefers.[44] Each of the fifty-eight *Expositiones* comments on the biblical passage progressively, that is, phrase by phrase. Medieval preachers followed two basic methods of organization and development in their sermons: the progressive exegesis of a complete pericope, phrase by phrase, and the focus on certain phrases, words, or images to develop themes.[45] The texts that employ sequential exegesis are most often called homilies; the thematically structured texts are generally called sermons. While Hildegard's progressive commentary follows the form of the homily, she differs from her predecessors in her technique of glossing nearly every word or phrase. In comparison, Bede and Gregory the Great tend to cite the whole of the biblical verse and then explain it from multiple

---

by Karlfried Froehlich and Margaret T. Gibson, 4 vols. (Turnhout: Brepols, 1992), IV, 224.

[44] *Expo. Euang.* 9, 210–11, ll. 23-28: "*Quod factum est in ipso*, id est in uerbo, scilicet in racionalitate, uidelicet in filio Dei, qui erat homo incarnatus, *uita erat*, quia filius Dei homo talis erat quod nichil ipsum nec tetigit, nec intrauit, sicut in angelum et in hominem fecit; quamuis etiam quod factum est aliter intelligi possit, quia omnia quae facta sunt in Deo uitam habent. *Et uita*, id est incarnatio filii Dei.*" In her commentary on the Athanasian Creed, Hildegard includes both interpretations of v. four: that *nihil* could not pertain to God and that all things have life in God; but she does not overtly differentiate the two. *Expl. Atha.* 109–33, at 118, ll. 250-60. John Scotus Eriugena, *Homélie sur le prologue de Jean*, ed. Edouard Jeauneau, SCh 151 (Paris: Cerf, 1969), 242, 244; Heiric, *Homiliae* I, 10, p. 84, ll. 92-109; I, 11, pp. 96–97, ll. 167-199; p. 96, ll. 177-78. The *Glossa* IV, 224, reads (interlinear): *haec vita, id est sapientia Dei*; the marginal gloss cites Augustine only for this.

[45] See Beverly M. Kienzle, "Introduction," *The Sermon*, 161–64. James E. Cross, "Vernacular Sermons in Old English," *The Sermon*, 561–96, at 563, explains that a homily follows the "sequential structure of the pericope" while the sermon "elaborates . . . on its dominant topic." Michael Casey observes that Cistercians generally did not follow the method of "sentence-by-sentence biblical commentaries." He prefers the term "talk" for chapter preaching and teaching, and the term "discourse" instead of sermon for preaching on major feast days. "An Introduction to Aelred's Chapter Discourses," *Cistercian Studies Quarterly* 45.3 (2010): 279–314, at 280–81.

perspectives. Gregory often moves sequentially through the passage and comments on clusters of the text a few lines at a time.[46]

Hildegard constructs her continuous narratives out of comments I describe as intratextual glosses.[47] The words or phrases
scilicet, id est, uidelicet ("namely," "clearly," "evidently," "that is,"
"in other words") frequently introduce each unit of commentary
and direct the listener, or the reader, to the interpretive narrative.
This method of keeping glosses in parallel with the scriptural passage differs from the usual medieval practice of placing glosses
outside the text on the manuscript page as either interlinear or
marginal notes.

Hildegard's sequential commentary often constitutes a dramatic narrative. The story that unfolds involves conflict and interaction, a crisis, a dénouement, and sometimes dialogue. It entails
narrative when Hildegard reports events and interaction between
the characters. She speaks as the narrator, retaining the third-
person voice of the biblical text, or in the voice of one or more
biblical characters, or in her own voice as expositor commenting
in the third person or as exhorter of her audience. Her method is
influenced by the structure of the biblical text itself; some of the
parables or episodes from Jesus' life unfold as a drama would
and Hildegard develops a drama in parallel. The biblical text and
her commentary constitute separable narratives, in some cases
seeming like parables based on parables.

Hildegard and Bernard of Clairvaux

The distinctive features of Hildegard's exegesis stand out from
the tradition of commentary by her predecessors but compare
with some of the preaching of her contemporary, Bernard of Clairvaux, notably his *Parabolae*, a collection of texts probably intended
for an early level of instruction in spirituality and the monastic
life. Like many of Hildegard's homilies, the *Parabolae* teach about

---

[46] Gregory the Great, *Homiliae in Euangelia*, ed. Raymond Étaix, CCSL 141
(Turnhout: Brepols, 1999), I.8, pp. 53–56.
[47] Kienzle, *Speaking New Mysteries*, 115–31.

spiritual growth and employ personified virtues that enter the action in order to aid the sinful soul to conversion.[48] The *Parabolae* may be compared to *exempla*, the short illustrative anecdotes medieval preachers employed to illustrate and lighten their sermons. However, the *Parabolae* stand on their own as independent narratives that convey a moral lesson in themselves, whereas *exempla* serve simply to support a more extensive text.[49] The *Parabolae* were probably delivered in the vernacular but taken down and preserved in Latin. They are considered close in form to their oral delivery, as are Bernard's *Sententiae*, short straightforward compositions with obvious outlining. They probably reflect the form and substance of the abbot's chapter talks, in contrast to the polished literary quality of his revised sermons.[50]

---

[48] On the *Parabolae* see Bernard of Clairvaux, *The Parables and The Sentences*, ed. Maureen O'Brien; includes *The Parables*, trans. and intro. Michael Casey; *The Sentences*, trans. Francis R. Swietek, intro. John R. Sommerfeldt, CF 55 (Kalamazoo, MI: Cistercian Publications, 2000); *The Parables*, "Introduction," 11–17, at 12–15. See also the extensive study by Mette Bruun, *Parables: Bernard of Clairvaux's Mapping of Spiritual Topography*, Brill Studies in Intellectual History 148 (Leiden: Brill, 2007).

[49] The *exemplum* represents a genre associated with and encompassed by the sermon. On the medieval *exemplum*, see Claude Brémond, Jacques Le Goff, and Jean-Claude Schmitt, *L'Exemplum*, Typologie des Sources du Moyen Âge Occidental 40 (Turnhout: Brepols, 1982); Kienzle, "Introduction," *The Sermon*, 145.

[50] See *The Sentences*, Introduction, 105–16. Bernard of Clairvaux's editors define *sententiae* as follows: *quae sive compendia sunt sive schemata orationum quas ipse habuit que edidit* (Bernard of Clairvaux, *Sancti Bernardi Opera*, 8 vols. [Rome: Editiones cistercienses, 1957–1977], VI. 2, *Ad lectorem* [n.p.]). The *sententiae* frequently have a simple numerical structure; the shortest *sententiae* constitute a list of the sermon's main points, with numbering to aid the preacher and the listener. On the *sententiae* see Jean Leclercq, *The Love of Learning and the Desire for God*, trans. Catharine Misrahi, 3d ed. (New York: Fordham University Press, 1982), 169–70, and Christopher Holdsworth's suggestion that the *Parabolae* and *Sententiae* are "the unrevised notes taken by some of [Bernard's] listeners," "Were the Sermons of St Bernard on the Song of Songs ever Preached?," *Medieval Monastic Preaching*, ed. Carolyn Muessig, 295–318, at 316. However, I think it just as likely that the *Sententiae* represent the sort of outline Bernard might have used as an *aide-mémoire*,

Bernard's *Parabola* I narrates, with a few direct allusions to
Scripture and notably to Luke 15:11-32 (the parable of the Prodigal
Son), the story of a wealthy and powerful king (God), who created
the human being, granted him free will, and forbade him to eat
from the tree of the knowledge of good and evil. The human in
the tale, who at first resembles his first ancestor, disobeyed, but
he thereafter took a course that varies from Adam's in Genesis:
he fled and began to wander through fields of vices, as does the
younger son in the Lukan parable. Bernard turns banishment
from the garden, as in Genesis 3, into the deliberate violation of
monastic stability. The ancient enemy and a host of vices vie for
the human against an army of virtues. Bernard enlivens the tale
by giving voice to the personifications of Hope, Prudence, Fortitude, Wisdom, and Charity.[51] The *parabola* provides insight into
monastic taste for stories that might have entertained converted
knights who had left feudal pursuits behind.[52]

Whereas Hildegard follows the scriptural text faithfully and
sequentially, constructing an elaborate allegory in parallel to it,
Bernard spins a Scripture-based story that is not a commentary.
Still both authors teach allegorically and morally about the spiritual life, and the *Parabolae* stand as an important contemporary
witness to the taste for Scripture-based storytelling in twelfth-
century monastic circles.[53]

---

composed before preaching, which Holdsworth, 315, also allows in Bernard's
preparation for preaching. Kienzle, "Twelfth-Century Monastic Sermon,"
The Sermon, 291–95.

[51] *Parabolae*, SBOp, VI. 93 2, 261–303, at 261–67.

[52] Otfrid of Weissenburg's *Evangelienbuch* constitutes a precedent for the
genre. Otfrid, a biblical scholar, directed Old High German verse renderings
of biblical narratives to a late tenth-century courtly audience. See discussion
of the *Evangelienbuch* and reproduction of a page in Margaret T. Gibson, *The
Bible in the Latin West* (Notre Dame: University of Notre Dame Press, 1993),
8, 40–41. See Bruun, *Parables*, 167–206, on this parable.

[53] Similar to Bernard's *Parabolae* and *Sententiae* are other collections of short
monastic texts such as Odo of Cambrai's *Homilia de uillico iniquitatis* on the
parable of the unjust steward (*PL* 160:1131–50), a copy of which was held at
Saint Eucharius at Trier (Josef Montebaur, *Studien zur Geschichte der Bibliothek*

Hildegard and Bernard: The Superior's Voice

Hildegard's *Expositiones* again merit comparison with the writings of Bernard of Clairvaux, notably the sermons in which he addresses behavior that hinders progress in observance of the Rule. This concept of a superior's accountability for the salvation of souls in his or her charge is deeply grounded in Benedictine spirituality and the Rule.[54] The responsibility for teaching weighed heavily on Hildegard; she expressed in her *Vita* that she "put a moat and a wall around" the sisters "with the words of the Sacred Scriptures, regular discipline, and good habits."[55] Moreover, her correspondence with abbesses and abbots demonstrates her strong feeling that a superior should inspire her sisters to desire to hear her words.[56] In the *Expositiones*, however, Hildegard does not identify herself as the superior as Bernard does in his sermons, where he reflects on his duties as abbot.[57] Nonetheless,

---

der Abtei St. Eucharius-Mathias zu Trier [Freiburg: Herder, 1931], 141), and the *sententiola* or *dicta* of Anselm of Canterbury, talks recorded by Alexander, monk of Christ Church, Canterbury. Alexander explains that Anselm spoke these various things *in commune* and that he, Alexander, took them down in various places. Others, which were borrowed or stolen, became lost. *Memorials of St. Anselm*, ed. by Richard W. Southern and Franciscus S. Schmitt, Auctores Britannici Medii Aevi 1 (London: Oxford University Press, 1969), 107. Jean Leclercq discusses monastic literary genres in *Love of Learning*, 153–90, and the informal *sententiae* and related texts on 168–70. See Bruun, *Parables*, 157–62, on the *similitudines* of Anselm and the *Parabolarium* of Galand of Reigny.

[54] *The Rule of St. Benedict in Latin and English with Notes*, ed. Timothy Fry, (Collegeville, MN: Liturgical Press, 1980), 2.6, 172, 173.

[55] *V. Hild.* 2.12, 37, ll. 29-32: *At ego per ostensionem Dei eis hoc innotui ipsasque uerbis sanctarum scripturarum et regulari disciplina bonaque conuersatione circumfodi et muniui. Life of Hildegard* 2.12, 60. Silvas, *Jutta and Hildegard*, 174, translates the passage as "I fenced them about and armed them," which overlooks the notion of digging (*circumfodere*).

[56] See John Van Engen, "Abbess: 'Mother and Teacher,'" in *Voice of the Living Light*, 30–51. Hildegard wrote that a certain abbess was bearing her burden well because her sheep wanted to hear God's admonishment through her teaching: *Epistolarium* 2, 150R, 339, ll. 2-4; *Letters* 2, 150R, 95.

[57] See Sommerfeldt, "Introduction," *The Sentences*, 105–14, at 105–9; Beverly Mayne Kienzle, "*Verbum Dei et Verba Bernardi*: The Function of Language in Bernard's Second Sermon for Peter and Paul," in *Bernardus Magister: Papers*

the *magistra*'s voice of responsibility carries over subtly into the homilies, several of which deal with the virtue of obedience.

Hildegard and Bernard: Writing Against Heresy

Both Hildegard and Bernard entered the church's battle against heresy with zeal. Hildegard's denunciation of heresy enters into a few *Expositiones*. Her strongest attacks on heresy are tied to preaching but are preserved in letters as well as in a *sermo* and an *admonitio*. Bernard railed against heresy in several of his *Sermons on the Song* and in his *Letters*. For the most part the sermons he and other twelfth- and early thirteenth-century Cistercians preached against heresy have not been preserved. Historians rely on letters and reports narrated by other people. Hildegard's letters on heresy and schism constitute important parallels to the letters of Bernard that address heresy in southern France. Her writings against popular heresy outnumber Bernard's.[58] The abbot's invective employs dense biblical imagery and skilled figures of speech, but Hildegard's language surpasses Bernard's in intensity by virtue of its apocalypticism and boldness. Her writing brings to mind later texts written by Henry of Clairvaux or Geoffrey of Auxerre and contemporary with Joachim of Fiore.[59]

Hildegard and Bernard: The Legends

Hildegard may have known Bernard's writings, but is there any other indication of contact between the two?[60] Hildegard's first biographer, Gottfried of Disibodenberg, recounts that Pope Eugene III sent a delegation to Disibodenberg to inquire into

---

Celebrating the Nonacentenary of the Birth of Bernard of Clairvaux, ed. John R. Sommerfeldt (Kalamazoo, MI: Cistercian Publications, 1992), 149–59.

[58] Beverly Mayne Kienzle, *Cistercians, Heresy and Crusade in Occitania, 1145–1229: Preaching in the Lord's Vineyard* (Rochester, NY: York Medieval Press/Boydell Press, 2001), 78–108.

[59] Kienzle, *Cistercians, Heresy and Crusade*, 205–6, and sources cited there.

[60] See Kienzle, *Speaking New Mysteries*, 36–38.

Hildegard's writing. Gottfried further relates that the Pope then requested a copy of the seer's work and read from it publicly, whereupon Bernard of Clairvaux and others urged him to confirm the "great grace" manifested in Hildegard. According to Gottfried's account, Eugene sent letters to Hildegard, granted her "permission (*licentia*) to make known whatever she had learned through the Holy Spirit and encouraged or urged (*animauit*) her to write."[61] Hildegard repeats and strengthens this story about twenty-five years later when she states in the *Vita* that Pope Eugene sent her letters and "instructed" (*precepit*) her to write what she saw and heard in her visions.[62] What Gottfried expresses as permission and encouragement from Eugene III, Hildegard presents as a papal mandate.

Scholars question the veracity of Gottfried's and Hildegard's accounts, but they generally agree that Hildegard wrote a letter to Bernard of Clairvaux in early 1147 and that he replied briefly. Additions were made to the letter around 1170 when Volmar compiled the definitive letter collection. Moreover, Hildegard sent a letter with part of the *Sciuias* to Eugene III, who spent the winter of 1147–48 (30 November–13 February) in Trier. From the letter and the autobiographical narrative one may conclude that Eugene III sent a delegation to Disibodenberg to investigate Hildegard's writings and bring her work back to him in Trier. Subsequently Eugene issued a charter of protection for Disibodenberg, but he made no reference to Hildegard or the women's community. Hildegard in turn wrote the Pope again to seek his approval and protection, but he sent no written reply. Instead, Volmar drafted a letter in Eugene III's name around 1170, when he also revised the letter from Bernard of Clairvaux.[63]

---

[61] See *V. Hild.* 1.4, 9–10; *Life of Hildegard*, 29–30.

[62] *V. Hild.* 2.2, 24, ll. 95-102; *Life of Hildegard*, 46.

[63] See John Van Engen, "Letters and the Public Persona of Hildegard," 375–418, at 379–89, on what he calls the "myth of authorization." Van Engen argues that the later letters reflect Hildegard's "self-understanding," which "claimed or imagined" approval from Bernard and Eugene. He clearly presents the case against any formal authorization for Hildegard to write.

What does Bernard's letter to Hildegard in its shorter, unrevised form reveal about his opinion of her? The abbot wrote:
"Besides, when there is inner enlightenment (*interior eruditio*) and
anointing that teaches about all things (*unctio docens de omnibus*),
what is there for us to teach or advise?"[64] The phrase *unctio docens de omnibus* alludes to 1 John 2:27: "And the anointing which
you received from him abides in you and you have no need that
anyone should teach you; but just as his anointing teaches you
about all things and is true and is not a lie, and just as it has taught
you, abide in him."[65]

It also echoes 1 John 2:20: "but you have anointing from the
Spirit and you know all things."[66] Bernard employs the notion of
unctio as teacher of all at least ten times in his various works, cit-
ing 1 John 2, and he evokes *unctio* even more often in the general
sense of teaching or anointing from the Spirit. Bernard at times
employs *eruditio* alone to contrast spiritual with "book" learning;
furthermore, he speaks of *spiritualis eruditio*, the equivalent of
interior eruditio, or the enlightenment of the inner person.[67] The
notions of *interior eruditio* and *unctio* represent spiritual enlightenment in the context of his writings.[68] Therefore, when the abbot

---

[64] *Epistolarium* 1, 1R, 6, ll. 12-13: *Ceterum, ubi interior eruditio est et unctio
docens de omnibus, quidnos aut docere aut monere?* The *apparatus biblicus* for the
letter does not identify the Johannine echoes. The text of the longer, later
letter is noted in the *apparatus criticus*.

[65] *Et vos unctionem quam accepistis ab eo manet in vobis et non necesse habetis
ut aliquis doceat vos sed sicut unctio eius docet vos de omnibus verum est non est
mendacium et sicut docuit vos manete in eo.*

[66] *Sed vos unctionem habetis a Sancto et nostis omnia.* Jean Leclercq, *Women
and St. Bernard*, CS 104 (Kalamazoo, MI: Cistercian Publications, 1989), 65–66,
notes that this text was "dear to Bernard."

[67] A CETEDOC search produced seventy-seven hits for *unctio** in Bernard's
works. Two of numerous examples for *eruditio* follow: (1) Ep. 108.2, SBOp, VII,
278: *Nec enim hanc lectio docet, sed unctio; non littera, sed spiritus; non eruditio,
sed exercitatio in mandatis Domini.* (2) In Ascensione Domini 6. 6, SBOp, V, 163:
*Nam de ignorantia, fratres, quaenam excusatio nobis, quibus numquam doctrina
caelestis, numquam divina lectio, numquam spiritualis eruditio deest?*

[68] The term *interior eruditio* echoes Hildegard's words in her letter to Bernard. *Epistolarium* 1, 1, 4, l. 17: *interiorem intelligentiam.* Leclercq, *Women and*

employed this scriptural allusion, he acknowledged Hildegard's gift from the Spirit.[69] While there is no evidence for any contact between Hildegard and Bernard beyond the exchange of these letters, later monastic legends report that the two figures did meet in Rupertsberg, where Bernard visited Hildegard. The fifteenth-century abbot Johannes Trithemius recounts that Bernard examined the seer's writings, acknowledged the gift of the Holy Spirit in them, and expressed unspeakable admiration for her work. A learned and devout monk who was present at the time reported to Bernard that many objected that Hildegard's writings were "womanly dreams" (*somnia muliebria*), the "phantasms of a ruined mind" (*destructi cerebri phantasmata*), or that they had been sent through demons (*fallaciter per daemonas immissa*). Bernard replied that people who were filled with vice could not recognize true revelations. He warned that anyone who said that the writings were sent by demons deserved to be judged in the same way as the haughty detractors of Christ who said that he worked miracles with the power of Beelzebub. The abbot of Clairvaux then assured Hildegard that God would protect her against the shameful actions of foolish men, and he promised that he would have the Pope read her volumes, just as he did those she had sent to Trier (*sicut etiam illa quae Treuirum misisti comprobanda*). In turn, Hildegard reportedly bestowed on the abbot of Clairvaux a relic from the body of Saint Rupert. The two wished each other well and Bernard then resumed his journey and performance of astonishing miracles.[70] This account from Trithemius denounces Hildegard's critics and legitimizes both her writings and a local relic. Moreover, it constructs a sort of

---

St. Bernard, 65–66, states that Bernard "respected the working of grace within" Hildegard, and that, in writing to Hildegard, Bernard was pointing out "the contrast between the power of the Spirit and his own inability."

[69] Van Engen, "Letters and the Public Persona of Hildegard," 382, describes the letter as "certainly ambiguous, probably condescending, and ironic."

[70] *Chronica Insignia Coenobii Spanheimensis, Johannes Trithemii Opera Historica* 251: *Dedit autem sancta Hildegardis viro Dei postulanti particulam reliquiarum sancti Ruperti, ducis Bingionum et confessoris.*

mutual benefit from the encounter: Hildegard gained Bernard's approval for her writing, and the abbot acquired a relic that must have contributed to the success of his miracle-working. The legend fills a lacuna in the historical record and describes a mutual admiration between two of the most important monastic figures of the twelfth century.

Interpreting and Translating the *Expositiones euangeliorum*

In conclusion, some explanation is needed on the technicalities of interpreting and translating the homilies. What follows will interest fellow translators above all, but it may prove helpful to those who find themselves asking about the original Latin texts as they read the English translation. The dual narratives in the homilies prove baffling at times;[71] hence the words of Scripture are italicized in this volume to help the reader distinguish them from Hildegard's commentary. A literal translation of the following verse and commentary on Matthew 2:7 will illustrate the running, sequential form of Hildegard's interpretation as it is found throughout the *Expositiones*:

> *Then Herod,* the devil, *secretly,* namely in his craftiness, *having called together the kings,* the seekers of creatures, *learned attentively from them,* seeking *the time,* clearly, the appetite for understanding, *of the star,* that is of God's gifts, *which appeared to them,* namely which was shown to them.[72]

Given that English does not show gender agreement as Latin does, the links between relative pronouns and antecedents are not obvious, as for *stellae* ("of the star") and *quae* ("which"), and

---

[71] Kienzle and Muessig, "Introduction," *Expositiones*, 159.

[72] *Expo. Euang.* 12, 221, ll. 45-48: "*Tunc Herodes,* diabolus, *clam,* scilicet in astutia sua, *uocatis magis,* inquisitoribus creaturarum, *diligenter didicit ab eis,* requirendo *tempus,* uidelicet gustum intellectus, *stellae,* id est donorum Dei, *quae apparuit eis,* scilicet qui eis ostensus est." See Hom. 12, p. 68.

gustum intellectus ("the appetite for understanding") and *qui* ("which"). Hildegard's audience would retain the gender and number of the Latin words and make connections that English does not permit. Moreover, the sisters would know the Scripture by heart and thus be able to process both channels of text. Hildegard's commentaries generally are built on a complex system of glossing within the text. A summary of the types of glosses Hildegard uses will illustrate not only her exegetical range but also the challenge to the reader and the translator. Occasionally Hildegard employs the simplest sort of gloss: a word that provides a synonym. These glosses fall into the category of literal exegesis, as they clarify the meaning of words or phrases. In the homilies on Mark 16:1-7, for example, the *magistra* defines the word *reuolutum* ("rolled back") with the phrase: *id est ablatum* ("that is, removed").[73] In other cases the gloss in one homily of a set is lexical while in the other homily it is not. In Homily 11 on Matthew 2:13-18 she explains *qui consurgens* ("and rising up") in verse 14 as *se erigendo* ("lifting himself up").[74] In contrast, for the previous homily (10) Hildegard adds an adverbial prepositional phrase to *qui consurgens* in accordance with her line of interpretation: *de tenebrosa natura ad rectitudinem* ("from shadowy nature to righteousness").[75] In Homily 11 the *magistra* glosses *ululatus multus* ("much wailing") with *uidelicet tristicia* ("clearly sadness"), again a lexical gloss, whereas the reading in Homily 10 for *ululatus multus* gives *scilicet calumpnia* ("namely, calumny") in accordance with the typological theme of leaving the Old Law behind.[76] Similarly, Hildegard mixes the allegorical and the lexical when she explains the phrase in Luke 16:9, *de*

---

[73] *Expo. Euang.* 28, 270, l. 28; *Expo. Euang.* 29, 273, ll. 15-16. *Glossa* IV, 135 provides no lexical gloss but interprets the stone as original sin (interlinear) and the Old Law, which was written on stone (marginal). Homs. 28–29, p. 128, 130–31.

[74] *Expo. Euang.* 11, 217, l. 11; Hom. 11, p. 65.

[75] *Expo. Euang.* 10, 215, l. 12. *Glossa* IV, 9 states that Joseph represents preachers who brought faith to the Gentiles (*gentes*). See Hom. 10, p. 63.

[76] *Expo. Euang.* 11, 219, l. 42; *Expo. Euang.* 10, 216, l. 38. *Glossa* IV, 10 situates the passage in the history of Israel, then provides an allegorical interpretation of Rachel as a figure for the church. See Hom. 11, p. 66; Hom. 10, p. 64.

mammone iniquitatis ("from the mammon of iniquity"), allegorically as *de pullulatione iniquitatis* ("sprouting up of iniquity") and
then clarifies the meaning of *iniquitatis* with the phrase: *id est
viciorum* ("that is, of vices").[77] The definition of *iniquitatis* provides
a lexical gloss at the same time that it extends to the tropological
interpretation of the pericope.

Hildegard often adds her commentary without an introductory
phrase such as *id est* in order to extend the meaning of the biblical
text in accordance with her allegory.[78] For Luke 16:7 the master
in the parable speaks to the debtor: *ait illi . . .* ("said to him").
No explicit subject or indirect object other than *illi* appears in the
scriptural text. Hildegard adds *creaturae* to the indirect object and
supplies Adam as the subject, reading: *"ait illi creaturae Adam"*
("Adam said to the creation").[79] Her commentary often adds a
noun following a demonstrative pronoun, thus assigning the
pronoun an adjectival function. For Luke 16:26 the *magistra* adds
predictis causis to the scriptural *Et in his omnibus* to read: *"Et in
his omnibus predictis causis"* (*"and in all these* aforesaid matters"),
so that the pronoun *his* ("these") then functions as an adjective
modifying *causis* ("matters").[80] Similarly, Hildegard adds nouns
or pronouns in the genitive to create partitive constructions, as
for John 6:7, *"ut unusquisque illorum modicum quid temperamenti
accipiat"* ("so that each one of them for the measure of temperament that he may receive"). The partitive genitives *illorum* ("of
them") and *temperamenti* ("of temperament") can be read within
the biblical text without interruption.[81]

Hildegard frequently supplements the scriptural text with
adverbial phrases or gerunds in the ablative. For John 6:5, *"cum*

[77] *Glossa* IV, 138 explains that mammon, a Syrian word in origin, means
the richness of iniquity: *mammona lingua syrorum: divitiae iniquitatis, quia de
iniquitate collectae sunt. Expo. Euang.* 2, p. 194; Hom. 2, p. 36.
[78] The following examples are taken from Kienzle and Muessig, "Introduction," *Expositiones*, 174–77. The translations here are literal.
[79] *Expo. Euang.* 1, 189, l. 58. See Hom. 1, p. 32.
[80] *Expo. Euang.* 37, 291, l. 65. *Glossa* IV, 139 has no note. See Hom. 37, p. 152.
[81] *Expo. Euang.* 4, 200, ll. 35-36. See Hom. 4, p. 43.

subleuasset ergo in laude felicitatis *oculos"* ("when he had raised
his eyes, therefore, in praise of blessedness"), the adverbial phrase
"in praise of blessedness" modifies the verb in the scriptural text,
subleuasset ("had raised").[82] Reflecting the usage of the Vulgate
Bible, Hildegard often employs the preposition *in* with a noun in
the ablative as an equivalent of an ablative of means. For example,
the Good Shepherd, represented by Faith, states: "illis clamabo,
ut in magno auxilio et in nouis miraculis ueniant" ("I will cry out
to them, so that they will come with great aid and through new
miracles").[83] The two prepositional phrases introduced by *in* both
have an adverbial function. When the *magistra* adds a gerund
in the ablative it often extends the meaning of the verb, like a
synonymous aorist, following the usage of the Vulgate. For Matthew 2:5 Hildegard adds *respondendo* ("responding") to *dixerunt
ei* ("they said to him") in order to read: "*dixerunt ei* respondendo
. . ." ("They said to him responding").[84] At times the meaning
of the gerund the *magistra* adds differs considerably from the
scriptural verb, as with Luke 2:5: "*ut profiteretur,* enarrando, *cum
Maria,* id est cum caritate" ("that he set forth, by relating, with
Mary, that is with charity"). The meaning of *enarrare* (to relate
or tell) remains consistent with the moral allegory of virtue and
vice that Hildegard constructs from Joseph and Mary's journey
to Bethlehem, but it is not synonymous with the idea of journey-
ing (*proficiscor*).[85]

For the most part Hildegard systematically uses glossing to
facilitate her allegorical or tropological interpretations. In *Expositio*
2 on Luke 16:1-9, for example, she glosses the phrase in Luke 16:8,
filii huius saeculi ("children of this world"), tropologically as: "id
est peccatores in seculo conuersantes" ("that is, sinners dwelling
in the world").[86] For Matthew 2:17, *tunc adimpletum est quod dictum*

[82] *Expo. Euang.* 4, 199, l. 20. See Hom. 4, p. 42.

[83] *Expo. Euang.* 31, 276, ll. 26-27; Hom. 31, p. 134.

[84] *Expo. Euang.* 13, 224, l. 27. See Hom. 13, p. 72.

[85] *Expo. Euang.* 8, 208, ll. 12-13. See Hom. 8, p. 53.

[86] *Expo. Euang.* 2, 193, ll. 68-69. *Glossa* IV, 138 reads: *Filii huius seculi, id est
tenebrarum.* Hom. 2, p. 36.

est per Ieremiam prophetam dicentem ("then what was said through
Jeremiah was fulfilled"), Hildegard provides a theological definition of prophecy: *quod dictum est* ("what was said") means that
which God uttered through the exhortation of the Holy Spirit.
She adds that no one could stand who wants to stand on his own;
but the one whom God sustains will stand because God is that
one's staff (*baculus*).[87]

The variety of intratextual glosses outlined above makes translation into English quite a challenge. No one approach works for
all cases, as Hildegard adapts her method to the structure of the
biblical text and to the interpretation she constructs. Moreover,
Hildegard's Latin is somewhat paratactical in that she places
thoughts together with no conjunctions or with a range of syntac-
tically weak connectors. Therefore, when translating, one at times
has to provide connections in English and at other times eliminate
some of the connecting words that are translated from Latin. The
frequent parenthetical comments introduced by *id est, hoc est, scilicet,* and *uidelicet*, which reflect Hildegard's explanatory pauses, are
sometimes omitted in translation and other times added when the
Latin parataxis is too jarring. Certain conjunctions, especially introducing temporal, purpose, and result clauses, ("when," or "so
that," Latin *cum, ut*) are often weak and simply equivalent to the
coordinating conjunction "and" (*et*). Those too are at times omitted in the translation or rendered as a simple "and" or "when."
Similarly, in Hildegard's usage it is often difficult to distinguish
the *quia, quod, quoniam* ("that") introducing indirect statement
from their use as causal conjunctions (because, since), or even
from the relative pronoun *quod* (which, that).

The approach to other sorts of words, and not only conjunctions, varies also according to the flow of Hildegard's interpretive

---

[87] *Expo. Euang.* 11, 218, ll. 35-39: "*Tunc adimpletum est quod dictum est per
Ieremiam prophetam dicentem,* scilicet quod a Deo dictum est in exhortatione
Spiritus Sancti, quia nullus stare possit qui per se stare uult, sed ille stabit
quem Deus sustentat, quoniam ipse baculus illius est." The *Glossa* does not
define prophecy here (*Glossa* IV, 10), but for Matthew 1:18-21, *Glossa* IV, 7 gives
a definition of prophecy: *Prophetia signum est praescientiae Dei.* Hom. 11, p. 66.

text. She incorporates certain words from the scriptural passage into her narrative but passes over or substitutes for others. When translating, repetition of certain elements of the scriptural text proves necessary to produce a coherent second text. Moreover, the translation uses fragments at times in order to prevent excessive repetitions of words from the scriptural text or to avoid making awkward or ambiguous connections merely for the sake of constructing a complete English sentence.

Given these particularities of Hildegard's commentary, a literal English translation from Hildegard's Latin generally would be awkward if not incomprehensible. On the other hand, a literary translation, smoothing out the rough spots and making dubious connections for the sake of good English prose, would both force the sometimes ambiguous meaning and misrepresent the quality of the Latin. Consequently, I lean more toward a literal than a literary rendering of the Latin in order to keep the homespun quality of the original, which is grammatically unsophisticated but poetically and theologically profound. Footnotes to the translation mark problematic passages as well as figures of speech, such as metonymy, and words, such as *uiriditas* (greenness) that signal important theological motifs.

Punctuating the English translation of the homilies poses a challenge to the translator. The Latin punctuation system is rather simple. The *punctus* is used throughout the Riesenkodex to indicate four forms of modern punctuation: full stop, comma, semicolon, and colon. Occasionally, the *punctus interrogativus* indicates sentences that contain a question. No punctuation signals the introduction of direct speech, and Scripture flows together with commentary.[88] It was necessary to add punctuation consistently in the Latin edition in order to aid the reader. How does one employ contemporary punctuation to separate the various voices in the scriptural text (the narrator, the author, or Jesus himself recounting a parable, the characters within historical narratives and parables) from the voice of Hildegard, who speaks not only

---

[88] See Kienzle and Muessig, "Introduction," *Expositiones*, 174–77.

as herself but in the voices of various biblical persons, including God, Jesus, Adam, and others?

First of all, the translations always mark Scripture with italics, so that Hildegard's words easily stand out from the biblical text because of the different typefaces used. Second, the identifications of specific chapters and verses are provided in footnotes only when they are not part of the gospel passage so as not to clutter a text already complicated by numerous glosses. Third, a scheme of suitable quotation marks has been devised. That system begins with the assumption that the italicized text of Scripture is equivalent to standard quotation marks (". . ."). Within that overarching system one must differentiate between the words of Hildegard, spoken in her own voice, and those in which she takes on the voice of someone else. Her commentary, when she explains and speaks in her own voice—that is, not assuming the voice of someone else such as Adam—is presented without quotation marks. However, when Hildegard takes the voice of a speaker in the text her words are enclosed in quotation marks (". . .") in all cases. Note that she alternates frequently from commentary to her own voice and that of someone else.

The words of the speakers in the scriptural texts require further layers of quotation. Single quotation marks designate the words of speakers within narrative passages of Scripture which are not parables. However, for parables, single quotation marks ('. . .') denote Jesus' voice when he narrates a parable such as the Great Banquet (Luke 14:16-24), or the Good Shepherd passage in John 10:11-16. The speakers within such passages have speaking parts themselves, and those are enclosed in standard quotation marks (". . ."). Their words are differentiated primarily by the typeface from Hildegard's extension of their voices; her words appear in roman type while the biblical words are regularly italicized. The two typefaces and levels of quotation will assist the reader in identifying what Hildegard herself says and the instances when she assumes the voice of a biblical personage.

Homilies 1 and 2

The Eighth Sunday after Pentecost

Luke 16:1-9

'A certain man was rich and had a steward. And charges were brought to the rich man against the steward, that he might have squandered the rich man's goods. So he summoned him and said to him: "What is this that I hear about you? Turn in the record of your stewardship, for you can no longer be steward."

Then the steward said to himself: "What shall I do, since my master is taking the stewardship away from me? I am not able to dig, and I am ashamed to beg. I know what I will do, so that, when I am removed from the stewardship, people may receive me into their homes."

After summoning his master's debtors one by one, he said to the first: "How much do you owe my master?" He answered: "A hundred jugs of olive oil." Then he said to him: "Take your bill, sit down quickly, and write fifty."

Then he said to another: "And you, how much do you owe?" He answered: "A hundred measures of wheat." He said to him: "Take your bill and write eighty."

The master praised the steward of iniquity because he had acted prudently. For the children of this age are more prudent in their own generation than are the children of light. And I tell you, make friends for yourselves from the mammon of iniquity, so that when you lack it, they will receive you into the eternal habitations.'

1. The Eighth Sunday after Pentecost, 1

'A certain man was rich and had a steward.' The one who created humanity, who is God and man, lacked nothing in the fullness of good; he *'had a steward,'* namely Adam, to whom he had entrusted Paradise and all creatures. *'And charges were brought to the rich man against the steward, that he might have squandered the rich man's goods.'* *'Charges were brought'* among the angels, because God sees our deeds in them and in other creatures, that Adam wanted to divide for himself, as it were, God's honor, which no one can divide. As the serpent said: *'you will be like gods,'*[1] which means, "God made you like himself, whence you are gods." Likewise human beings later made themselves somewhat like gods by means of idols.

'So he summoned him and said to him: "What is this that I hear about you?"' as when God said: *'where are you?'*[2] when Adam disobeyed the divine command, and when God again spoke: *'for who told you that you were naked, unless you have eaten from the tree from which I had commanded you not to eat?'*[3] "*Turn in the record of your steward-ship*, since you will be judged according to your deeds and will leave *the land of the living.*"[4] "*For you can no longer be steward*, because you cannot excuse yourself, that you have not done evil."[5] Therefore, *'the earth is cursed by your deed. In labors you will eat from it all the days of your life; it will sprout thorns and thistles for you, and you will eat the herbs of the field. In the sweat of your face you will eat your bread'* "because you first initiated the evil and bitter deed." And he made *pelts*[6] *for them, and banished Adam.*[7]

'Then the steward,' namely Adam, to whom God had entrusted Paradise and all of creation, *'said to himself,'* clearly, in his con-

---

[1] Gen 3:5.

[2] Gen 3:9.

[3] Gen 3:11.

[4] Pss 26:13; 51:7; 141:6; Isa 38:11; 53:8; Jer 11:19; Ezek 26:20; 32:23-27, 32.

[5] In this first homily Hildegard adduces citations from Genesis as glosses for the words of the rich man, just as she does with the words of the house-holder in Matt 20:1-16, Homily 22.

[6] Gen 3:21.

[7] Gen 3:24.

science, when he was leaving Paradise then in a wretched state: "*What shall I do, since my master*, namely God, *is taking the steward-ship away from me?*: evidently the honor given to me in innocence in Paradise, expelling me because I disobeyed his command." "*I am not able to dig*, that is, not able to make the creatures subject to me in obedience, as they were subject to me in Paradise, although I am not able to forget the honor that was given to me by God." "*And I am ashamed to beg*, that is, to supplicate, with mourning and wailing, the creatures once subject to me." "*I know*, in my soul's perception, *what I will do, so that when I am removed from the stew-ardship*, that is, when I have lost the honor that I had in Paradise these creatures which were first subject to me, *will receive me into their homes*, namely, into their cohabitations, so that we may live and dwell together on earth."

'*After summoning his master's debtors one by one,*' that is, after Adam was expelled, he summoned each and every one of the creatures that from its nature owed service to God and enjoined them in subjection to him. '*He said to the first: "How much do you owe my master?"*' that is, to the flying creatures and to the other creatures of this type, which were created before the human: "*How much* service do *you owe*, in the capacity of your nature, to the one who is my Creator?" '*He answered: "A hundred jars of olive oil."*' The creature told the capacity of its nature: "A superabundance of fullness for places with the excellence *of oil*, because we fly near the earth below and in the clouds above, just as also oil floats above other liquids." '*Then he said to him: "Take your bill, and sit down quickly, and write fifty."*' Adam '*said*' to the creatures, namely to the ones that fly: "Take up this nature of your flight; descend to me *quickly*, since you fly rapidly; trace the circles of your flight; leave the middle course of that flight's possibility and be with me in the midst of the air, reaching to me, I who have the five senses of the body."

'*Then he said to another: "And you, how much do you owe?"*' that is, to the herds: "And you, herds and similar animals, which walk upon the earth, *how much* service *do you owe* in your nature?" '*He answered: "A hundred measures of wheat,"*' that is, the herds '*an-swered*': "The fullness of the circle of the earth in its best fruit, since we take our nourishment from the earth." *'He said to him: "Take your bill and write eighty."'* Adam *'said'* to the creatures: "Take up the circle of your nature, in which you roam over the earth; that is, trace the circles of your travel, lest you go forth more than necessary, according to what I, the human being, order you by God's power, through my five bodily senses. By those I encompass three creations, namely the skies, the air, and the earth. [Five and three] number eight, because I too must toil in the eight beatitudes."[8]

'The master praised the steward of iniquity.' Clearly, God commended Adam on this, because at some time he was going to raise himself to heavenly things, since God knew beforehand that the same understanding which had led Adam to this and turned him toward sins, would lead him back again to knowing God, even though at that time he was a *'steward of iniquity.'* Clearly, first as a steward in Paradise, he was in the innocence of justice; when, however, he disobeyed God's command, he became a steward of sin in iniquity, because he ignored God's command. *'He praised him, because he had acted prudently'*; although he had turned himself away from the light through disobedience, having no other consolation, he then associated himself to the other creatures in darkness, that is, in the world. *'For the children of this age,'* namely human beings, *'are more prudent in dealing with their own generation than are the children of light.'* Adam, when he lost joy, prudently drew out for himself the tears of wandering; and after being expelled from Paradise he also prudently associated himself with other creatures by necessity. And for this reason human beings appear *'more prudent'* than the fallen angels, who were created in the light of brightness and truth. When they lost heavenly glory they neither attached themselves nor inclined themselves to search for God's grace by any happiness, but instead remained obstinate in the inextinguishable darkness of unhappiness. And in this way humans are more prudent than those in their own generation, that is, their own children, who beget and are begotten in this age, when here also they can perform good or evil.

[8] Cf. Matt 5:10.

'*And I,*' namely Christ, '*tell you,*' human beings: "*Make for yourselves friends*, namely, good angels and humans, in justice and
truth, so that they may hold you in esteem for good deeds. Do
this *by mammon of iniquity*, namely with the work of perversity
and sin, *so that when you lack it they may receive you into the eternal
habitations*. When physical strength so fails in you that you must
pass on from this world, *they will receive you* with good report
and praise of reward before God. They whom you have led in
this age from unfaithfulness to faith and from sin to righteousness and thus into the eternal habitations, will hasten to you with
supreme mercy and welcome you into the heavenly and unfailing
homeland which you lost because of Adam."[9]

2. The Eighth Sunday after Pentecost, 2

'*There was a certain man who was rich, who had a steward.*' The
one who made the human being *in his image and likeness*[10] '*was
rich,*' having no need on heaven or earth. The *steward* [denotes]
the human will under his power; the will leads and coaxes the
human being according to what pleases him. '*And charges were
brought before him against this steward, that he might have squandered
the rich man's goods.*' Evil report went out from the will, as much
before humans as before God, when it stooped toward evil. It
had esteemed [divine] commands lightly through the pleasure
of this world.

'*So he summoned him, and said to him: "What is this that I hear about
you? Turn in the record of your stewardship for you can no longer be
steward."*' Evidently '*he summoned*' the human will through baptism and the gospel precepts, and said to the human by the Holy
Spirit's admonition: "Why does evil report raise itself up about

[9] Note that the voice of Hildegard becomes assimilated to the voice of
Christ here, as she exhorts her audience in the second person plural. This
dramatic technique is all the more interesting since this homily may be one
of four delivered at Disibodenberg in 1170, some twenty years after she had
left to found Rupertsberg. See Kienzle, *Speaking New Mysteries*, 44–45.

[10] Gen 5:3; cf. Gen 1:26, 27.

you, so that you worship evil and iniquity more than the good? *Turn in the record* of your will, in which you have performed evil; for *you can no longer* satisfy your will in shameful actions, as you did before."

'*Then the steward said to himself: "What should I do, since my master is taking the stewardship away from me?"*' Clearly, the human will '*said*' to itself that it must then turn itself toward some other and better behavior: "*What should I do* now in other deeds, *since my master*, whom I was supposed to serve but did not, *is taking the stewardship away from me* in the cultivation of my inordinate desires? *I am not able to dig*, that is, to seek out and fulfill the small and even the least commands, when before I could not keep the great ones. *And I am ashamed to beg*, that I would seek other paths than I considered before in my practice. *I know*, in rationality, *what I will do, so that when I am removed from the stewardship, they will receive me*." Clearly, since the outset of the beginning of good has such a rapid journey in rationality, it may even be necessary that the human being keep himself together in sadness, as happened to the Apostle Paul.[11] "*When I am removed* from my evil custom by divine inspiration, the good and righteous people, they who also sinned before, and afterwards repented, *will receive me* into their homes, that is, into their community."

'*After summoning his master's debtors one by one, he said to the first: "How much do you owe my master?"*' '*After summoning,*' by the admonition of good counsel, those who had sinned as he himself did in disobedience of God's commands, '*he said*' to one who had abnegated faith, which is the foundation of good deeds, and thus had sinned also against God and had not loved his neighbor: "In which things have you sinned against God's commands?" '*He answered* with compunction: "*A hundred jars of olive oil*,"' that is: "I sinned beyond measure, when I did not worship the Lord; neither did I show the honor due to him. Hence I did not fulfill the commands of mercy." '*Then he said to him: "Take your bill, and write quickly fifty."*' Divine inspiration said to him: "Learn another

---

[11] Hildegard perhaps alludes here to Rom 8:8-9.

custom in your deeds and restrain your pleasures quickly, and believe that you will receive remission of sins by serving God in your five senses, when you amend the sins you first committed through them."

'Then he said to another, evidently with an admonition: *"And you, how much do you owe?"'* that is, "You who have committed greater bodily sins, *how much do you owe* to absolve your sins by repentance?" *'He answered: "a hundred measures of wheat,* that is, an abundance and excess of evil deeds, as it were, the worst circles in the wheat of the law, when in the fatness of the flesh I became a disobeyer of the law."' 'He said to him: "Take your bill, and write eighty."'* God *'said'* to the will through supernal inspiration: "Take the deeds you did with good counsel, and believe that you will be saved by the eighth beatitude, if you have been willing to suffer *persecution* and tribulation *for righteousness.*[12] Since you sinned in the four elements, God will seek you in the fourth vigil, when you will be saved by the eighth beatitude."

'The master praised the steward of iniquity.' In other words, God *'praised'* the will, since it demonstrated its conversion to the angels and to the saintly souls, when it abstained from the depraved custom in which it was a *'steward of iniquity'*, when it took delight in sins. In another sense the *'steward of iniquity'* can be understood as a priest, because sins are consigned to him in people's confession, so that he may minister to them when he absolves and removes them by penance.[13] Therefore, the Lord *'praised him because he had acted prudently,'* because although the human will had first turned itself away from the good, it finally converted itself prudently to another path to the good, where it would discover its Lord.

---

[12] "The eighth beatitude" refers to Matt 5:10, "Blessed are they who suffer persecution for righteousness' sake because theirs is the kingdom of heaven."

[13] Note that Hildegard offers two possible readings here for "steward of iniquity," introduced by "vel alio modo." Jean-Baptiste Pitra mistook this for the beginning of another homily. See "Introduction," *Expo. Euang.* 160; and *Expositiones quorumdam evangeliorum quas divina inspirante gratia Hildegardi exposuit,* ed. J.-B. Pitra, in *Analecta Sanctae Hildegardis opera Spicilegio Solesmensi parata,* Analecta Sacra 8 (Paris : A. Jouby et Roger, 1882), 320–22.

'*For the children of this age are more prudent in their own generation than the children of light.*' The sinners living in the world '*are more prudent*' because, when sinners reject and leave their sins behind in repentance, with their entire progeny of penitents, by this they become more prudent than the evil angels, who were created in light and who persuade humans of evil. When sinners do penance for evil actions, so that they receive glory from their repentance, the evil angels, whose persuasions led them to those iniquities, are then confounded, since they do not seek to have any repentance for their fall. '*And I,*' "who bring about the remission of sins for sinners," '*tell you,*' the penitents: "*Make friends for yourselves from the mammon of iniquity, so that when you lack it, they will receive you into the eternal habitations.*" "Make virtues for yourselves from the sprouting of iniquity, that is, of vices, so that you may associate virtues to yourselves by repentance, and leave behind the burning lust of vices. In that way, when you lack vices, and you do not want to sin further, they will receive you, repentant and renewed in the good, into life's pastures, where there is no lack of security or fullness of eternal joys."[14]

---

[14] Hildegard ends this second homily as well with a direct exhortation, addressing her audience with second-person plural forms.

Homilies 3 and 4

The Last Sunday before Advent

John 6:1-14

Jesus went across the Sea of Galilee, which is the Sea of Tiberias. And a very great multitude was following him, because they saw the signs he was doing over those who were sick. Therefore Jesus went up on the mountain and there sat down with his disciples. Now the Passover, the feast of the Jews, was at hand.

After Jesus raised his eyes and saw that a very great multitude came toward him, he said to Philip: 'Where will we buy bread so that these people may eat?' But he said this to test him, for he knew what he was going to do. Philip answered him: 'Two hundred denarii worth of bread would not suffice for them so that each one would get a little.'

One of his disciples, Andrew, Simon Peter's brother, said to him: 'There is a boy here who has five barley loaves and two fish. But what are these among so many?' Jesus then said: 'Make the people sit down.' Now there was much grass in the place; therefore, the men sat down, about five thousand in number.

Jesus then took the loaves; and when he had given thanks, he distributed them to those who were seated; so also the fish, as much as they wanted. When they had eaten their fill he told his disciples: 'Gather up the fragments that were left over, so that they may not be lost.' So they gathered them up and filled twelve baskets with fragments from the five barley loaves, which were left over by those who had eaten.

When the people saw what Jesus had done, the sign, they said: 'This is truly the prophet who is to come into the world.'

3. The Last Sunday before Advent, 1

Jesus, in his passion, *crossed the Sea of Galilee,* that is, through the anguish and tribulation of this world, *which is the Sea of Tiberias.* This pertains to the righteous and highest region; after he had risen from the dead every group of people is drawn toward it and was reaching toward it. *And a very great multitude of believers was following him,* that is, his footsteps, *because they saw the signs he was doing over those who were sick.* There was one heart and one soul[1] for them, *because they saw,* both with faith and the sight of the eyes, *the signs,* namely, when the Holy Spirit descended in tongues of fire[2] upon the believers, and the many other miracles Christ *was doing* through his disciples and others of the faithful. He sent his grace from above to those who were at first infirm in faith,[3] so that afterwards they were healed by baptism.

Therefore, Jesus went up on the mountain and there sat down with his disciples. Clearly, *Jesus* entered persuasively with the precepts of the law and new testimonies into the sanctification of the church, which appears exalted in the whole world, and he reigned in honor and comeliness with all who have believed and do believe in him. *Now the Passover, the feast of the Jews, was at hand,* that is, the communion of the body and blood of Christ, the innocent lamb, was continually frequent and near;[4] the good, great and splendid ardor of faith and of good deeds was being born and shining in the hearts of those who believe and who confess their sins.

After Jesus raised his eyes and saw that a very great multitude of believers came toward him, he said to Philip: 'Where will we buy bread so that these people may eat?' The Savior, therefore, raised the intent for knowledge in the church, and in the glory of honor *saw* through his mercy *that a very great multitude* of believers came toward him, through baptism and martyrdom and other good examples. *He said* through his own inspiration to the simple, lawful precepts

[1] Acts 4:32.
[2] Acts 2:3.
[3] Latin *infirmi in fide* is alliterative.
[4] Latin is awkward: *in assidua frequentatione propinquitatis.*

of the Old Law: "From which deeds of the law or precepts of the ancient sacrifices will we call forth or reveal the ones who are righteous and holy in their deeds, from whom they may draw an example of belief and holiness?"

But he said this to test him; that is, Jesus *said this* examining and discussing the precepts of the Old Law in their significations. *For he knew what he was going to do;* in that he was going to draw out many wonders and significations for the salvation of believers, just as indeed it had been prefigured by the ram caught in the thorns.[5]

Philip answered him, that is, Christ: '*Two-hundred denarii worth of bread do not suffice for them, so that each one may receive a little.*' "In other words, the entire sum of life's rewards, which was promised to righteous and holy people both by the prophets and the Old Law, does '*not suffice for*' those who follow your footsteps in the church. Those who have received baptism may gather '*a little*' virtue and example in their mind by those significations, because they want to have much greater things, going from strength to strength."[6]

Andrew, one of his disciples, Simon Peter's brother, said to him: 'There is one boy here, who has five barley loaves and two fish.' Those proven in the oneness of faith—those who had followed Christ's footsteps by faith and deed, the believers strongest in virtuous strength, and the brothers of Christ—were made into the strongest stones[7] when they fulfilled his will everywhere in the divine precepts. The pure[8] in deeds most devotedly embrace the oneness of faith in the church, so that in the five senses they are most righteous and holy people, loving the barley[9] of the narrow and difficult way.[10] They imitate Christ, true God and human, in the pure and

---

[5] Cf. Gen 22:13.

[6] Ps 83:8. Hildegard employs direct speech here, following Philip's voice in the gospel text.

[7] Cf. 1 Pet 2:5.

[8] Hildegard plays on the Latin words here: *puer* (boy) and *puri* (pure).

[9] An example of metonymy: the coarse grain stands for the harsh life of monasticism.

[10] Cf. Matt 7:13-14.

discerning living of the spiritual life, as monks and virgins, completely renouncing the world.[11] '*But what are*' the deeds of discretion and the way of life of worldly rejection '*among so many*,' who
labor in the church, because these virtues '*do not*' yet '*suffice*' for
them. In the end-time, far greater powers will arise in prophecy
and in the sufferings of the saints, when indeed far greater evils
will winnow them like wheat.[12]

Jesus then said to those following him: '*Make the people sit down*':
in other words, "Arrange upright and good repose for believers
in the church through my precepts." *Now there was much grass in
the place.* Clearly, there were still many mockeries in the culture of
unfaithfulness that people had seen first in Judaism and pagan-
ism in the practice of the people. *Therefore, the men sat down, about
five thousand in number.* Evidently, the virtues preeminent among
human beings who are fortunately preordained for life arranged
themselves in the church. They produce through the five senses
of believers an innumerable abundance of good deeds.

*Jesus then took the loaves, and when he had given thanks, he distrib-
uted them to those who were seated.* When he drew righteous and
holy people to his grace by virtues through the precepts of the
law, and when he had revealed his gifts through his grace,[13] he
gave and set them forth as an example for believers, when for
the name of Christ they humbly prostrated themselves to the
earth, as it were. *So also from the fish, as much as they wanted.* By his
inspiration those who, like monks and virgins, have approached
the angelic order, who are the greatest example for the faithful of
contempt for the world, as much as desire for the church requires
in a holy way of life.

*When, however, they had eaten their fill, he told his disciples: 'Gather
up the fragments that were left over, so that they will not be lost.'* Jesus

---

[11] This and other intratextual references indicate, along with manuscript
evidence, that Hildegard possibly delivered these homilies to the monks and
or nuns at Disbodenberg in 1170. See Kienzle, *Speaking New Mysteries*, 44–45.

[12] Cf. Luke 22:31.

[13] The Latin has *cum* three times, *ubi* once. The translation omits one *cum*
to make a complete sentence.

said to all in the church with their ranks, who were capable in perception and intellect, such as the doctors of the churches: "Keep aside and instruct those in the church who are more simple and live simply, such that they may think that whatever small and least things suffice for their salvation; and in this, they seem like fragments of bread, as if weak and cast away. But you, instruct them with gentleness of words, so that they *will not be lost* by the negligence of oblivion;[14] make them bear *fruit a hundredfold*."[15]

Therefore, they collected and filled twelve baskets with fragments from the five barley loaves, which were left by those who had eaten. Clearly, the doctors also instructed with divine precepts the ones who were proceeding into the church simply and in weakness, who were not daring to lift themselves to higher things, as do certain people in the world who live simply. The preachers' and the apostles' words accomplished this, when they led the simple as well as the weak, like the fragments of bread, to that faith the apostles had taught when *their voice went out over all the earth.*[16] The most righteous people existing in the five senses take up the narrow way[17] with barley loaves,[18] because those living in the world fear the stronger and greater bread-baskets of life. The holier people run strongly to undertake the life of God's mandates, but content with their simplicity, they lead life in humility.

When the people had seen what Jesus had done, the sign, they were saying: 'This is truly the prophet who is to come.' Those who worship Christ in faith through baptism and through many other wonders in the church *had seen* in good knowledge, in good intellect, and in the good taste for the sweetness of virtues, *what Jesus had done* in humanity, in suffering, and in the Holy Spirit's gifts, *the sign* through prophecy and the Gospel, as from the commentators. *They were saying* in a clear voice, in the praises of belief: *'This is*

---

[14] Note the echo of the Rule of Benedict: RB 7.60.

[15] Luke 8:8.

[16] Ps 18:5.

[17] Cf. Matt 7:14.

[18] Hildegard repeats this use of metonymy, with barley representing the religious life.

the one' who fulfilled all the prophets in himself, *'who is going to come'* prevailing by his miracles in the fullness of time, so that all his deeds, which were foretold many ages ago as going to come, would be fulfilled. He will accomplish them until the last day, when the world will be completed in its course.

4. The Last Sunday before Advent, 2

Jesus went across the sea of Galilee, which is also the Sea of Tiberias. By the Holy Spirit's admonition, the Savior *went* beyond the rottenness of vices in their transformation: that is, when the human being leaves evil behind and begins good; clearly, when he sighs for the love of things in heaven, where all the virtues direct themselves. *And a very great multitude* of virtues *was following him* in good report, *because they saw the signs he was doing over those who were sick.* Clearly, *they saw* the holy intention, the conversion of this person, *which he was doing* for holy admonition, when he restrains vices, as he converts people to the good, such that the converted sinner may be a praiseworthy human being.

Therefore Jesus went up on the mountain, and there sat down with his disciples. Counseling and assisting by the Holy Spirit's admonition, he *went up* onto this height, so that the human being may be renewed by the virtues, *and there sat down* in the dwelling of repose with the virtues. *Now the Passover, the feast of the Jews, was at hand.* Clearly, joy was near, the joy of illumination, the happy feast, that is, the clarity in which the human being confesses sins.

After Jesus raised his eyes and saw that a very great multitude came toward him, he said to Philip: 'Where will we buy bread, so that these people may eat?' *After* the Savior raised blessed knowledge in praise of happiness *and saw* in inquiry that *a very large multitude* of virtues *came toward him,* doing brilliant deeds in the human being through his grace and reaching toward him, *he said* in his admonition to Innocence: *"'Where* will we seek constraints, so that they may persevere in the virtues?'"*[19] *But Jesus said this to test him,* that is,

---

[19] The language of perseverance recalls RB Prol. 50, 7.36, and 58.3.

moderating and fashioning Innocence. *For he knew* in his secrets *what he was going to do* in that person, how he would raise him up and press him down, lest he ascend on high beyond measure, and lest he descend into the abyss beyond measure, since God knows what the human being can accomplish.

Philip answered him: 'Two hundred denarii worth of bread would not suffice for them, so that each one of them could get a little.' Innocence answered the Savior: "Constraints into the height and depth of those reaching out in the fullness of heavenly rewards *would not suffice* in their hearts, *so that each one of them could receive a little* moderation through discretion."

Andrew, one of his disciples, Simon Peter's brother, said to him: 'There is a boy who has five barley loaves and two fish.' Clearly, the oneness of the virtues and the constancy of the brothers,[20] which is the companion of the strongest fortitude, *said to him:* "'*There is*' a beginning here, the good for which all believers must strive, namely, constraints on the strongest curbs in the five senses, when the human being leaves behind evil habit and directs himself toward any virtues; and evidently, spiritual desire in God and in the human being, when the human despises earthly things and reaches out to heavenly things with total exertion of mind and body. '*But what are these'* constraints and the hunger for spiritual desires among *so many* virtues, since the human has so strong and so steep a desire for God that he is hardly restrained by this humility, so that he may recognize that he is human and like other people?"

Jesus then said, 'Make the people sit down.' By the Holy Spirit's admonition the Savior *then said* to the virtues: "Seize and subdue by your constraint '*the people,'* clearly, those who are human but yet want to surpass humans in ascent of virtue without the measure of discretion. Hold discretion with humility, lest exceeding their capacity they fall into a lower place."

---

[20] This may indicate that Hildegard delivered these homilies to the monks at Disbodenberg in 1170. The accent on unity of the brothers points to the possibility of a conflict Hildegard was called to resolve, as she was at other monasteries. See Kienzle, *Speaking New Mysteries*, 44–45, 48.

Now there was much grass in the place; evidently, human temptations in presumption and mockery, when they ought to know and understand that they are weak human beings. *So the men sat down, about five thousand in number*, constrained and subdued in humility by divine scourges and chastisements, tested by earthly and heavenly things, *in the number* of blessedness, holding by their five senses an abundance of the heavenly host, well disposed in virtues.

Jesus then took the loaves, and when he had given thanks he distributed them to those who were seated. Evidently, he took up the human being's constraints, by which he had humbled him, so that he would not exalt himself unsuitably. When he had extended his grace to these things, he divided them with humility and discretion for those who had restrained themselves uprightly and well, and who had imposed upon themselves a measure of moderation. *So also the fish, as much as they wanted*; that is, the spiritual desires and insightful considerations by which people contemplate moderately and temperately those things that are around them, according to the amount they endure.

When, however, they had eaten their fill, he said to his disciples, 'Gather up the leftover fragments, so that nothing may be lost.' When *they were* well-disposed by discretion and right measure, *he said* to the virtues, because they embrace him everywhere: *'Gather up the leftover fragments.'* In other words, note down and store away the good deeds that remain, because they seemed somewhat unbearable to human beings, and even greater than what people think they could endure. The *'fragments'* [denote] the sufferings and constraints, as much of the soul as of the body, by means of which virtuous humans strove to direct themselves toward the virtues but were scarcely able to attain them. *'Lest they be lost'* in praise, evidently so that they not lack praise before God and human beings.

So they gathered them up and filled twelve baskets with fragments from the five barley loaves left over by those who had eaten. They were noting and preserving those constraints; they completed and led to the fullness of the sacraments ten talents, plus two among the faithful servants to whom the precepts of the law and the

Gospel were given to fulfill; and they cling to them through the entwinements of mysteries, when, in the fragments of sufferings and constraints, the faithful so restrain themselves, that nothing is overlooked by them. The faithful impose constraints of the heaviest weight on their own five senses. With abundant constraint, they drove their body back to servitude[21] and *crucified their flesh with its vices and inordinate desires,*[22] while inwardly they endured many sufferings in their hearts.

When the people had seen what he had done, the sign, they said: 'This is truly the prophet who is to come into the world.' When they had put aside human intellect and had brought themselves to the divine by other virtues, with an eye of good will, they *had seen the sign,* namely, in those who imitate him with total effort through the most powerful virtues; in other words, lest the ones remaining in check under his power take a turn downwards through immoderation. *They said* with sighing and moaning hearts: *'This is truly the prophet,'* knowing all the things that are necessary for the salvation of human souls, *'who is to come'* at the onset of good when the human being first begins to do good, and at its consummation when he brings it to a good end, such that praise and thanksgiving are brought forth to God by human beings among people throughout the ages.

[21] Cf. 1 Cor 9:27.
[22] Gal 5:24.

Homilies 5 and 6

The Eve of
the Lord's Birth

Matthew 1:18-21

When Jesus' mother Mary was betrothed to Joseph, before they came to live together, she was found having [a child] in her womb through the Holy Spirit. Her husband Joseph, since he was a righteous man and did not want to hand her over publicly, wanted to divorce her secretly. When he was pondering these things, the angel of the Lord appeared to him in a dream. The angel said to him: 'Joseph, son of David, do not be afraid to take Mary as your wife. For what has been conceived in her is from the Holy Spirit. She will give birth to a son, and you will call his name Jesus. He will save his people from their sins.'

5. The Eve of the Lord's Birth, 1

When Jesus' mother Mary was betrothed to Joseph, before they came to live together in willful marriage, *she was found having [a child] in her womb through the Holy Spirit.* God considered righteous the first arrangement whereby he himself united Adam and Eve. He contemplated and wished the mother of his son to be betrothed to a man, so that he would protect her faithfully and caringly, and so that she would be subject to him. It was just that every woman

46

who had an infant should have a husband to protect her. There is justice in this, and humility follows in submission to it. For if Mary did not have a protector and if, as it were, she needed no husband to protect her, pride would have snatched her easily. Clearly, by the intent of the union, she was given the name "mother" in the presence of God and his people.[1]

Her husband Joseph, since he was a righteous man and did not want to hand her over publicly, wanted to divorce her secretly. Joseph was *her husband* in the betrothal and the union of the bond, and a *righteous man*, because he sought after no falsehood in all his desires. His will was pure, because he did not wish to be a transgressor of the law, that is, to act against the law, as it were, because he saw that she had a child in her womb and that the child was not his. He was astounded, knowing she was chaste and yet pregnant and not knowing by whom. On account of the people's gossip he wanted to go away from her, so that no one would know whether he was alive or dead.

When he was pondering these things, the angel of the Lord appeared to him in a dream, not while he was awake, because he was wavering on these things, and he did not have the spirit of prophecy. The angel *said to him: 'Joseph, son of David, do not be afraid,'* because Joseph feared he would be defamed on account of her. The angel said: *'Take Mary as your wife,'* only in the bond of betrothal. *'What has been conceived in her is from the Holy Spirit. She will give birth to a son, and you will call his name Jesus. He will save his people from their sins.'* Now when Joseph heard the angel's words, at once he saw with faith, and he believed that the Savior would be born.

6. The Eve of the Lord's Birth, 2

When Jesus' mother Mary was betrothed to Joseph, before they came to live together. Now this betrothal first occurs in the baptism of any faithful soul whatsoever, which by accomplishing good deeds,

---

[1] Latin: *mater nominata.* This homily sets out one of the few (six at most) commentaries in which Hildegard explains the literal sense of the pericope. See Kienzle, *Speaking New Mysteries,* 95–96.

becomes the mother and a member of Jesus' [body] through the salvation of illumination.[2] For the faithful soul is betrothed through baptism to Joseph, that is, to Wisdom, which knows every good thing in earthly and heavenly realms.[3] It is found in some people of the world, in a mind that, instructed by the inspiration of the Holy Spirit, meditates on every heavenly thing. *Her husband Joseph*, clearly, Wisdom, in a bond of blessing, since Wisdom is righteous in all things, does not wish to hand over the soul to worldly things, because Wisdom meditates on the heavenly things above it. But he *wanted to divorce her secretly*; in those things it desires, Wisdom wants to test for itself whether or not it will be able to complete what it began.

But when Wisdom handles these matters within itself, the admonition of heavenly inspiration appears in secret quiet,[4] as *the angel of the Lord in a dream, saying: 'Joseph, son of David,'* that is, the one whom no one can vanquish, *'Do not be afraid to take Mary as your wife'*; "in other words, *'take'* without any hesitation the faithful soul. With trust, lead her with you to the things that you know in God, because she has been joined to you by holy baptism." *'For what has been conceived in her is from the Holy Spirit,'* namely, what the soul holds in her mind is from divine inspiration.[5] *'She will give birth to a son, and you will call his name Jesus.'* Clearly, the soul will accomplish this with a full and perfect deed, because by this it will be saved before Jesus. *'He will save his people from their sins'* when he frees the thoughts, speech, and all members of his body

---

[2] Hildegard introduces the image of the Body of Christ here and returns to it in the closing sentence of the homily.

[3] Here Mary represents the faithful soul and Joseph designates Wisdom. On Hildegard's allegories of the soul, see Kienzle, *Speaking New Mysteries*, 199–205, 240–43.

[4] Hildegard omits the verb used in the Scripture, *apparuit*, from *apparo, -ere*, but uses the same verb in the present tense: *apparet*, indicating clearly her application of this moral lesson to her contemporaries.

[5] At this point, Hildegard ceases to speak through the voice of the angel and turns to third-person discourse to conclude the homily.

from the snares of sins and leads them to God by a faithful and salutary transferring.[6]

---

[6] For the Latin *salubri translatione ducit* the direct object is understood from the preceding clause: the "thoughts, speech, and all members" of Christ's body, and the verb with its modifying phrase indicates the transferring of the soul to God. The term recalls Joseph's unwillingness to hand Mary over publicly (*traducere*), interpreted here as Wisdom's reluctance to hand over the soul to worldly matters (*secularia*).

Homilies 7 and 8

The Lord's Birth

Luke 2:1-14

A decree went out from Caesar Augustus that the whole world should be enrolled. This first enrollment was carried out by Quirinius, governor of Syria. And all went out, so that they would declare themselves in their own cities. Joseph went up from Galilee from the city of Nazareth to Judea, to the city of David, which is called Bethlehem, because he was from the house and the lineage of David, so that he would declare himself with Mary, who was betrothed to him, his pregnant wife. It happened that while they were there the time came that she should give birth. She gave birth to her first-born son, wrapped him with cloths, and laid him to rest in a manger, because there was no place for them at the inn. And shepherds were in the same region, guarding and keeping watch by night over their flock. And behold, an angel of the Lord stood near them and the brightness of God shone around them, and they feared with great fear. And the angel said to them: 'Do not fear, for behold, I announce to you good news of great joy that will be for all people, for today in the city of David is born to you a Savior, who is Christ the Lord. This will be a sign for you: You will find the infant wrapped in cloths and placed in a manger.' And suddenly with the angel there was a multitude of the heavenly host praising God and saying: 'Glory to God in the highest and on earth peace to people of good will.'

7. The Lord's Birth, 1

A decree went out from Caesar Augustus that the entire world should be enrolled. In other words, the ancient plan *went out* from the heav-

50

enly Father that all creation should go forth. *This first enrollment was carried out by Quirinius, governor of Syria.* Clearly, the creation *was carried out* through the Word of the Father, because the Word was the head of all creation and was also to be incarnated. *And all went out, so that they would declare themselves in their own cities*; in other words, each and every creature *went out* so that they might carry out their initial condition in accordance with their nature, as it had been appointed for them in their own capacity, that is, by walking, swimming, or flying.

Joseph went up from Galilee from the city of Nazareth to Judea, to the city of David, which is called Bethlehem, because he was from the house and the lineage of David, so that he would declare himself with Mary, who was betrothed to him, his pregnant wife. Clearly, the human being *went up* to that height away from other creatures, because he was placed over them. The human understood all things, because he had rationality, since God had created him in his image and likeness.[1] The human *declared himself* to God, from whom he went away after being created and to whom he returned once he had been redeemed. Rationality was given to him, so that with it he might discern when he ought to listen to God's command.

It happened that while they were there the time came that she should give birth. She gave birth to her first-born son and wrapped him with cloths. Clearly, since the human had discretion through rationality, he brought forth a good intention at the outset when he perceived the Lord's command by hearing and when he heeded God's command. *And she laid him to rest in a manger, because there was no place for them at the inn.* [God] placed the human in upright desires when the human humbled himself to good will, because he did not yet have the secret place for the evil that was begun.

And shepherds, that is, solicitude for the mind,[2] *were in the same region*, namely in God's understanding,[3] *guarding and keeping*

---

[1] Gen 5:3; see Gen 1:26-27.

[2] Latin *sollicitudo animi*, an objective genitive. Hildegard seems to use *animus* here as the rational faculty that makes ethical decisions.

[3] The antecedent for the Latin *in comprensione sui* is ambiguous. It seems to have God as its understood antecedent.

watch by night over their flock, standing guard protectively over all human deeds, so that they would not sin through knowledge of evil.

And behold, an angel of the Lord stood near them and the brightness of God shone around them, and they feared with great fear. The angels' protection was present for them, and consequently they knew the angels; and the gifts of God *shone around them*, with the result that they knew good things, and they were very anxious over what they were going to do.

And the angel said to them: 'Do not fear, for behold, I announce to you good news of great joy that will be for all people, for today in the city of David is born to you a Savior.' The angel revealed in revelation: "There will be honor for all your deeds in thought and act. What is born in you is salvation, because you have been made *in the image and likeness of God,*[4] in order that you perform good deeds with firm fortitude."[5]

'This will be a sign for you,' revealing true things: *'You will find the infant wrapped in cloths,'* evidently good intention in upright desires, *'and placed in a manger,'* that is, in good will.[6] *And suddenly with the angel there was a multitude of the heavenly host praising God.* When the human was created and placed in Paradise under the angels' protection [there was] a great miracle in the whole heavenly host, *'praising God'* about[7] the human; because divine works shone forth in him, since rationality was supposed to work in him. For the angel is rational only in praise, but the human in both praise and deed. Once they had seen the human, the angels knew God to a greater extent.

And the angels were saying, 'Glory to God in the highest and on earth peace to people of good will.' God is glorious on high with the

---

[4] Gen 1:26; see Gen 1:27; Gen 5:3.

[5] The Latin employs alliteration here: *forti fortitudine.*

[6] This is an instance where Hildegard extends the speech of the speaker, the angel, in order to develop her tropological allegory, but she does not actually assume the angel's voice.

[7] The Latin *super* as a preposition here relates the cause for praise.

angels, and in heaven *peace* was given, because Adam was in good will before the Fall.

8. The Lord's Birth, 2

A decree went out from Caesar Augustus that the entire world should be enrolled. A certain arrangement was made by self-will, that it would be extended through the entire body. *This first enrollment was carried out by Quirinius, governor of Syria*; evidently this first extension *was carried out* by carnal appetite. *And all went out, so that they would declare themselves in their own cities*; clearly, the virtues and vices turned themselves, each to its own capacity.

Joseph went up from Galilee from the city of Nazareth, into the city of David, which is called Bethlehem, because he was from the house and the lineage of David, so that he would declare himself with Mary, who was betrothed to him, his pregnant wife. Good Desire *went up* from what is customary, that is, from the care it has in Rationality, because from the creation it knew good and evil.[8] It *went up* into the hidden way[9] of knowing God, which is the soul's salvation, and said that it was betrothed to Charity for bringing forth virtues.

It happened that while they were there the time came that she should give birth. When Good Desire so dwelled with Charity, the splendor of good works appeared. *She gave birth to her first-born son, wrapped him with cloths, and laid him to rest in a manger, because there was no place for them at the inn.* Charity brought forth Obedience, the foremost virtue, embraced it, and placed it in Humility, because there was no place for Vanity.

And shepherds were in the same region; that is, there was anxiety in the same self-will over whether the human would perform good deeds, *guarding* with abstinence, *and* with prayers *keeping watch*, that is foresight, *over their flock*, so that the human would preserve his good deeds, *by night*, that is, when the human turns away from sins.

[8] Gen 3:22; see Gen 3:5.
[9] See Matt 7:14.

And behold an angel of the Lord stood near them and the brightness of God shone around them, and they feared with great fear. God's grace surrounded them and God's aid sustained them, but they were still afraid as to how they might defeat the devil. *And the angel said to them: 'Do not fear, for behold, I announce to you good news of great joy that will be for all people, for today in the city of David is born to you a Savior.'* God's grace pointed out: "Do not doubt. Great virtue is in the breath of life, because it is common to all humankind. In you holy Rationality has been born, which is Christ the Lord, coming from God, in defense of all holiness." *'This will be a sign for you: You will find the infant wrapped in cloths and placed in a manger.'* "Clearly, through revelation, you will find Obedience, hold it in your embrace, and *'place it'* in Humility."

And suddenly with the angel there was a multitude of the heavenly host praising God and saying: 'Glory to God in the highest and on earth peace to people of good will.' With God's grace, a multitude of virtues will quickly come about *'praising God'* with the sweetest sound, revealing in human knowledge that God *is able to do everything,*[10] and to lead the sinner back to life, when the sinner has dwelled in earthly matters. *'People'* may have quiet amidst the turbulent adversities of vanities, since they would willingly do good things if they were not shackled by their own fragility. Nonetheless, God will be a peacemaker among these people.

[10] Eph 3:20.

Homily 9

The Lord's Birth

John 1:1-14

In the beginning was the Word, and the Word was with God, and the Word was God. In the beginning the Word was with God. Through him all things were made and without him nothing was made. What was made in him was life, and the life was the light of humans. And the light shines in the darkness, and the darkness has not comprehended it. A certain man was sent from God, whose name was John. He came for testimony, that he might bear witness about the light, so that all would believe through him. He was not that light, but he came to bear witness about the light. That was the true light that enlightens every human, coming into this world. He was in the world, and the world was made through him, and the world did not know him. He came into his own, and his own did not receive him. Whosoever received him, he gave them the power to become children of God, those who believe in his name. They were born not from blood, nor from the will of the flesh, nor from the will of a man, but from God. And the Word was made flesh, and dwelled among us, and we saw his glory, glory as of the only begotten Son from the Father, full of grace and truth.

The Lord's Birth

In the beginning was the Word. Clearly, at the origin of the world, there was Rationality, which is the Son.[1] Although the *Word* is the

---

[1] Hildegard uses Rationality here as the Son of God, the *logos*, but also as the rational faculty in the human being. See the Topical Index in this volume for other examples.

55

beginning of all creatures, nonetheless, the Word is not called the beginning,[2] yet the same Word sounded the beginning, which is *Fiat.*[3] *And the Word,* that is, Rationality, which is the Son, *was with God,* because God is Rationality.[4] God was neither made nor created, but has always existed. Rationality, however, created all things; *and the Word was God,* because God is truly rational. But in the human and the angel rationality has a starting point, while in God it lacks a starting point. *In the beginning the Word was with God.* Evidently Rationality was at the origin of the world, which is *Fiat,*[5] in such a way that Rationality and God are one and not divided.[6]

Through him all things were made and without him nothing was made. Heaven, earth, and the other things that are in them *were made* because God said, '*Fiat.*'[7] Without Rationality, that is, without the Son, contradiction *was made.* God made the angel rational, but because rationality in an angel contradicted God, God himself did not make it, but allowed it to be made. Nonetheless, this may be understood in another way, namely that *nothing* was made without the Son. God cannot be brought to an end, but the notion

[2] The concern for the Word's name has precedent in Augustine and others, who explain why the Son is called "Verbum." However, Augustine and Heiric of Auxerre state that the Father and Son are called "beginning." See Augustine of Hippo, *In Iohannis euangelium* I, 11, p. 6, ll. 1-17; Heiric of Auxerre, *Homiliae* I, 10, p. 82, ll. 39-48; *Homiliae* I, 11, p. 93, ll. 93-108. Hildegard also deals with this verse in *Diu. operum,* p. 251, ll. 84-96, and p. 252, ll. 116-17.

[3] Gen 1:3, 6.

[4] For this highly debated pericope I include a few key explanations and references to earlier sources, notably Augustine and Heiric of Auxerre. For a full discussion, see Kienzle, *Speaking New Mysteries,* 272–77, and the sources cited there, as well as the edition of the *Expo. Euang.,* 209–15.

[5] Gen 1:3, 6.

[6] This notion of indivisibility echoes previous exegetes, notably Heiric of Auxerre, who is influenced by Eriugena when he asserts: "There is one principle/beginning and not two, one God and not two." See John Scotus, *Homélie sur le prologue de Jean,* 240; Heiric of Auxerre, *Homiliae* I, 10, p. 82, ll. 52-53; *Homiliae* I, 11, p. 93, ll. 103-108. On the notion of having no origin and being indivisible, see also *Diu. operum* I, u. 4, c. 105, p. 250, ll. 75-76, and I, u. 4, c. 105, p. 251, ll. 79, 82, 90.

[7] Gen 1:3, 6.

that God wanted himself to be brought to an end was *nothing*, because this could not happen.[8] The angel found that which is nothing; the human later followed the angel and did the same thing through disobedience.[9]

What was made in him, that is, in the Word, namely, in Rationality, clearly, in the Son of God, who was incarnate as a human, *was life*, because the Son of God was human, of such a kind that *nothing* either touched him or entered him, as it did in the angel and the human. Nonetheless, *what was made* may be understood in a different way, that all things that were made have life in God.[10]

---

[8] The Latin (*Expo. Euang.* 9, p. 210, l. 19) reads: *Deus non deleri potest, sed quod ipsum deleri voluit, nichil erat, quia hoc fieri non potest.* God willing himself to be destroyed would be a contradiction and therefore the equivalent of nothingness.

[9] Hildegard offers two readings for John 1:3a and 1:3b, "All things through him were made," and "without him nothing was made." She proclaims that all things were made when God uttered *Fiat*. Augustine specifies what "all things" comprehend, including the fly, which the Manicheans claimed to be the Devil's creation. Augustine, *In Iohannis euangelium* I, 5, p. 3, ll. 11-15; I, 9, p. 6, ll. 24-26; I, 13, p. 7, ll. 11-16; I, 13, p. 8, ll. 35-42. On the fly see *In Iohannis euangelium* I, 14, p. 8, ll. 1-22. For John 1:3b Hildegard explains that *nihil* means contradiction. Heiric of Auxerre gives a similar reading when he interprets *nihil* as negation. Hildegard allows that this phrase may be understood in another way, namely, that without the Son *nihil* was made. She probably has Augustine in mind where he equates *nihil* with what God did not make: sin and idols, as in 1 Cor 8:4: *nihil est idolum.* Augustine, *In Iohannis euangelium* I, 13, p. 7, ll. 3-11. Augustine equates *nihil* with what God did not make. Hildegard explains *nihil* as evil and sin in the *Diu. operum* I, u. 4, cap. 105, p. 252, ll. 139-40.

[10] For John 1.4: "what was made in him," Hildegard explains first that "what was made" *in ipso* was made by Rationality, by the Son of God incarnated. That "was life" (*uita erat*), because the Son of God was human. Hildegard also asserts that *nihil* neither touched nor entered Christ, as it did the angel and humankind, a comment that relates back to *nihil* as the contradiction or disobedience of sin. She then introduces another meaning of the phrase with wording similar to her comment on the preceding verse. In her commentary on the Athanasian Creed, Hildegard includes both interpretations of John 1:4: that *nihil* could not pertain to God, and that all things have life in God, but she does not overtly differentiate the two as in the *Expositiones. Expl. Symb.* 118, ll. 250-60; *Expl. Atha.* 43. Augustine distinguished two

And the life, which is the incarnation of God's son, *was the light of humans*, because he shone for them, and the darkness never entered him. *And the light shines in the darkness*, when the human fell. This light does not shine in nothingness, namely in that which is nothing, because the devil is not redeemed but shines in the fallen human. *And the darkness has not comprehended it*; in other words, the human fell and did not comprehend the incarnation. The Lord's incarnation was pure, since Christ was born without the original sin through which humans draw Adam's guilt.

A certain man was sent from God into the arid earth, without the sweat of the will, that is, of carnal pleasure, because God so wanted it. *His name was John*, because God's grace worked wonders in him, and because he was going to reveal the grace that was going to come into the world, without the vicissitude of habits, speaking the truth as a flying arrow was flying. *He came for testimony, that he might bear witness about the light, so that all would believe through him.* He worked by revealing and performing miracles. It would not be possible for him to touch the light unless the filth were removed from it, because he himself was a miracle working a miracle and resplendent in holiness from *the light* of life. This was done, therefore, so that the same miracle might give faith to humans, because his testimony was true. *All would believe through him*, on account of the miracles that became apparent in him. When a messenger is righteous and upright, his words are believed that much more confidently.

He was not that light into which the darkness never entered, but that light was such that very great miracles worked in it, which never appeared in human seed. *But he came to bear witness about the light*, namely, what truth and uprightness were in that light, which was pure and true without human vicissitude.

---

readings of v. 4, the first punctuated after *est: Quod factum est, . . .* , and the second after *illo: Quod factum est in illo.* He rejected the second way of reading, stating that stones, for example, are made but are not life, as the Manicheans assert. Hildegard defines life in terms reminiscent of Augustine's definition of life as wisdom and reason (*sapientia* and *ratio*). See *In Iohannis euangelium* I, 16, pp. 9-10, ll. 9-25; p. 19, ll. 241-45.

That was the true light that enlightens every human coming into this world, pure and righteous, because that very light is true, and it has no likeness with the people in darkness, since humans come into this world in darkness and sins.

He was in the world, yet he was not made from the world like other human beings. *And the world was made through him*, when the Father's word sounded, '*Fiat*,'[11] and therefore he was both the light and the righteous Lord. *And the world did not know him*, because he had no likeness in sins with the world, whereupon humans did not know him coming, staying, and going in the world.

He came into his own, the things he had created and thus were his own, so that he went up and surpassed in all things and above all things. *And his own*, the ones he had created, *did not receive him*, because they were unwilling to receive his honor and miracles. Therefore, knowledge and sensitivity and the likeness of those did not receive who they were and how they were, because they were unable to grasp him.

Whosoever received him were enlightened by him, knowing him. *He gave them the power* to perform good works because they were born from him, not in likeness but in faith, and *the power to become children of God*, in uprightness and righteousness, because they were touched and enlightened by him, since they were announcing him. They preached and they made known his miracles *to those who believe in his name*, so that they would believe that he was the Word working through all things and that they, like a wheel in the light of the Holy Spirit's fire, were led before others by miracles. Therefore, they know him, because they, too, like the wind, were led around by prophecy and other miracles.[12]

They were born not from blood, namely, of the coagulations in lust, *nor from the will of the flesh,* clearly, of a woman giving consent, *nor from the will of a man*, evidently the one doing that, *but from God*. When blood flows in this way there will be coagulation. This coagulation is *from the will of the flesh*, because it will be flesh, and

[11] Gen 1:3, 6.
[12] The Latin verbs involve circular motion: *circumducti sunt* and *circumacti sunt*.

from the will of a man displaying his own strength. It is their will,
because both the will of the flesh and the will of a man bring
these together into one, like a mill going around. And this forma-
tion does not show that children of God are made, but they are
curdled like cheese.[13] This birth is absent from becoming *children
of God* because in the end they are formed from the Holy Spirit's
wind, and from the fire of the Holy Spirit's inspiration, and from
prophecy, and so they are children of God.

And the Word was made flesh. The same Word that fashioned
flesh from earth with the breath of life introduced itself into complete flesh and slept with a sleep similar to Adam's sleep without
sin, when another flesh was made from him into a woman. Thus
the Word was made flesh, and the human grew, *and dwelled among
us,* just as Eve with Adam, before sin. No vicissitude was in them,
but they were whole, just as God had created them, and therefore
evil had not yet entered them, just as the Word dwells in us and
loves people in kindness and truth. However, when the craftiness
of the serpent entered Adam their blood was spread into poison,
and that sin sprouted from their blood and both *from the will of
the flesh* and *from the will of a man.*

Then they abandoned God and brought themselves to an end,
so that afterwards no flesh could become righteous or just, except
the infant whom the Virgin conceived from a heavenly wind, and
who himself overcame and from himself was strengthened and
grew.[14] Neither anger, nor pride of ill will, nor the taste for manly
sweat, nor any evil was in him. This little girl, pure and chaste,
without the shaking of a tempest, was pure flesh,[15] and therefore,
the Word brought himself into her and grew as a human.

And we saw in faith and miracles *his glory* in many revelations
of heavenly miracles. He was without sin and he did not open his

---

[13] This notion and the terminology appear in the *Causae et curae* 105, 149–50,
several places in *Sciuias*; and in Gregory the Great, *Moralia in Iob* 9.52, p. 511,
ll. 6-9. For further references, see the *apparatus fontium, Expo. Euang.* p. 213.

[14] See Luke 2:40.

[15] Hildegard uses the Latin diminutive *puellula* to refer to Mary.

mouth to deceit,[16] or for the revenge of anger, or for any storm of the flesh by which the human is shaken. *Glory as of the only begotten Son from the Father*, as this glory was like that of an only begotten son, whom a father loves very much and to whom he gives great glory, so that henceforth, there will be no such son. For just as God created no human but one from dust, for that reason the second Adam is from God. The first Adam was made by God, but this Word was made in God, an only son. *Full of grace and truth*, it says; he was full of grace, whereupon he brought grace to humankind, and truth without any falsehood, because no falsehood touched him and no vicissitude was able to come down into him as into Adam. For Adam handed his children into perdition and disinherited them. The second Adam was of such a sort that he led all the children of humankind to righteous moderation by himself, and this pure Adam set himself against all evils as well as all swells of iniquities, which the *ancient serpent*[17] began. When the human fell, the Son of God touched him with this sweetness, so that he would say: "Rise up, and say that you are a sinner and have transgressed God's command, which is penitence." With it he may make reparation for the perverted voice of the serpent that said: '*Eat and you will be like gods*'.[18]

[16] Isa 53:7.
[17] Rev 12:9.
[18] Gen 3:5.

Homilies 10 and 11

The Eve of
the Epiphany

Matthew 2:13-18

The angel of the Lord appeared in a dream to Joseph, saying: 'Rise and take the child and his mother and flee into Egypt. And be there until I tell you. For it will happen that Herod will search for the child to destroy him.' And rising up he took the child and his mother by night and departed into Egypt. And he was there until the death of Herod. What was spoken by the Lord through the prophet was fulfilled: 'Out of Egypt I have called my son.' Then Herod, seeing that he had been tricked by the wise men, became very angry. And he sent and killed all the male children who were in Bethlehem and all its region from two years of age and under, according to the time that he had sought after from the wise men. Then was fulfilled what was said by the prophet Jeremiah, saying: 'A voice in Ramah was heard, wailing and much lamentation. Rachel weeping for her children refused to be consoled.'

10. The Eve of the Epiphany, 1

The angel of the Lord appeared in a dream to Joseph, saying: 'Rise and take the child and his mother and flee into Egypt.' Clearly, the foreknowledge of God gave a sign to the patriarchs and prophets

in spiritual darkness, *saying: "'Rise'* from your sleeping and shadowy nature and *'take'* holiness in your desire and good knowledge and incline toward the unbelief of the peoples, so that they
might turn to righteousness." *'And be there until I tell you,'* that
is, until the gifts of the Holy Spirit work in them to put the devil
to shame. *'For it will happen that Herod will search for the child to
destroy him.'* From the outset the devil *'will search for'* holiness,
through diabolical plots with craftiness, in order to destroy it
completely. *And rising up, he took the child and his mother by night
and departed into Egypt.* [They rose up] from their shadowy nature
toward righteousness amidst great difficulties in order to convert
unbelievers. *And he was there until the death of Herod*; in other
words, until the Devil was put to shame, so that faithful humans
cast him out and chose God through the law. *What was spoken by
the Lord through the prophet was fulfilled: 'Out of Egypt I have called
my son.'* *What was spoken* by the Creator through God's mouth
and inspiration was completed. "From unbelievers and sinners
I chose believers, who are my children in faith; from pagans I
made Jews and from Jews I made Christians." *Then Herod, seeing
that he had been tricked,* that is, deceived, *by the wise men,* namely
the wise who resisted him, *became very angry* in astonishment
and trouble. *And he sent and killed all the male children who were in
Bethlehem and all its region from two years of age and under, according
to the time that he had sought after from the wise men.* By breathing out his plots, through the calf at Horeb[1] and through other
idols, he *killed* the simplicity they held for God in the law given
by God and in its meanings, from prophecy and the law and in
wisdom, like wise men. According to what he saw established
by the wise in divine worship he made idols and mockeries, and
magic arts and shrines, like Jeroboam who made two calves in
Dan and in Bethel.[2]

　　*Then was fulfilled what was said by the prophet Jeremiah, saying:
'A voice in Ramah was heard, wailing and much lamentation.'*[3] *What*

---

[1] See Exod 32:2.
[2] See 1 Kgs 12:28-29.
[3] Jer 31:15.

was said through a divine oracle was manifested: that God was
angered by vanities of this sort. Before God indignation and calumny were *'heard'* in complaint. *'Rachel weeping for her children,'*[4]
namely Wisdom, which says: "Who is this who rejects God and
venerates the devil?" Wisdom remembered the honors with which
the human had been created but yet rejected God. *'She refused to
be consoled'*[5] about the iniquity in which they were at that time;
they appeared lost, because they are not wholly in ruin. She was
looking toward God, seeking and begging that at last he restore
them into the bosom of his redemption through his own Son. For
concerning every matter that cannot be recuperated or restored,
it is necessary that a human of whatsoever sort have consolation
when nothing else can be done. Concerning a matter that will be
able to be recuperated or amended it is evident that as long as
it has not been amended the human will not be consoled. Thus,
until such time as one has the matter in mind one does not forget
it and attain consolation by its recuperation. Hence *'Rachel refused
to be consoled,'*[6] because they were to be redeemed through the
redemption of Christ's blood. She refused to hand [them over] to
oblivion, because they were to be redeemed. For when anyone is
in the distress of captivity the friends are not able to be consoled,
because they await that one's liberation.[7] But if someone has died,
they receive consolation, because they are not able to have the
person any more and they despair over the person, as was written about David also, who mourned his ill son but did not weep
for him once he was dead.[8]

[4] Jer 31:15.
[5] Jer 31:15.
[6] Jer 31:15.
[7] Because Hildegard speaks here in very general terms about human
situations she facilitates a translation with gender-inclusive language. At
other times her interpretation builds tightly on the identity of a male biblical
character (or group) and it is difficult to achieve a translation using inclusive
language.
[8] See 2 Sam 12:15-23.

11. The Eve of Epiphany, 2

The angel of the Lord appeared in a dream to Joseph, saying: 'Rise and take the child and his mother and flee into Egypt.' The admonition of the Holy Spirit admonished the human secretly, saying: "*'Rise'* by intellect and *'take'* knowledge and the substance of good works and go down into this affliction, so that you correct your sins. *'And be there until I tell you,'* evidently until God reveals his grace to you." *'For it will happen that Herod will search for the child to destroy him.'* Perhaps it will occur that the devil will toil to destroy the knowledge that is in the human.

And rising up he took the child and his mother by night and departed into Egypt, and he was there until the death of Herod. Lifting himself up, he afflicts himself with grief and moaning until the devil sees that he cannot overcome him and thus leaves him. *What was spoken by the Lord through the prophet was fulfilled: 'Out of Egypt I have called my son.'* Clearly, as God says: "From the affliction and darkness of sin I will lead forth the soul of one who believes in me, and that one will not die in eternity,[9] because I am the life, in whom darkness is never found. For to one who looks toward me from his sins I shall give life, as I did to Adam, whom I formed from clay."[10]

Then Herod, seeing that he had been tricked by the wise men, became very angry. The devil, understanding that he was deceived by the enlightenment of that mind, was thoroughly frightened. *And he sent and killed all the male children who were in Bethlehem and all its region, from two years of age and under, according to the time that he had sought after from the wise men.* Turning himself to others, because when he is not able to conquer one he turns to others, he deceives some good people, some devout people, and some chaste people who were upright and [doing] good works in knowledge of good and evil, because they were simple and unaware, as it is written: *There are ways that seem upright to humans.*[11] When they do not do many and great sins, in accordance with the enlightenment of

[9] See John 11:25.
[10] See Gen 2:7.
[11] See Prov 16:25; RB 7.21.

their minds they think that they are holy and do not find others like themselves, and the devout spurn the harsh, and the chaste vainly seek glory because of their chastity. *Then was fulfilled what was said by the prophet Jeremiah, saying*: evidently what was said by God in the Holy Spirit's exhortation, that no one is able to stand who wants to stand by his own effort, but the one whom God sustains will stand, because God is his staff.

   '*A voice in Ramah*,' namely of miseries, '*was heard*' above, '*wailing and much lamentation*,'[12] that is, distress and sadness when Pride oppressed Innocence by striking it.[13] '*Rachel weeping for her children*,'[14] evidently holiness, because the eyes of its knowledge brought forth weeping. She had lost '*her children*' even as the children, who were supposed to possess an inheritance, were disinherited; but the innocent lamb demanded them back with his own blood. '*She refused to be consoled*,'[15] because when humans rise up in repentance after the Fall, holiness leads them back to life with very great efforts. Since they are not forgotten before God they will rise up in repentance, even though holiness is not able to find them now in upright innocence, as innocent as they were at first.

---

[12] Jer 31:15.

[13] Pride striking Innocence is reminiscent of the *Psychomachia*, a fifth-century poem by Prudentius that widely influenced medieval art and literature, including the *Speculum uirginum*, a twelfth-century guide to the spiritual life. See Kienzle, *Speaking New Mysteries*, 204–5, 222–23.

[14] Jer 31:15.

[15] Jer 31:15.

Homilies 12 and 13

The Feast of
the Epiphany

Matthew 2:1-12

When Jesus was born, in the days of Herod the king, behold wise men from the East came to Jerusalem saying: 'Where is he who was born king of the Jews? For we have seen his star in the East and we have come to worship him.' But hearing this, Herod the king was troubled and all Jerusalem with him. And assembling all the leaders of the priests and the scribes of the people, he inquired from them where Christ would be born; and they told him: 'In Bethlehem of Judah. For so it is written by the prophet: "And you, O Bethlehem, in the land of Judah, are by no means least among the rulers of Judah. For from you will go forth a ruler who will govern my people Israel."' Then Herod, secretly, after summoning the wise men, diligently ascertained from them the time when the star appeared to them. And sending them into Bethlehem: 'Go, inquire diligently about the child; and when you have found him, report to me so that I too may come and worship him.' When they heard the king they went away. And behold the star they had seen in the East went before them, coming all the way until it would rest above where the child was. But seeing the star, they rejoiced exceedingly with great joy. And going into the house, they found the child with Mary, his mother. And going forward, they worshiped him; and after opening their treasures, they offered him gifts: gold, frankincense, and myrrh. And after receiving an answer in a dream that they should not return to Herod, they went back along another road into their own region.

12. The Feast of the Epiphany, 1

When Jesus was born in the days of Herod the king, behold wise men came from the East to Jerusalem saying: 'Where is he who was born king of the Jews?' In other words, when the Word of the Father, through which all things were created and freed,[1] had gone forth creating creatures, such that through him were created the four elements that nourish every creature that praises God, and at the origin when the devil also was created, who wanted to rule himself and to fulfill his own will, pagans and Jews *came* to search for *Jerusalem*.[2] They were questioners of things, with knowledge of good and evil, having been created and breathed out by God, because all wisdom is from the Lord God. They *came to Jerusalem*, where humans had made dwellings, repose, discipline, and law for themselves according to their faith, *saying*: "By what law should he be worshiped, *'he who was born'* before the ages and before creatures, *'king'* of all who praise him? *'For we have seen his star in the East,'* in the eyes of the hearts' knowledge,[3] *'we have seen'* his gifts going forth from divinity, such as the strength in Samson or the wisdom in Solomon. *'And we have come'* seeking *'to worship him,'* so that we may know that there is none except him."

But hearing this, because he perceived by his own knowledge, *Herod the king,* clearly, the devil, who exercised his power in the world, *was troubled and all Jerusalem with him.* He *was* in distress, that God was demanding it,[4] who was more glorious and more powerful than he. Those who were living in their own law, which they had constituted for themselves by their own observance,

---

[1] See John 1:3.

[2] In this homily Jesus is the Word, newly incarnate, but also the child, innocence; the wise men represent pagans and Jews who come to seek him, and Herod stands for the devil, who attempts to thwart their search.

[3] Hildegard uses the plural here: Latin *in oculis cordium*.

[4] The Latin reads *quia Deus requirebat*. The pagans and Jews were seeking God in the newly incarnate Son. Hence, one might expect a passive form here: "God was being sought." The active verb *requirebat* seems to indicate that God was the power behind their asking; therefore, God was the one demanding or asking them to seek.

were *troubled,* as was the devil, pondering whether they would dwell uprightly in righteousness or not.

And assembling all the leaders of the priests and the scribes of the people, he inquired from them where Christ would be born. Clearly, the devil assembled in astonishment the chiefs and leaders who gave the laws for different worship, those who observed that same worship, those who arranged that worship, and those who simply practiced it at that time; *he inquired* cleverly *from* the worshipers *where* the one whom they wanted to consider greater would be born.[5]

And they, that is, those who had wisdom of this world, *told him,* in accordance with what they thought, *'in Bethlehem of Judah,'* that is, in the four elements that praise him among created things. *'For so it is written by the prophet,'* evidently, found and perceived by rationality: *"And you, O Bethlehem in the land of Judah,"*[6] that is, the four elements in the practice and sustenance of creatures praising God, *"are by no means least* in your strength, because you will be great *among the rulers,* that is, among the angels in miracles and in reports of those praising God, because they worship God with the angels in praise, and you will praise him most excellently. *For from you will go forth a ruler who will govern my people Israel,* namely, one who will be human, born from a virgin, saving and also ruling humans. He *will govern* uprightly those who are rational and who are mine, seeing God on account of their rationality."

Then Herod secretly, after summoning the wise men, diligently ascertained from them the time when the star appeared to them. The devil, in his craftiness, *after summoning* the questioners of creatures, demanded the taste for understanding the gifts of God, who was revealed to them.

---

[5] Hildegard uses the word *cultura* three times as well as the verb *coluerunt* (worshiped) and *cultoribus* (worshipers), which seems to indicate that she is referring not to culture or observance in general but to worship, and specifically to idol worship, which she associates with the devil and his temptations and with the time before Christ. See Homily 25, 114–15.

[6] See Mic 5:2; John 7:42.

And sending them into Bethlehem: 'Go and inquire diligently about the child.' He sent them away with the poison of deception into the four elements, in which there is nourishment for creatures, speaking even as Balaam did,[7] and others like him. "Search, with many investigations concerning the innocence that you will seek. *And when you have found him, report to me, so that I too may come and worship him.* In other words, *when you have found* innocence, by the appetite for rationality, return *to me* with carnal appetite, *so that I too may come* through dissimulating deceptions, as if I were to slay him with honor, by fornication, avarice, and similar things." *When they had heard the king,* that is, the devil in their knowledge, *they went away,* seeking these things with much worldly wisdom.

And behold the star they had seen in the East went before them, coming all the way until it would rest over the place where the child was. The taste for the gifts of God *they had seen* with the eyes of knowledge proceeding from divinity *went before them* in Abraham and in Moses by the commandments of the law, *where* childlike innocence *was* held on high by obedience. *But seeing the star, they rejoiced exceedingly with great joy. But* with their knowledge, *seeing* the gifts of God in circumcision, *they rejoiced* in the wisdom of rationality such that their souls tasted heavenly things.

And going into the house, they found the child with Mary, his mother. And going into the law of righteousness, *they found* innocence with virginity[8] in the observance of the law, which foreshadowed the incarnation of Christ. *His mother* clearly [stands for] innocence, because virginity confers the innocence that Cain lost by shedding his brother's blood; whence afterwards the innocent Christ arose for saving the people. *And going forward, they worshiped him and, after opening their treasures, they offered him gifts.* In the experience of faith *they worshiped,* knowing God in truth; *and after opening* their desires, they persisted in prayer with hope, binding themselves fast in love of God with the sacrifice of burnt offering.

[7] See Num 31:16.

[8] Hildegard uses *uirginalitas* here, in contrast to *uirginitas* below. See Kienzle, *Speaking New Mysteries*, 229–32.

And after receiving an answer in a dream that they should not return to Herod, they went back along another road into their own region. In other words, through salutary inspiration through that very desire, in the shadow of prophecy, they returned not to heresy, which comes from the devil, but to themselves and toward the choice of a heavenly reward through the living God, because the god they had previously worshiped was false and dead.

13. The Feast of the Epiphany, 2

When Jesus was born in Bethlehem of Judah, in the days of Herod the king, behold wise men from the East came to Jerusalem, saying: 'Where is he who was born king of the Jews?' Jesus, who is the Savior of the world, is *born* in the sighing and tears of the repentant human being who confesses his sins.[9] At the time of temptation by the devil, who leads to evil ways the humans who serve him and his pomp, *behold* the perception of God, when a human is converted to God by the birth of God's grace.[10] In spiritual joy, in the vision of peace, God receives a repentant human. With God's grace the human is *born* in repentance through God's gifts, because God has the power to forgive sins for those who confess them. *'For we have seen his star in the East and we have come to worship him.'* "We have experienced good report at the birth of the grace of his miracles, *'and we have come'* with good intention to make known the one who brings these things about in a sinful human being."

But hearing this, Herod the king was troubled and all Jerusalem with him. Clearly, the temptation of the devil, who reigns in iniquity, understood in fright all the trust the repentant human ought to have then in the quiet of peace. The devil inflicts him with many temptations during his repentance.

---

[9] Here Jesus is the Savior, Herod represents the devil, and the other personages stand for qualities that play a role in the process of repentance. The wise men slowly emerge in the text as "Knowledge of God."

[10] Latin: *in ortu* means at the birth, rising of the sun, dawning, or origin. Since Hildegard is commenting on the actual birth of Jesus, "birth" seems the best translation.

And assembling all the leaders of the priests and the scribes of the people, he inquired from them where Christ would be born. Deceitfully investigating those who prophesied the gospels,[11] since prophecy preceded the gospels, as well as the commentators and teachers of the faithful,[12] *he inquired* through his guile how it could be that the sinner would rise up through repentance, as if it were impossible that the sinner would rise up to salvation.

And they told him: 'In Bethlehem of Judah, for it is written by the prophet: "And you, O Bethlehem, [in the land] of Judah, are by no means least among the rulers of Judah."'[13] The teachers of the truth answered: "In repentance,[14] which knows sin by confessing in humility, are found the multiple occasions of God's grace. Repentance, rising up from earthly matters by confession, is clearly great among the virtues, as are chastity, continence, holiness, and the like. *'For from you will go forth a ruler who will govern my people Israel.'"* God's grace says: "Because repentance crushes the devil in the abyss,[15] a savior, who rules in heaven and on earth, will forgive sins for the *people* whom I touch and who look upon God among the virtues."[16]

Then Herod secretly, after summoning the wise men, diligently ascertained from them the time when the star appeared to them. The devil, *summoning* Knowledge of God as if a friend, deceitfully sought

[11] Latin: *prophetae euangelicorum.*

[12] This is one of several references to commentators on Scripture, *the expositores*, with whom Hildegard implicitly places herself at times. See Kienzle, *Speaking New Mysteries*, 78–80, and Homily 47, p. 178, where she names "Gregory, Ambrose, Augustine, Jerome, and others like them."

[13] See Mic 5:2, John 7:42.

[14] Here and elsewhere in the homily Hildegard uses the Latin *penitentia*, which refers not only to the feeling or state of penitence but also to the resolve to change one's life. "Repentance" seems to convey that more clearly than "penitence" would.

[15] Hildegard uses this image in *Sciuias* 2.7.5, p. 303. See Kienzle, *Speaking New Mysteries*, 191–92.

[16] The Latin here reads: *"populum meum* quem ego tango, dicit gratia Dei, Israel, qui in uirtutibus Deum inspicit." The *qui* follows Israel and refers back to *populum meum*, understood as *Israel*, and not to either *gratia*, which would require the feminine *quae*, or to *Dei*, which would be grammatically correct but not make sense.

from Knowledge of God with an evil notion the beginning and intention of good report, which *appeared* in the attempt at finding.[17]

And sending them into Bethlehem, he said: 'Go, and inquire diligently about the child.' And *sending them* deceptively to repentance, *he said*: "Lift yourselves up with vainglory *'and inquire'* with a false choice how these things have been done, so that he wishes to be innocent. *'And when you have found him, report to me so that I may come also and worship him.'* In other words, when this has been shown to you, join yourselves to me with dissimulating pride, such that he thinks he is so holy that no one may be like him."

And when they had heard the king they went away. When Knowledge of God had been there, namely when they had understood the devil's temptation in its evil deception, *they went away* scrutinizing what the human's repentance would be in his innocence. *And behold the star they had seen in the East went before them, coming all the way until it would rest over the place where the child was. They had seen* good report at the birth of God's grace; it *went before them* in upright perception and wisdom, *until* when sought after *it would rest* with the stability of perseverance *over* innocence in the human. *But seeing the star, they rejoiced with great joy; seeing* upright report in simplicity without vainglory, *they rejoiced with* unfeigned faith.[18]

And going into the house they found the child with Mary, his mother. And going into the chamber where the sinner abandoned his sins and holiness rose up *they found* innocence with the shining and salutary material of holiness. *And going forward, they worshiped him.* Evidently, making these things manifest, *they worshiped* with praises the one who brought about these things in the sinner. *And after opening their treasures,* evidently with good will at the outset of their deeds, which signifies great merit, *they offered him gifts: gold,* that the human begins to know God; *frankincense,* that he reveals his sins in confession, *and myrrh,* that he prostrates his entire self in constraint.

---

[17] Hildegard may be referring to the humans' attempt to find repentance or to the attempt the devil made to find good report, or to both.
[18] Hildegard uses alliteration here, echoing 1 Tim 1:5: *fide non ficta.*

And after receiving an answer in a dream that they should not return to Herod, along another road they went back into their own region. After the manifestation of the Holy Spirit *that they should not* revert evilly to the devil's temptation, *they went back,* living well and uprightly in the living God to the righteousness through which the righteous human will have an inheritance.

Homilies 14 and 15

The Sunday in the Octave of the Epiphany

Luke 2:42-52

When Jesus had reached the age of twelve they went up to Jerusalem according to the custom of the feast day. And when the feast days were ended, as they were returning, the boy Jesus remained in Jerusalem and his parents did not know. But supposing him to be in the company, they went a day's journey, and they searched for him among their relatives and acquaintances. Not finding him, they returned to Jerusalem seeking him.

And it happened after three days that they found him in the temple, sitting in the midst of the teachers, listening to them and questioning them. And all who heard him were amazed at his understanding and his answers. And seeing him they were astonished. And his mother said: 'Son, why did you do this to us? Behold your father and I, sorrowful, were searching for you.' And he said to them: 'Why is it that you sought me? Did you not know that it is necessary for me to be among the things of my Father?' And they did not understand the word that he spoke to them.

And he went down with them and came to Nazareth, and was obedient to them. And his mother kept all these words in her heart. And Jesus increased in wisdom and stature and grace before God and humans.

14. The Sunday in the Octave of the Epiphany, 1

When Jesus had reached the age of twelve they went up to Jerusalem according to the custom of the feast day. In other words, when the

miracles of Christ's incarnation had been carried out by the twelve
prophets, in that they had completed their prophecy about him,
the faithful who were announcing that he was going to become
human *went up* into the peace of redemption, toward which they
gazed, in accordance with the most brilliantly splendid foretelling,
that the Son of God was made human.[1] *And when the feast days
were ended, although they set out to return, the boy Jesus remained in
Jerusalem, and his parents did not know.* Clearly, when the prophets
had carried out all the signs that were supposed to foretell about
Christ, they then ceased prophesying on the incarnation of the
Lord. Once incarnate, he himself performed the work of redemption, because the Jewish people in the Old Law did not know that
he was the Son of God in human form.

*But supposing him to be in the company, they went a day's journey
and they began to search for him among their relatives and acquaintances. Not finding him, they returned to Jerusalem, seeking him.* Turning this way and that in their pondering, they thought that he was
like other holy people. They were seeking him in the profundity
of the prophets, *and they searched for him* with their knowledge
and intellect. Not finding that he resembled the others in any
likeness, *they returned* to the redemption of peace; with scrutiny,
they sought out among philosophers and wise men what would
be evident in him.

*And it happened after three days that they found him in the temple,
sitting in the midst of the teachers, listening to them and questioning
them.* It came to pass after the revelation of the prophets, the wise,
and the prudent, *that* by revealed signs and supernal sanctity[2]
they found him in the very great teaching of the Father's precepts.
He was *listening to them,* in the argument with which he convinced
them, *and questioning them* as to who their God was. *But all who
heard him were amazed at his understanding and his answers.* Clearly,
human understanding trembled with new hearing *at his* unparal-
leled wisdom *and his answers* to the confounding inquiries. *And*

---

[1] In this homily Hildegard interprets the pericope in light of the "Old Law"
and the prophets who anticipate and search for the incarnate son of God.

[2] Hildegard employs alliteration here: *in superna sanctitate.*

seeing him, that is, all his knowledge of the Scriptures, *they were astonished,* such that they could not marvel fully at these miracles.

And his mother said to him: 'Son, why did you act this way to us?' In other words, the Old Law *said* to him: "Incarnate one in human form, we have waited and expected you for a long time." *'Behold, your father and I, sorrowful, were searching for you,'* namely, Abraham and the Old Law, with many desires and sorrows, *were searching,* as it is written: *Would that you would break open the heavens and descend!*[3]

And he, the incarnate Son of God, *said to them: 'Why is it that you sought me'* "and doubted?" *'Did you not know that it is necessary for me to be among the things of my Father?'* In other words, *'did you not know'* the ram caught in the thorns and the burning bush that Moses saw,[4] and as it was written: *Behold a virgin will conceive and will bear a son,*[5] and: *'It is necessary for me to be among the things of my Father,'* "because I, the word of the Father, will fulfill his will in my flesh"?[6] *And they did not understand the word that he spoke to them.* Evidently Abraham and the Old Law did not understand that the Word of the Father was a human being, since they saw him signified not in flesh but only in a shadow.[7]

And he went down with them and came to Nazareth and was subject to them. On account of humanity *he went down* from the Father's bosom in humility *and came* into circumcision and the law *and was subject* to all things established by the precepts of the law. *And his mother kept all these words in her heart.* The Old Law kept hidden within itself, in its books and significations, all the signs that were done with him and through him.

And Jesus increased in wisdom and stature, toward perfection in prophecy and law, *and grace,* when the *fullness of time*[8] came in

[3] Isa 64:1.

[4] See Gen 22:13; Exod 3:2.

[5] Isa 7:14.

[6] Hildegard includes all these signs within one sweeping question.

[7] Latin *umbra,* a term that appears frequently in Augustine and other patristic writings. See the *apparatus fontium* to the *Expo. Euang.* 227.

[8] Gal 4:4.

the Gospel, *before God and humans,* that is, *before* divine fortitude, so that it would be known by all that he was God and human.

15. The Sunday in the Octave of the Epiphany, 2

When Jesus had reached the age of twelve they went up to Jerusalem according to the custom of the feast day. In other words, when the time was accomplished that Rationality in the human reached the age of discernment such that a human knows good and evil, the admonition of the Holy Spirit and of Wisdom *went up* to faith *according to the custom,* which is just.[9] *And when the feast days were ended, although they set out to return, the boy Jesus remained in Jeru-salem, and his parents did not know.* Clearly, when the good begin-ning of the brilliant deed that began there was finished,[10] they ceased admonishing, saying: "See what you do now, because I led you to a good beginning." Rationality *remained in* faith and lays up treasure within itself, determining inwardly what it is going to do. And they *did not know* the brilliance and perfection of its deeds, because it had not yet arrived at the end of its work.

But supposing him to be in the company, they went a day's journey and began to search for him among their relatives and acquaintances. Not finding him, they returned to Jerusalem, seeking him. [Rationality] reckoned along the usual path of self will, regarding whether it did good deeds and considering the vices and virtues, and whether it was between the vices or virtues. They were *not find-ing* the human at work, but only reckoning with himself what he wished to do. They looked back to the faith to which they had led him, *seeking* him, because it is not good for a human to keep silent about his good works and to be useful only to himself. Let him do good things openly, offering examples also to others.

---

[9] Hildegard interprets the pericope here as the process of human ratio-nality coming to make the ethical choice between good and evil and being guided by Wisdom and the Holy Spirit (Mary and Joseph).

[10] Hildegard uses the repetition of prefixes to emphasize her point: *inicium* (beginning) and *incepit* (began).

And it happened after three days that they found him in the temple, seated in the midst of the teachers, listening to them and questioning them. When this admonition was completed accordingly, because the human is rational and receives faith and also has the will for accomplishing the good, *they found him seated* in good deeds, as it is written: *Lord, let my prayer be directed* to you *like the incense in your sight*,[11] that is, beginning to do good to all, following the examples of other holy persons, inquiring after good things, and running after the saints.

All who heard him were amazed by the good edification of holy deeds. When good report goes out about *his understanding* of new sanctification *and his answers*, they believe that it is as they hear in good report.[12] *And seeing his conversion they were amazed*, because joy arises from that. *And his mother*, clearly, Wisdom, *said to him: 'Son, why did you act this way to us?'*; "that is, placing yourself in hiding. I do not want you to conceal your treasure, but to proceed openly in good deeds. *'Behold your father and I,'* namely the Holy Spirit's admonition, which inspired you to the good, clearly, Wisdom, who nourished you gently, *'would be sorrowful'* if you dishonored us, that is, if you bore our work to no avail. *'We were searching for you'* because we do not want you to dishonor us in this way, that we would not be recognized in you."

And Rationality in the human *said to them: 'Why is it that you were seeking me?'* "I fear that if I go about openly, vainglory will impede me." *'Did you not know that it is necessary for me to be among the things of my Father?'* "In other words, the admonition of the Holy Spirit reveals that I will always be in humility. It is necessary for me to flee pride and boasting."

And they did not understand the word that he spoke to them, because they did not want him to cast himself upon the ground and hide his good works, such that others would not be edified from them; but rather that he have humility and fear in them, but still allow them to shine forth discreetly. It is as if they said: "Our work has

[11] Ps 140:2.
[12] Hildegard uses the present tense for the commentary, even though the Scripture is in the imperfect.

been revealed, and we have not fallen. We desire that you also act in this way and do not doubt; because a person sometimes mistrusts God's grace, such that he conceals the gift of God within himself and hides it too much, and God does not want this."

And he went down with them and came to Nazareth and was subject to them. In other words, when a human abandons his own will he enters into evident good deeds, and he is *subject to them* in great fear. *And his mother,* that is, Wisdom, *kept all these words in her heart,* that is, she kept fear, anxiety, and obedience in her memory.

And Jesus increased in wisdom and age and grace before God and humans. Clearly, the human *increased* in a multitude of good deeds, because he was steadfast in righteous deeds, namely in their fullness; because in the secret place of the heart one is good in the presence of God and humans when one dwells openly with them in good deeds.

Homilies 16 and 17

The Second Sunday after the Epiphany

John 2:1-11

There was a wedding at Cana in Galilee, and the mother of Jesus was there. Jesus and his disciples were also invited to the wedding. And when the wine ran out, Jesus' mother said to him: 'They have no wine.' And Jesus said to her: 'What is it to me and to you, woman? My hour has not yet come.' His mother said to the servants: 'Whatever he tells you, do it.'

Now there were six stone jars placed according to the purification rite of the Jews, each holding two or three gallons.[1] Jesus said to the servants: 'Fill the jars with water.' And they filled them all the way to the brim. And Jesus said to them: 'Now draw it out and bring it to the steward.' And they brought it. But the steward tasted the water become wine and did not know where it came from, although the servants who had drawn out the water knew.

The steward summoned the bridegroom and said to him: 'Everyone serves the good wine first, and when they become inebriated, then that which is inferior. But you have kept the good wine until now.'

Jesus performed the first of [his] signs at Cana in Galilee and manifested his glory, and his disciples believed in him.

---

[1] Note the numbers two and three instead of twenty and thirty, as in the RSV.

16. The Second Sunday after the Epiphany, 1

There was a wedding at Cana in Galilee, and the mother of Jesus was there. When God formed Adam and Eve, in that punishment when God gave them the divine command and in the transgression when they disobeyed God's command, the humanity of the Savior *was there*, because Christ was going to be born from Adam and Eve's descendants since Adam was the physical source of the entire human race.

Jesus and his disciples, that is, the Savior through his incarnation, the prophets, and all who spoke about his incarnation, *were also invited to the wedding*, namely, to the creation of the human, whom Christ was going to redeem. *And when the wine ran out, Jesus' mother said to him: 'They have no wine.'* Clearly, when the appetite and veneration for the divine were tepid, when Adam was exiled from Paradise, Jesus' humanity admonished the word of the Father: "In their knowledge *'they have no'* appetite for the divine." *And Jesus said to her* responding: "'*What is it to me,*' because all things were created through me, *'and to you, woman?'* In other words, humanity is present to me, inasmuch as I created all things, and to you, inasmuch as you were my covering.[2] *The spirit certainly is willing, but the flesh is weak.*[3] *'My hour has not yet come'* when I will transform all creatures into the eternity of steadfastness."

His mother said to the servants, in other words, Christ's humanity declared to those who serve God by observing the law: *'Whatever'* "in divine commandments" *'he tells you'* "in a revelation of faith," *'do it'* "by fulfilling it, because it is good, true and upright."

Now there were six stone jars placed according to the purification rite of the Jews, each holding two or three gallons. In the descendancy of Adam, whom God had formed, *there were six* things to be observed: clearly, the five books of Moses, and sixth, the Gospel, which the Holy Spirit breathed out like fire from a rock.[4] [The

---

[2] Latin *indumentum* often refers to the human nature or flesh of Christ.

[3] Mark 14:38; Matt 26:41.

[4] Hildegard seems to have in mind Moses drawing water from the rock (Exod 17:6), echoed by Paul in 1 Cor 10:4, when she expresses the Holy Spirit's inspiration of the gospels as breathing fire from a rock.

six were] *placed* as a sign, so that through the Scriptures the filth of sins would be purged from humans who praise God. *Each was holding* two or three measures, because *by the very same measure which they measure out will it be returned to them.*[5] *Two* [designate] love of God and neighbor; *three* represent divinity, as in Noah; circumcision, as in Abraham; the Lord's incarnation, as in Moses.

Jesus said to the servants: 'Fill the jars with water.' Jesus said, with the power of his breath:[6] "'*Fill*' the Old and New Testaments '*with water*' of wisdom, so that humanity may know God." *And they filled them* with diverse knowledge *all the way to the brim*. When the human by circumcision and by law could do nothing further they desired that the word of the Father would be incarnated, and they then exclaimed: *Would that you would break open heaven and descend!*[7]

And Jesus said to them: 'Now draw it out and bring it to the steward.' And Jesus admonished: "'*Now draw out*' in me what you do not have in yourself, and show it to the Old Testament, because when a human begins to know God he afterwards works for the good, and then embraces God in the law." *And they brought it*, when they gave good report.

But the steward tasted the water become wine and did not know from where it came. Evidently the Old Testament understood the Father's wisdom when *the word was made flesh*[8] and did not know how the Son of God was incarnated, because the Jews refused to believe that God was human. *However, the servants who had drawn out the water knew.* The observers of the law understood; they who had examined the Father's wisdom were seeing it through the law.

The steward summoned the bridegroom and said to him: 'Everyone serves the good wine first; and when they become inebriated, then that

---

[5] Matt 7:2; Mark 4:24.

[6] The Latin here and again below, *in inspiratione*, seeks to evoke Gen 2:7b: *et inspiravit in faciem eius spiraculum vitae*. With this language Hildegard underscores Jesus' eternality and presence at the creation as well as his power to work miracles.

[7] Isa 64:1. Hildegard cites this in another instance to express a historical desire for Christ's incarnation.

[8] John 1:14.

which is inferior.' The Old Testament, marveling that the word of the Father *was made flesh,*[9] in amazement *summoned* Adam and Eve, who were in the first wedding of human creation *and said* in astonishment:[10] "All nations reveal[11] their flowering and splendid virtues in their youth; when they grow old in their labors, they then diminish." For Abel, Abraham, and Moses brought forth many good things in the law; but at present there is failing in nearly all these things. *'But you have kept the good wine until now.'* "In your descendants *'you have kept'* the greatest virtue after the law up to the last days, because God is called man, and nothing is more splendid."

Jesus performed his first sign at Cana in Galilee and manifested his glory, and his disciples believed in him. Clearly, *Jesus performed the first sign* of humankind's redemption in punishment when Adam was exiled from Paradise, revealing that he changed Adam's death into life and the law into the Gospel through himself; *and* all who *believed in him* through faith were glorifying his incarnation.

17. The Second Sunday after the Epiphany, 2

There was a wedding at Cana in Galilee and the mother of Jesus was there. In the joy of new offspring,[12] when a human recognizes and rebukes himself, he judges his own evils zealously and, being transformed, leaves his sins behind. The good example of the bearer of God the Savior *was there* in the joy of new offspring.

Jesus and his disciples were also invited to the wedding. Jesus was *invited,* with good intention, to assist through the power of di-

[9] John 1:14.

[10] Here and above Hildegard uses words from the same root: *obstupendo* and *in stupore.*

[11] This sentence offers a simple example of grammatical agreement in Hildegard's commentary, as the third-person singular of the text is transformed into the plural of her narrative: "*Omnis homo . . . ponit*" becomes "*cunctae nationes . . . ostendunt.*"

[12] Perhaps Hildegard has in mind Deut 30:9, where God promises abundance of many sorts to those who keep the commandments. The person who repents experiences a new birth of self.

vinity, with the footprints he sowed,[13] so that the human would accomplish a good deed when he recognizes himself. *And when the wine ran out, Jesus' mother said to him: 'They have no wine.'* When the virtue of perfection *ran out* in humans, good examples *said* in perceiving what was lacking: " *'They have no'* virtue of perfection, unless you, God, give it to them."

And Jesus said to her: 'What is it to me and to you, woman?' And the Savior *said* to good example: " *'What is it to me'* in giving *'and to you'* in seeking what is said: 'You, flesh, will seek and I will give.' *'My hour has not yet come,'* that is, the *'hour'* of perfection, so that you may be perfected before you come into eternity."

His mother said to the servants: 'Whatever he tells you, do it.' [Good example] gave counsel to the virtues: *'Whatever'* "in divine orders" *'he tells you,'* "fulfill the commands that were given to you."

Now there were six jars of stone placed according to the purification rite of the Jews, each one holding two or three gallons. In the joy over new offspring *there* was hardness in humankind, five in the senses and the sixth in self will. [They were] given *according to the* honor of those who praise God, beholding him on high, and they diligently embraced measures: *two,* so that they abandon themselves in his will,[14] *or three,* clearly in love, fear, and perfection.

Jesus said to the servants, that is, the virtues*: 'Fill,'* "resounding in praises," *'the jars,'* "clearly, the form of humankind," *'with water,'* "that is, with the good journey." *And they,* the angels and peoples, *filled them all the way to the brim*; clearly, they reached God with their praises. *And Jesus said to them,* with the power of his breath: *'Draw it out'* "with praise" *'and bring it to the steward,'*

[13] Here Hildegard combines the biblical images of footprints (*vestigia*) and sowing (*semino, -are*); instead of sowing a particular virtue, the footsteps, as paths to virtue, are sown. Perhaps she is playing with the closeness in sound between forms of *semino* and the word *semita, -ae,* footpath, which would connect in meaning to *vestigia.*

[14] Latin *in uoluntate sua* seems to refer to God's will, as opposed to the self-will Hildegard just mentioned in the homily. She does occasionally use a reflexive to refer to the subject of discourse (God).

"dividing it for all people." *And they brought it*, so that it would be accomplished in this way.

But the steward tasted the water become wine, and did not know from where it came. All people understood the good journey in the human, that is, when it was completed by a good deed, but did not understand from which gifts of God *it came. But the servants, who had drawn out the water, knew*; that is, the virtues that minister and carry the gifts of the Holy Spirit on the good journey.

The steward summoned the bridegroom and said to him: 'Everyone serves the good wine first; and when they become inebriated then that which is inferior.' [All people] *summoned* with praises the human who recognizes himself, *and* astonished *said to him*: "Human custom, attempting in haste what it could do in uprightness, extends the virtue of perfection so that it may be known by all. When all have seen this, it serves *'that which is inferior'* on account of unjust report. *'But you have kept the good wine until now.'* In the scrutinizing of scrutiny[15] *'you have kept'* perfection for the best part in repentance,[16] when humans are converted to the good."

Jesus performed the first sign at Cana in Galilee and manifested his glory, and his disciples believed in him. A human is pierced by compunction when he judges himself through divine inspiration, passing through sins into penitence, *and has manifested* in the "new man" that he came to heal sinners.[17] Those who followed his footsteps in repentance praise him.

---

[15] The Latin is repetitive and alliterative: *in scrutinio scrutationis*.
[16] See Luke 10:42.
[17] See 1 Tim 1:15.

Homilies 18 and 19

The Third Sunday after the Epiphany

Matthew 8:1-13

When Jesus had come down from the mountain, many crowds followed him. And behold a leper, arriving, worshiped him, saying: 'Lord, if you wish, you are able to cleanse me.' And extending his hand, he touched him saying: 'I will to cleanse you.' And immediately his leprosy was cleansed. And Jesus said to him: 'See that you tell this to no one; but go and show yourself to the priest and offer the gift that Moses commanded as testimony to the people.' When, further, he had entered Capernaum a centurion came up to him, questioning him and saying: 'Lord, my servant is lying paralyzed at home and is terribly distressed.' And Jesus said to him: 'I will come and heal him.' And responding, the centurion said: 'Lord, I am not worthy that you should enter under my roof. But only say the word and my servant will be healed. For I also am a man under authority, having soldiers under me; and I say to this one: "Go," and he goes; and to another: "Come," and he comes; and to my slave: "Do this," and he does it.'

Jesus, hearing this, marveled; and to those following him he said: 'Amen I say to you, I have not found so much faith in Israel. I say to you that many will come from the east and the west and will sit at table with Abraham, Isaac, and Jacob in the kingdom of heaven. But the sons of the kingdom will be cast down into the outer darkness. There will be weeping and gnashing of teeth.' And Jesus said to the centurion: 'Go, and as you have believed, so may it be done for you.' And the servant was healed in that hour.

18. The Third Sunday after the Epiphany, 1

When Jesus had come down from the mountain, many crowds fol-
lowed him. When the fullness of the Holy Spirit felt compassion
and *came down* from divinity, the virtues *followed* in obedience.
And behold a leper, arriving, worshiped him, saying: 'Lord, if you will,
you are able to cleanse me.' The vicissitude of the vices in humankind, which the *ancient serpent*[1] won over for himself, knowing
that it was not clean, subjected itself to him, *saying: 'Lord,'* "you
who inspire all good things," *'if you will, you are able'* "by your
power" *'to cleanse me,'* "so that I may be touched by your gentleness, because I am unrighteous."[2]

And extending his hand, he touched him, saying: 'I will cleanse you.'
Pouring out his gifts, the Holy Spirit anointed *him, saying*: "I am
able to *'cleanse you,'* since you have called upon me." *And im-*
mediately his leprosy was cleansed; clearly the serpent's gullet was
strangled in the human.

And Jesus said to him: 'See that you tell this to no one, but go and
show yourself to the priest and offer the gift that Moses commanded
as testimony to the people.' The fullness of the Holy Spirit *said* to
the vicissitude of vices: "Take heed that you not lead my gift
into vainglory, as if you were holy; *'but go'* on the right journey
'and show yourself' to the one who renews humankind *'and offer'*
repentance by the gift of baptism through the sign of the dove."

When he had entered Capernaum, that is, visiting for the purpose
of taking possession of and removing vices,[3] with the result that
they ceased, *a centurion came up to him, questioning*; clearly, Repentance beseeched *him,* humbly *saying: 'Lord, my servant is lying*
paralyzed at home and is terribly distressed.' In other words, Igno-

---

[1] Rev 12:9.

[2] Hildegard uses the phrase *uicissitudo uiciorum.* I have kept the alliteration in the translation. It is this quality of variability in the vices that speaks
here. The following section of commentary repeats the sounds of "s," and I
have tried to preserve those in the translation by using "vicissitude" rather
than the more common word, "variability."

[3] Latin: *in possessionem subtractionis,* is difficult to render into English.

rance is sleeping, weary in its heart's habitation,[4] *'and is terribly distressed'* by a great stench of vices.

And Jesus said to him, in other words, to Repentance: *'I will come and will heal him'* through inspiration, by touching him. *And responding, the centurion said: 'Lord, I am not worthy that you should enter under my roof. But only say the word and my servant will be healed.'* Recollecting, Repentance *said:* "Due to weariness, *'I am not worthy that you should enter'* my intelligible understanding, as it is written: *Day and night your hand is heavy over me; I am turned in my hardship, while the thorn is inserted."*[5] "Look upon the holiness of the saints who were redeemed through the Father's Word; I plead for help from them, because your divinity is too great for me; and clearly Ignorance *'will be healed'* by their merits."[6]

'For I also am a man,' "that is, I have transgressed," *'under authority, having soldiers under me,'* "that is, with the potential from you, namely my own will"; *'and I say to this one: "Go," and he goes; and to another: "Come, and he comes;" and to my slave: "Do this," and he does it.'* "I turn my will where I wish; because if I have one will in weariness, I put aside that will, and I command another, and it comes; and I say to the custom of perverse deeds: *'Do'* your perverse custom, and it accomplishes it."

Jesus, hearing this, marveled, and to those following him he said: 'Amen I say, I have not found so much faith in Israel.' Knowing [this], the fullness of the Holy Spirit *marveled* joyfully at the holy deeds that imitated him,[7] and *said:* "In truth," *'I have not'* "seen such a

---

[4] For the Latin phrase here: *"puer meus,* scilicet ignorantia, *iacet* dormiendo *paraliticus,* id est tedio affectus," *affectus* may be either the nominative past participle agreeing with the preceding *paraliticus* (affected by weariness), or the genitive of the noun *affectus, -us* (m) (with weariness of devotion/emotion). In either case it is clear that Hildegard intends to say that *ignorantia* is weary, and I have translated accordingly.

[5] Ps 31:4; Latin *conversus sum in aerumpna mea: dum configitur spina.*

[6] Ignorance and Repentance appear in this homily both as personified characters and as abstract qualities. When personified, they are capitalized. On such variations in the *Expositiones,* see Kienzle, *Speaking New Mysteries,* 216–17.

[7] Latin *ipsum* seems to refer to Jesus and not to the Spirit.

mirror among those who wanted to be holy, as the hypocrites also
in the devil." *'I say to you that many will come from the east and the
west and will sit at table with Abraham, Isaac, and Jacob in the kingdom
of heaven.'* "In other words, *'I say'* to good deeds *'that many will'*
arise from Adam's fall and among the tax collectors *'and will sit'*
in power, who worship the true Trinity and do penance by my
brilliant work." *'But the sons of the kingdom will be cast down into the
outer darkness.'* "Evidently demons and those who imitate them
with false holiness and hypocrisy, and who want to be prudent in
their own presence, but are foolish, will be despised when I neither touch them by my grace nor want to see them, because they
did not know themselves." *'There will be weeping,'* "because they
fled my joy in their ignorance," *'and gnashing of teeth,'* "because
they refused to speak my words, and therefore they also will not
be nourished by the food of life."

*And Jesus said to the centurion: 'Go, and as you have believed, so
may it be done for you.'* And [the Spirit] *said* to Repentance: *'Go'* "on
this journey, as you have begun, when you recognized yourself in
your ignorance"; *'so may'* "the help you sought" *'be done for you.'*
And the servant was healed in that hour. Virtue was restored, and
Ignorance turned to good and upright knowledge, when divine
grace shook it beneficially.[8]

19. The Third Sunday after the Epiphany, 2

*When Jesus had come down from the mountain, many crowds fol-
lowed him.* When Jesus came to humankind, that is, the breath
knowing good and evil,[9] which God sent to humankind from the
height that arouses all things, all the creatures with the elements
served and perceived him.

*And behold a leper, arriving, worshiped him, saying: 'Lord, if you
wish you are able to cleanse me.'* Carnal appetite, recognizing itself
and sighing, was honoring the breath of humanity, namely the

---

[8] Note how this final sentence functions as a summary of the narrative.
[9] Gen 3:22; see 3:5.

soul, and said with a moan: "Since you are my master, *'if you wish'* to stand in battle for me, *'you are able'* to absolve me from pleasure."

And extending his hand, he touched him. Taking up the shield of protection, he shattered carnal appetite. *'I want to cleanse you'* "from pleasure, to do battle for you." *And immediately his leprosy was cleansed.* The sweetness that it had in taste was checked. *And Jesus said to him: 'See that you tell no one, but go and show yourself to the priest and offer the gift that Moses commanded as testimony to them.'* Divine inspiration persuaded it: "Take heed; manifest to no creature that you have been vanquished and made righteous; but go up and show gratitude to the appointer and lawgiver, *'and offer'* in devotion the good knowledge rationality inspired, so that the name of God may be manifested in you."

When, however, he had entered Capernaum, a centurion came up to him. When the soul *had entered* the tabernacle of bodily darkness the body's five senses came lamenting to the soul, namely, what the human seeks, what one understands, what one undertakes, what one does, and what one achieves, with which one may look around everywhere like the four beasts, as it is written: *Their backs are filled with eyes.*[10] The centurion *said: 'Lord, my servant is lying paralyzed and terribly distressed.'* [In other words, the senses said:] "O soul, my knowledge *'is lying'* prostrate in carnal grief, such that it often sleeps in oblivion, and *'is terribly distressed'* through the apertures of the ancient serpent's[11] persuasions."

And Jesus said to him: 'I will come and will cure him.' In compassion, the human's breath *said to him: 'I will come'* "with a heavenly host and shatter knowledge." *And responding, the centurion said: 'Lord, I am not worthy that you should enter under my roof.'* Recollecting themselves, the five senses *said*: "Soul, to whom I must be obedient, *'I am not worthy'* on account of my inconstancy; but be sparing, lest I perish; *'that you should enter'* my body with such a host of virtues." *'But only say the word and my servant will be*

[10] Ezek 10:12.
[11] See Rev 12:9.

healed,' "that is, touch my flesh, *'say the word'* of correction with discretion, kissing my flesh with your greenness, *'and my servant will be healed'* by the good, in both parts, such that with your medicine you touch my flesh, and with your greenness you heal with discretion."[12]

'For I also am a man under authority, having soldiers under me and I say to this one: "Go," and he goes; and to another: "Come," and he comes; and to my slave: "Do this."' *'For I also am'* "a worker of rationality," *'having under me'* "the capacity for working and discerning; I abandon one vice, such that I refuse that one; and another that I love embraces me. I show other things to sin, and it accomplishes what I want. Whence, O soul, be sparing to me and to yourself, and we will exist with peace."

But hearing this, Jesus marveled, and to the ones following him he said: 'Amen I say to you, I have not found such faith in Jerusalem.' Understanding this, the soul was terrified and *said* to its strength: "In wisdom's truth, which holds heavenly and earthly things in its embrace, searching thoroughly, *'I have not found'* moderation in the depth of the austerity where I am, like a nail deeply driven, such that I could not be sparing to the flesh, because I am the breath coming from God; but Wisdom moderates all these things, as it is written: *Wisdom cries out*[13] *in the streets.*"

'But I say to you,' asserting *'that many'* among the virtues *'[will come] from the east,'* where they glow with divine things, *'and the west,'* those who have fallen into sins, so that the former condescend to the flesh, and the latter lift themselves up from vices. *'And'* at last *'they will sit,'* having made the journey, *'at table with Abraham,'* obedient in faith, *'and Isaac,'* rejoicing in hope, *'and Jacob,'* fleeing the devil, *'in the kingdom of heaven,'* that is, in contemplation of God. *'But the children of the kingdom will be cast down into the outer darkness.'* Those who are soiled beyond measure in sins and are living according to their own will and not humbling themselves according to obedience *'will be'* driven out *'into'* dis-

---

[12] Hildegard employs lovely images here with *uiriditas*—the kiss and the touch of greenness—to refer to the healing power of the Holy Spirit.

[13] Prov 8:1.

tant places of imprudence where they will find neither wisdom's wine nor discretion's grain. *'There will be weeping and gnashing of teeth,'* with no consolation of purgation *'and gnashing'* of useless matters, such that none there will root up[14] any benefit, but they will utter forth only empty gnashing.

And Jesus said to the centurion: 'Go, and as you have believed, so may it be done for you.' The soul *said* to the five senses: *'Go'* "to repose, desiring, instructing, and teaching me; I will be subject to you for the purpose of discretion." *And the servant was healed in that hour.* Humanity's knowledge *was healed* in repose, tempered in this way with the help of discretion.

---

[14] Latin *riment*, from *rimor*, an agricultural verb meaning "to turn over or root up," and also "to search, investigate."

Homilies 20 and 21

The Feast of
the Purification of
the Blessed Virgin Mary

Luke 2:22-32

After the days of Mary's purification were fulfilled according to the law of Moses they brought Jesus to Jerusalem in order to present him to the Lord, as it is written in the law of the Lord: 'that every male opening the womb will be called holy to the Lord,' and in order to offer sacrifice according to what is said in the law of the Lord: 'a pair of turtledoves or two young pigeons.'

And behold there was in Jerusalem a man named Simeon, and this man was just and God-fearing, awaiting Israel's consolation. And the Holy Spirit was upon him. And he had received a response from the Holy Spirit that he would not see death unless he first saw Christ the Lord. And he came in the Holy Spirit into the Temple.

And when his parents brought in the boy Jesus, so that they could do for him according to the law's custom, Simeon received him in his arms, blessed God, and said: 'Now you dismiss your servant, Lord, in peace, according to your word; because my eyes have seen your salvation, which you have prepared before the face of all peoples: a light for revelation to the Gentiles and glory to your people Israel.'

20. The Feast of the Purification of the Blessed Virgin Mary, 1[1]

After the days of Mary's purification were fulfilled according to the law of Moses; that is, when the rituals of the Old Testament *were* at their consummation, the old observance was changed for the better through the inspiration of the prophets who were speaking about the Gospel. For just as a woman is in silence after birth, until she brings the infant to the temple, so was the Old Testament hidden in secret until the New, when the Son of God was incarnated. *They took Jesus to Jerusalem in order to present him to the Lord*; namely, according to the Lord's will, the holiness that was in the ancient law *brought* Jesus, that is, the Savior, to the vision of our peace, so that once incarnated he would appear as a human being in God. *As it was written in the law of the Lord, 'every male opening the womb will be called holy to the Lord'*; in other words, *as it was* predestined by that inspiration,[2] where it is said: *And it will be just as a tree that is planted by a waterfall,*[3] Adam, the first male, *'opening'* the earth, was sanctified through the breath of life. And as Adam rose up from the earth's wholeness, so also Christ went out from Mary's wholeness and was holy. *In order to offer sacrifice according to what is said in the law of the Lord, 'a pair of turtledoves or two young pigeons.'* In other words, he gave virtuous constancy by inspiration, as it is written: "He shall be called Emmanuel,"[4] that is, fear and love of the Lord, the beginning and the end of good deeds.

And behold there was in Jerusalem a man named Simeon, namely, the prophets, who were also worshiping earthly things. They would see that the Son of God was going to come in flesh, since

---

[1] The first of these two homilies is another of the few examples in which Hildegard provides some literal interpretation of the text, although here her emphasis is on the typological or salvation-historical reading. See Kienzle, *Speaking New Mysteries*, 149–50.

[2] Hildegard uses the Latin *inspiratio* here and in several other instances in this homily.

[3] Ps 1:3.

[4] See Isa 7:14.

they were without doubt. *And this man was just and God-fearing,*
awaiting Israel's consolation; that is, [the prophets were] without
guile, simple men for God's honor,[5] *awaiting* with the joy of faith
that the Son of God was to be incarnated. *And the Holy Spirit was*
upon him, because he was neither doubting nor duplicitous.

And he had received a response from the Holy Spirit that he would
not see death unless he first saw Christ the Lord. Clearly, the Spirit
responded to his desire, that the prophecy would not fail before
the Son of God would be incarnated, as it is written: *The scepter will*
not be taken away from Judah.[6] *And he came in the spirit* of prophecy
into the temple; clearly, for the open revelation of the church, which
they saw in the spirit. *And his parents brought in the boy Jesus so that*
they could do for him according to the law's custom. Believing *Jesus*
pure from every contagion, the patriarchs, *according to the custom*
that was given through divine inspiration, converted circumcision
into baptism before God for the salvation of the peoples.

Simeon *received him in his arms* in the grasp of faith, *and blessed*
God; clearly, the prophets praised *God*, who did these wondrous
things, believing what they did not see, and keeping in faith what
they did see. *And he said* in faith: *'Now you dismiss your servant,*
Lord, in peace according to your word.' "Clearly, you who rule all
things will now remove the law that served carnally; *'according*
to' your incarnated Son it was transformed for the better, and
for that peace, as it is said: *Glory to God in the highest and on earth*
peace to all humankind."[7] *'Because my eyes have seen your salvation,*
which you have prepared before the face of all peoples,' "that is, our
knowledge through the institutions of the law has perceived[8] the
Son whom you sent for the salvation of all and raised up for the
sight of all"; the Son, clearly greater than all humankind, as it is

[5] Hildegard interprets Simeon with the plural noun, "prophets"; the
Latin verbs *colebant, uiderent, erant,* and the adjective *simplices* are plural to
indicate that.

[6] Gen 49:10.

[7] Luke 2:14; see Luke 19:38.

[8] The Latin verb is plural, *senserunt,* to agree with *uiderunt,* even though
the subject of the gloss is singular: *scientia.*

said:[9] *Beautiful in form before humankind's children.*[10] *'A light for the revelation of the Gentiles and glory to your people Israel,'* because he was made human, he will lead those who were in the darkness of idol worship to the catholic faith, that is, all who wish to look upon him in faith, as much in this age as in the future.

21. The Feast of the Purification of the Blessed Virgin Mary, 2

After the days of Mary's purification were fulfilled according to the law of Moses they brought Jesus to Jerusalem in order to present him to the Lord. After the days were completed in truth, that she might be purified from every contagion of womanly union, she remained a virgin. Clearly, a man and woman are accustomed to be united by marriage; they were created from both earth and water. Those who vow virginity by good example *brought* virginity to the vision of true peace and salvation in order to fulfill the virginity they vowed. *As it is written in the law of the Lord, 'every male opening the womb will be called holy to the Lord.'* According to the example held from the Lord's incarnation, which was without blemish, one would be able to open the womb, if one wished, but would close it in a manly way because virginity is virtuous and holy to God. *And in order to offer sacrifice according to what is said in the law of the Lord: 'a pair of turtledoves or two young pigeons,'* that is, victory's praise *'according to what is'* promised in the Lord's incarnation: innocence and chastity, or holy deeds, martyring themselves in battle with vices.

And behold, there was in Jerusalem a man named Simeon. One who ought to be such in virginity *was* in a vision of salvation, a mirror in which he may behold and protect himself, lest the hawk rush in upon him.[11] *And this man [was] just and God-fearing,* that is, on

[9] Hildegard ceases at this point to extend the words of Simeon and sums up in third-person discourse.

[10] Ps 44:3.

[11] The hawk image (Lev 11:16; Deut 14:15; Job 39:13, 26) appears also in Hildegard's letters: *Epistolarium* 1, 16R, p. 50, l. 21, and 52R, p. 129, ll. 29-30, the last also dealing with virginity.

righteous paths, such that he would not unjustly love the spirit
sometimes and unjustly love the flesh at other times, but he would
embrace the straight path in the sun lest he cast down the crown
of integrity he placed upon his head. [He was] *awaiting Israel's
consolation*, that is, *awaiting* with desire the joyful life that ought
at once to be confessed and praised. *And the Holy Spirit was upon
him*; by its gifts he expelled vices from himself. *And he had received
a response from the Holy Spirit, that he would not see death unless he
first saw Christ the Lord.* By his appetite he drew inwardly toward
himself, so that in his conscience he would not fail but would be
so filled with virtues that he would not fail from hunger, which
neither knows nor has a taste for the good, but he would rise
from virtue to virtue,[12] seeing Christ, such that he could not be
saturated with his sweetness.

And he came in the spirit into the Temple; that is, *in the spirit* of his
own heart *he came* into the sweetness of the sight of God, so that
he would love God above all things. *And his parents brought in
the boy Jesus in order to do for him according to the custom of the law.*
Clearly, good examples by doing well *brought in* virginity, which
must be pure, preparing in holiness and praise the honor of the
Lord's incarnation, which they imitate in virginity.

He received him in his arms and blessed him; that is, grasping *him*
with full desire, because they who used to weep for God in the
world will rejoice in eternal life. *He said: 'Now you dismiss your
servant in peace, Lord, according to your word.'* Evidently *he said* in
prayer: "Take away my flesh's servile deed and the heat of concupiscence according to the honor of your son, who has shown
us chastity, so that I[13] have rested in peace, freed from the devil."
*'Because my eyes have seen your salvation which you have prepared
before the face of all peoples; a light for revelation to the Gentiles and
glory to your people Israel.'* "In other words, my heart's knowledge
recognizes a shining gem in the gentleness of your sweetness, *'before'* desire, because virginity is bright and shining in its chastity

---

[12] Ps 83:8.
[13] Latin *requiei*, first person singular, perfect tense.

over the other virtues; a dawning in manifestation against the carnal laws of those who live in carnal union, and the singular reward for all who follow in virginity."

Homilies 22 and 23

Septuagesima Sunday

Matthew 20:1-16

'The kingdom of heaven is like a householder who went out early in the morning to hire laborers for his vineyard. After agreeing with the laborers to a denarius per day, he sent them into his vineyard. He went out at about the third hour and saw others standing idle in the marketplace and said to them: "You go into my vineyard too, and whatever will be just, I will give you." They also went. He went out again at about the sixth hour and the ninth hour and did the same. At about the eleventh hour he went out and found others standing and said to them: "Why do you stand here idle all day?" They said to him: "Because no one has hired us." He said to them: "You go into the vineyard, too."

Then when evening came, the owner of the vineyard said to his steward: "Call the laborers and pay them their wages, beginning from the last up to the first." Therefore, when they who had arrived about the eleventh hour came they [each] received a single denarius. But the first ones coming believed that they were going to receive more. Yet they each also received a single denarius. And receiving it, they grumbled at the householder, saying: "These last worked one hour, and you made them equal to us who have borne the day's burden and the heat."

And responding to one of them, he said: "Friend, I do you no wrong. Did you not agree with me for a denarius? Take what is yours and go. I wish, however, to give to this last as to you. Am I not allowed to do what I want? Or is your eye evil because I am good?" Thus the last will be first and the first last. For many are called, but few indeed are chosen.

22. Septuagesima Sunday, 1

'*The kingdom of heaven,*' clearly of mysteries, '*is like a householder,*' the one who is God and human, '*who went out early in the morning,*' when he created heaven and earth on the first day, and when he said, *Let there be light*,[1] '*to hire laborers in his vineyard,*' in other words to lead diverse creatures into the world.

'*And having agreed with the laborers to one denarius per day, he sent them into his vineyard.*' On the second day, when he divided *waters from waters*,[2] he *agreed* with the creatures that existed at that time on the function[3] they would carry out in the world for each day they were going to fulfill.

'*He went out at about the third hour and saw others standing idle in the marketplace, and said to them: "You go into my vineyard too, and whatever will be fair, I will give you."*' On the third day he said: *Let the waters that are under heaven come together into one place, and let the dry land appear.*[4] When creatures still were not working, he said to them: *Let the earth bring forth vegetation*, and so on;[5] "*and whatever will be just, I will give you* for your function, according to the nature of your creation." '*They also went*' to fulfill the divine command by their function.[6]

'*He went out again at about the sixth hour, and the ninth hour, and he did the same.*' On the fourth day he said: *Let there be lights in the firmament of heaven*,[7] and the rest that follows. Clearly, on the fifth day he said: *Let the waters bring forth swarms of living creatures*,[8] and the following things. He enjoined his creation to his work.

---

[1] Gen 1:3.

[2] Gen 1:6.

[3] Latin *ex officio suo*. Hildegard uses *officium* to designate the duty or function of the various creatures.

[4] Gen 1:9.

[5] Gen 1:11.

[6] In the first homily Hildegard adduces citations from Genesis as glosses for the words of the householder. Those are indicated in italics, as with other Scripture, but not with quotation marks, in order to differentiate them from the words spoken in the parable itself.

[7] Gen 1:14.

[8] Gen 1:20.

'At about the eleventh hour he went out, and he found others standing and said to them: "Why do you stand here idle all day?"' On the sixth day he said: *Let the earth bring forth a living creature in its kind,*[9] and what follows: *Let us make humankind in our image and likeness.*[10] In other words, *he found* creatures ready for work *and said to them*: *"Why do you stand here* idle, that is, doing nothing after you were created?" *'They,* namely those creatures and the human, *said to him: "Because no one has hired us,* showing us what work we could do."' God *'said to them: "You go into the vineyard too*; that is, into the world, to work in accordance with what I appointed for you."'

'Then when evening came, the owner of the vineyard said to his steward: "Call the laborers and pay them their wage."' After all things had been created, as it is said: *And on the seventh day God completed his work that he had done;*[11] God *said* to Adam: *"Call* the various creatures, as it is written": *Therefore, when the Lord God had formed from the dirt all the living creatures of the earth and all the birds of the sky, he led them to Adam, to see what he would call them.*[12] *"Pay them, beginning from the last up to the first."* "In other words, enjoin their functions on them with their names,"[13] because, although the creatures were in air full of light, he was enjoining on them the functions they were going to do. However, in Adam's transgression they went with him into the whirlwind, from the beasts and herds, which were created with humankind, because they were made after other creatures, up to those that were created first. It is as if he said: "Assign functions first to those that are more like you and dwell with you on earth and also were created with you, according to their nature; and then show their functions to those that preceded first in creation and are unlike you in their nature."

[9] Gen 1:24.

[10] Gen 1:26.

[11] Gen 2:2.

[12] Gen 2:19.

[13] Hildegard rephrases the words of the householder in accordance with her interpretation, then switches to third-person discourse to explain, and finally returns to direct speech in God's voice.

'*Therefore, when they who had arrived at about the eleventh hour had come, they each received a single denarius.*' Those who had come forth with humankind in the last creation, namely on the sixth day, each received particular functions according to their nature, with the result that wild creatures were in the forest but domestic ones in the farmland with humankind.

'*But the first ones coming believed that they were going to receive more, but they each received a single denarius also.*' Led first to Adam were the ones who had come forth first in creation, such as birds and the like; in their opinion they would have greater potential in these things than would the herds, since they could both fly in the air and walk with humankind on earth. Clearly, '*they each received*' one function according to their nature: birds the function of flying, and fish that of swimming, just as the one function of walking on land was assigned to beasts. '*Receiving*' their functions, '*they grumbled*' in their opinion '*against*' their Creator, '*saying: "These last,* who were created after us, like the herds, *labored one hour*, because coming forth in their creation, they had supported no other creature to be created after them, as the prior creatures did; and *you made them equal to us*, in the full and not half function of their nature; *equal* on the pastures of the earth alone, because the birds, herds, and remaining creatures all feed at once from the earth alone."' "*We have borne the burden*, in our estimation, of flying and walking, what we were going to do, the time of our proceeding forth, and *the heat* of the sun, the moon, and the vicissitude of the other creatures following us."

'*And responding to one of them*, clearly to creation, which is one from one Creator, *he said*: "*Friend*, by carrying out my order, *I do no wrong to you*, but I assign you your function according to a just measure, lest you go beyond your capacity by rising or descending more than was assigned to you, and not according to your capability."' "*Did you not agree with me for a denarius,* that is, to that duty which I enjoined to you by what I said: *Let there be*,[14] that you would carry out my command?" "*Take what is yours and*

---

[14] Gen 1:3; 1:6.

go; in other words, *take* the duty [enjoined] by your nature and fulfill it." "*I wish, however, to give to this last as to you.*" "*I wish to give* that which was created afterward and that treads upon the earth the potential to carry out its function, *just as to you*, who were created first and fly in the air." "*Am I*, who am the Creator, *not allowed to do what I want* in that very creation, such that it says rebelliously: *Why did you make me thus?*[15] *Or is your eye worthless because I am good?* Is your knowledge foolish when you want more than is suitable for you *because I am good*, who created you rightly and beautifully?"

'*Thus*,' in this way as it was made here, '*the last*,' those creatures that came forth later, such as the herds, '*will be first*,' at the outset of work, because the herds first began to walk with and dwell with humankind, and for their meat, pelts, service, and in all ways they are more useful to human beings than birds are. '*And the first*,' clearly, those that came forth first in creation, '*will be last*' in their function, because birds are not as useful for human usage as are herds, which were created with humankind on the sixth day. '*For many are called, but few indeed are chosen.*' In other words, many and diverse creatures were called at creation to come forth in their variations so that they fulfill their functions according to what was appointed for them; but the human being alone was chosen by God, that he be made in God's *image and likeness*[16] and predestined for heavenly things.

23. Septuagesima Sunday, 2

'*The kingdom of heaven is like a householder who went out early in the morning to hire laborers in his vineyard.*' The entire fastening[17] in the human being is the rationality that is in the human; it '*went out*' in the knowledge of perception to lead the body's five senses

[15] Rom 9:20.

[16] See Gen 1:26; 5:3.

[17] Latin *compago*. See *Diu. operum* 1.2.46: *omnes compagines membrorum hominis*. Peter Dronke discusses this term in the *Diu. operum* and suggests the translation "fastening" (of the limbs), *Diu. operum* xxiv.

into faith in the salvation of souls. *'After agreeing with the laborers to a denarius per day he sent them into his vineyard.'* In other words, rationality promises hope for life to the five senses, which they will always have; it *'sent them'* to faith in the salvation of souls.[18]

'He went out at about the third hour,' that is, at work, *'and saw others,'* clearly at another variation of work greater than that of opinion, *'standing idle in the marketplace,'* that is, in deliberating over choosing what they wanted to do, *'and said to them'* admonishing: *"You go into my vineyard, too,"* evidently into faith in the salvation of souls, and *"I will give you whatever is just* in remuneration." *'They also went'* to work.

'He went out again at about the sixth hour,' namely when the work was completed, *'and the ninth hour,'* when the human is already weary from work, *'and did the same,'* calling them to work. *'At about the eleventh hour he went out and found others standing, and said to them again: "Why do you stand here idle all day?"'* Clearly, in the absence of work *'he found'* them weary and deliberating, and admonished them *'again':* "Why do you stand in deliberation, in knowledge of good and evil, but not occupied with work?" *'They said to him: "Because no one has hired us."'* They agreed with rationality: "We do not know the reward for work." He said to them, again admonishing: *"You go into the vineyard too,"* in other words, by means of good deeds into faith in the salvation of souls.

'Then when evening came, the owner of the vineyard said to his steward: "Call the workers and pay them wages beginning from the last up to the first."' When the end of whatever labors arrived, rationality of faith in the salvation of souls *'said'* to the merit that will administer the reward for deeds: *"Call* the body's five senses and other vicissitudes of work, and give them praise and honor according to what they have merited before God and humankind: *from* those who repented from their evils, when knowing their sin they refused to sin, whereby they became innocent, *up to* those who, out of simplicity and innocence, did not know how to

---

[18] The repetition of this phrase, *in fidem saluationis animarum*, at key summary points perhaps indicates a memory device for Hildegard and her audience.

sin, or because they completed the righteous and upright deeds they began." *'Therefore, when they who had arrived at about the eleventh hour came for remuneration, they each received a single denarius.'* Clearly, those who failed to work and fell away to sin *'received'* only the hope of a heavenly reward.[19]

'But the first ones coming believed that they were going to receive more.' They who, from the body's innocence, did not know how to sin, *'believed that they were going to receive more'* because they had not sinned since they did not have the appetite for sin. *'Yet they each received a single denarius also,'* that is, *'they received'* only heavenly hope. *'And receiving it, they grumbled against the householder,'* that is, against rationality in their hearts, saying: *"These last labored one hour"*; in other words, in their opinion, after their sins they did good things with single steadfastness and vigor. *"And you made them equal to us"* in remuneration, *"who have borne the burden of the day"* in oppression *"and the heat"* in ardor of thoughts and body.

'And responding to one of them, he said: "Friend, I do no wrong to you."' Rationality *said* to Taste, which is the leader, as it were, of the other senses: "You know by tasting,[20] and I perceive; *I do no wrong to you* in remuneration." *"Did you not agree with me to a denarius?*—in other words, that you would be rewarded through heavenly hope alone." *"Take what is yours* in heavenly hope, *and go* into the dwellings you have there." *"I wish, however, to give to this last as to you,* that is, *to give* to the one who knows how to sin, and stops sinning, *as to you,* who do not know how to sin, due to the simplicity of innocence." *"Am I not allowed to do what I want,"* judging these things with upright judgment? *"Or is your eye worthless, because I am good?"* "Is your heart's intention countering these things unjustly *because I am* a discerner, not wandering unstably?"

'Thus the last will be first,' that is, those who in appetite for sin stopped sinning, and those who became innocent through repentance, when they have persevered in good things. *'And the first,'* evidently those who went along in the simplicity of innocence *'will*

---

[19] Hereafter Hildegard uses the phrase *spes superna*. The translation "heavenly hope" keeps the alliteration.

[20] Latin *sapis*, means both to taste and to know.

be last,' when, through the burden of anxieties and the heat of the body's passion, they strive toward the good goal of perseverance. *'For many are called, but few indeed are chosen.'* Rationality leads the human being's five senses to God's righteousness, *'but'* rarely are found any who do not grumble against ecclesiastical institutions and ordinances. Nevertheless, both the former and the latter will receive a denarius, clearly the hope of reward, albeit differently.

Homilies 24 and 25

The First Sunday of Lent

Matthew 4:1-11

Jesus was led into the wilderness by the Spirit so that he would be tempted by the devil. And when he had fasted forty days and forty nights, afterward he was hungry. And the tempter approached and said to him: 'If you are the Son of God, tell these stones to become loaves of bread.' Responding, he said: 'It is written: "Humankind does not live by bread alone, but by every word that proceeds from the mouth of God."'

Then the devil took him into the holy city, set him on the pinnacle of the temple, and said to him: 'If you are the Son of God, throw yourself down. For it is written: "He gave his angels charge of you; and on their hands they will bear you up, lest you strike your foot against a stone."' Jesus said to him: 'Again, it is written: "You shall not tempt the Lord your God."'

Again, the devil took him to a very high mountain, and showed him all the world's kingdoms and their glory. And he said to him: 'All these I will give you if you will fall down and worship me.' Then Jesus said to him: 'Be gone, Satan! For it is written: "You shall worship the Lord your God and him only shall you serve."' Then the devil left him; and, behold, angels came and ministered to him.

24. The First Sunday of Lent, 1[1]

Jesus was led into the wilderness by the Spirit, where there was no activity of humans or animals. This happened by divine plan so that the malevolent tempter could carry out his wish and his temptations in Christ more freely, and the tempter would be frightened more greatly by the work of creation, and he could not accomplish his iniquities so freely.[2] He *was led* by the Holy Spirit, from whom also he was conceived; *so that he would be tempted by the devil,* that is, *tempted* by hearing alone when the devil was speaking to him, not in another way. However, his very goodness so conquered the devil that neither before nor afterward was the devil vanquished in this way by a human. Hence, even the devil was ever afterward uncertain about Christ, because he found no appetite for human sin in him.

And when he had fasted by the power of the Holy Spirit he ate, drank, and slept not at all and did not show any human function in himself.[3] *Forty days and forty nights* he demonstrated his power and the new institution of the faithful, his future people. Just as God demonstrated his power by the flood for forty days and forty nights and destroyed evil people, so that afterward a new people would rise up in purity, so also Christ manifested his power and defeated the devil, and made a new people rise up in the sanctification of faith. Moreover, since four times ten are forty,

---

[1] In both homilies Hildegard enters into the drama intensely as *magistra*, narrator, and interpreter. The proportion of her commentary compared to the scriptural text is higher than in other *Expositiones*. On the performative aspects of these homilies, see Kienzle, "Performing the Gospel Stories: Hildegard of Bingen's Dramatic Exegesis in the *Expositiones euangeliorum*," chap. 5 in *Visualizing Medieval Performance: Perspectives, Histories, Contexts*, ed. Elina Gertsman (Burlington, VT: Ashgate, 2008), 121–40.

[2] Hildegard runs together three clauses with a somewhat ambiguous result. In "Performing the Gospel Stories," 114, I interpreted this second clause as the devil trying to tempt Jesus away from the work or act of creating, but this seems incorrect since it is apparent in the remainder of the homily that the creation has taken place. Therefore, the devil seems to be frightened by created works, which reveal the power of God.

[3] Latin employs an *ut* result clause here.

we should understand the four elements for four, and we should note the Ten Commandments of the law for ten, such that what we would abandon by the four elements we would emend by correcting with the Ten Commandments.[4] And he fasted before he was tempted, so that the power of divinity would be seen in him, and through it the devil would be incited to tempt him, while he wondered who this man was who had such great fortitude in himself, as if to say: "What? Might he be another Adam?" During these forty days and nights the devil frequently came to Christ and withdrew; he did not presume to tempt him fully, like a bird that often flies to one thing and flies back again and would catch it freely if it dared. *Afterward he was hungry,* because he stooped then to weary humanity and gave the devil a sort of free rein to tempt him.

And the tempter approached with Christ's permission; he saw him working spiritual and not carnal things, and for that reason *approached* him. The *tempter* was spirit, not assuming an aerial body, and not transfiguring himself into any other form of any creature, but only remaining thus as he is; he shows himself in form as a very black shadow. He saw such great power in Christ that he dared not transform himself deceitfully into another form. Therefore, he is called the tempter, because he, not Lucifer, was the one who tempted Adam; because he fell from there he was not moved from the place of perdition in hell. There is such great vehemence for malice in him that if he were permitted to get out he would destroy the air in another region. Hence, he is constrained by divine power to such a degree that he cannot carry out his own will by his wickedness, but he only sends out others for deceiving humans.

And so he said to him, namely to Christ, with his permission: '*If you are the Son of God,*' that is, "because you do not act like a human." He knew that God was going to have a Son, and he knew this from the prophets, but he did not know how it would happen, because Christ acted like a spirit then and not

---

[4] Hildegard uses first-person plural verbs here four times.

like a human. On account of that the devil was doubting, because although he saw him as a man, nonetheless he found no
sin or appetite for sin in him, and he did not know his father
but saw that his mother was a virgin. For in the subtlety of his
nature the devil himself knew that God would in no way allow
a human to perish in this manner, but would at some time with
his reason send forth some plan to rescue him. Therefore, when
he had seen such great power in Christ, he thought that God,
for the purpose of delivering humankind, had engendered this
new man by some marvelous and secret means, as also he had
fashioned Adam wondrously. For the devil was thinking that
if he vanquished Christ he could also destroy some part of the
kingdom of God, because he was from among those spirits who
violently send their temptations to humankind. *And he said: 'Tell,'*
with one word, *'these stones,'* which were present there, *'to become
loaves of bread.'* The tempter did not tell Christ to make bread
from nothing but to change a created thing into another mode,
so that he would know more truly if he was the God of creation.
And the devil urged that what was contrary to God's righteousness be done, because it would be against God's righteousness
if Christ changed some creature into another mode, as the devil
always urges to be done. However, the fact that the Son of God
changed water into wine was not contrary to nature, since wine
is both wet and liquid just like water; therefore, water changed
only its taste.[5] If the stones, however, had been made into loaves
of bread they would have lost their entire nature, and the loaves
of bread would have also, because bread is the first and most
vital food for the hungry.

Responding, he said: *'It is written: "Humankind does not live
by bread alone,*[6] that is, by eating bread, *but by every word* of God,
which I am," *that proceeds from the mouth of God,'* namely, other
creatures that were created through the word of God, when God

---

[5] An obvious reference to John 2:1-11, although Hildegard does not discuss
this matter in her homilies on that pericope.

[6] Deut 8:3.

said: *'Let there be light,'*[7] and *'let there be stars,'*[8] and the remaining
created things, because the human lives with these and with the
elements. But he adduces Scriptures, and through this he brings
human beings to rationality, because rationality in humans finds
the Scriptures, so that through rationality as through the Scriptures they may know God. For whatever the devil says, he says
these things by himself, and he does not deem it worthy to take an
example from anyone, so that he alone may seem to do all things.

Then the devil took him into the holy city; clearly, the devil in his
temptation had made a sort of whirlwind around Christ, with
Christ's permission. And the devil touched it, and he bore Christ
with him by that lightness without weight, just as also Christ
himself was transfigured on a mountain, and as he ascended
to heaven. And the devil led Christ with him above this, which
appeared there like an edifice. However, the evangelist does not
name this city, but calls it only *holy*. For when Christ had fasted,
immediately there in the wilderness God the Father pointed
ahead to the church with the temple of holiness and with the
edifice of the virtues, which were to be fulfilled in the church
through Christ. But the devil, since he was a spirit, saw those
things appearing in spirit, knowing that the things he saw there
look toward Christ; and he tempted him with his devices, as if
through vainglory he could prevent those magnificent works in
Christ in any way. As it was foretold, he touched the whirlwind,
which he had stirred up around Christ by his temptation in order
to tempt him, and thus, with his permission, sensing no weight in
Christ, *he set him on the pinnacle of the temple*, which he saw appear
there. While he had done that, rejoicing greatly, he supposed that,
if Christ had consented to him in this, he would also consent to
him in another matter.

And the devil spoke to him again: *'If you are the Son of God,'* because
you are so strong, *'throw yourself down* with confidence.' *'For it is
written: "He,"* that is your Father, *"gave his angels charge of you; and*

---

[7] Gen 1:3.
[8] Gen 1:14.

in their hands they will bear you up," because they will not dare to let go, *"lest you strike your foot against a stone."*[9] *Jesus said to him,* rejecting his temptation: *'Again, it is written: "You shall not tempt the Lord your God*[10] *who I am."'*

Again the devil, touching the whirlwind mentioned above, as he had done before, *took him* with his permission *to a very high mountain,* which also appeared there in the wilderness by those wonders, spiritually and not physically, through God the Father's will, so that he showed forth the greatness and exaltedness of those miracles, which were going to exist in the church through Christ, since the works and wonders of God appear great and splendid above all things. For no mountain could be found on earth so high that the whole earth, from wherever you will, could be seen with bodily eyes. *And the devil showed him all the world's kingdoms,* which were among diverse nations, *and their glory,* namely the things that were in the kingdoms, in accord with the fact that the world, that is, human beings, seek worldly pomp. *And he said to him,* tempting again, as if he might be able to conquer him then at least: *"'All these* things that you see in worldly pomp, *I will give you,* because they are mine, *if you will fall down,* prostrated to the earth, *and worship me* as God.'" *Then Jesus said to him: "'Be gone, Satan,* back into your place, which was prepared for you, because you find no place in me.'" *'For it is written: "You shall worship,* prostrated, *the Lord* of all creatures, the God of all the living, and *your God,* who I am; *and him only shall you serve,* and not alien and false gods, offering the service owed to him."'[11] *Then* instantly in that very hour *the devil left him,* such that he would never dare afterward to tempt him further. *And behold, angels,* that is citizens of heaven, *came* as they had done before, since they allowed these temptations to be carried out this way in Christ at that hour, according to his will; *and ministered to him,*[12] worshiping him and knowing him, as well as fulfilling his will.

[9] Ps 90:11-12.
[10] Deut 6:16.
[11] Deut 6:13.
[12] Mark 1:13.

25. The First Sunday of Lent, 2

Jesus was led into the wilderness by the Spirit so that he would be tempted by the devil. In other words, the Word of the Father, through whom all things were created, *was led into* the substance of creatures, before creatures were distinguished by species and before they could function at anything. He *was led* by the Holy Spirit, which brings all things to life, because the Father is eternity, the Son is the one by whom all things are created, the Holy Spirit is the one by whom all things are brought to life. *So that he would be tempted by the devil,* that is, *tempted* by evil, when the devil deceived the human and the other creatures with him. *And when he had fasted forty days and forty nights,* that is, after humankind's fall, neither glory nor honor nor praise was offered to God, as was due. *Forty days,* because after Adam's expulsion his children, all the way up to Noah, did not fully worship God in the four elements through the light of the awareness of Him. *Forty nights,* since they became sullied by the four elements just as by the nights of sin when they had not yet learned the ten commandments of the law; before the flood the devil had accomplished all his evils in humankind in the circle of the four elements, from Adam's fall all the way to Noah. God purged the earth of those creatures, which he allowed to perish when he said: *'I regret that I made*[13] the human race.' *And afterward Jesus was hungry* for righteousness, when after the flood he restored anew the human being, when righteousness began to shine forth in Noah. *And the tempter approached,* that is, the devil approached human beings through many vanities, because when he saw righteousness appear after the flood he began to make idols and many delusions against that very righteousness. *And the devil said to him,* who created all things: *'If you are the Son of God,'* "through whom all things were made and in whom righteousness appears," *'tell these stones to become loaves of bread.'* In other words: "Perform by your command just as when *he commanded and they were made,*[14] because I influenced the making of many idols." *Stones*

[13] Gen 6:7.
[14] Pss 32:9; 148:5.

[signify] hardness: "Humankind rejects you and refuses to honor you as God." *Loaves of bread* [meaning]: "Make some form of worship so that you also will be worshiped like God. I brought about the worship of my law in idols. Do likewise, so that you will at least be known as God." The devil said this ridiculing God.

Responding, the Word of the Father *said*: *'It is written: "Humankind does not live by bread alone, but by every word that proceeds from the mouth of God."'* [15] In other words, in the true Scripture the Creator is known through the creation, and it is understood that the Highest created it, but not by that created substance alone that the human uses frequently, or that which is subject to him and serves him. Let this suffice for his salvation, that he believe that these visible things were created by God. [16] This he is not able to see with bodily eyes, or to touch with his hands, or to comprehend with sensual perception; it proceeds invisibly from the mouth of God, born ineffably so that they may truly believe that he is the Son of God and the Son of Man.

Then the devil took him into the holy city, namely to the Jewish people, to whom the sanctity of the law was given. When Christ was incarnated and when he sent forth the words of his preaching the devil set many traps for him through the Jewish people. He *set him on the pinnacle of the temple,* that is, at the height of heaven, where the Jews tempted him and beseeched him that *a sign from heaven* [17] *be made. And the devil said to him* through the Jews, *'If you are the Son of God,'* "that is, since you make many signs around the earth in earthly matters, make also signs from heaven that are unknown to us, and *'throw yourself down,'* that is, descend in renown to humans."*For it is written,* in the Scripture, which you yourself established: *"He,* clearly God your Father, *gave his angels charge of you; and on the hands* of their labors, *they will bear you up,* carrying you this way, because they are very excellent creatures, assisting God, as also humankind and other creatures serve him; *lest you,*

[15] Deut 8:3.

[16] This passage belongs to the wider context of Hildegard's writings against heresy, and specifically against the Cathar belief that Satan created matter. See Kienzle, *Speaking New Mysteries,* 245–88.

[17] Luke 11:16.

placed in any negligence, *strike your foot against a stone,*[18] that is any hardness. Your footsteps are gentle and mild, such that no force is able to harm you." Jesus said to him, of course, to the devil: *'Again, it is written* in the true Scripture: *"You shall not tempt* in the presumption of pride *the Lord your God,*[19] *whom you shall worship as Creator."'*

Again, after this temptation, *he took him to a very high mountain.* Clearly, the devil *took* Christ among his faithful members to a mountain of error, which in its height extends all the way to the edge of the windstorm in Antichrist. *And he showed him all the world's kingdoms and their glory,* through the false deceptions by which he will assail faithful persons in the last days. The majority of humankind will turn from all the kingdoms of earth toward Antichrist; then after being deceived they will enter into that worship. *And he said to him: 'All these I will give you if you will fall down and worship me.'* Clearly, the devil through his deceptions said to Christ, that is to Christ's faithful ones, who are his members: *'I will give you all these things'* "that you see—human beings who worship me as God and desert you—so that with me you may be worshiped by them, if you desert the worship of the Christians, since the church, already thrown down, will not be able to stand further. No one worships you any longer, because they have abandoned you to turn toward me."

Then Jesus said to him: 'Be gone, Satan!' In the last days, when the Antichrist will be confounded by his zeal, Jesus will say to the devil: *'Be gone'* "into the place of your damnation, which you have earned; you have fallen below! *'For it is written'* in the Scripture of truth: *You shall worship the Lord your God,* and no other, *and him only shall you serve,*[20] because no one is like him." *Then the devil left him* and will raise no further power against God; *and, behold, angels came and ministered to him* in the fullness and perfection of charity and in celestial harmony and praise, since they will praise God without end.

[18] Ps 90:11-12.
[19] Deut 6:16.
[20] Deut 6:13.

Homilies 26 and 27

Sabbath before the Third Sunday of Lent

Luke 15:11-32

'A certain man had two sons, and the younger of them said to his father: "Father, give me the share of the property that belongs to me." And he divided the property between them. And not many days later, having gathered everything, the younger son set out away from home to a distant land, and there he squandered his property by living lustfully. And after he had spent everything a great famine came upon that region and he began to be hungry. And he went away and joined himself to one of the citizens of that region, and he sent him out to his farm to feed his swine. And he desired to fill his stomach with the pods that the pigs were eating, and no one gave him anything. And turning inward, he said: "How many hired servants in my father's house have plenty of bread, but I am dying here from hunger. I will rise up and I will go to my father. And I will say to him: 'Father, I have sinned against heaven and before you. I am no longer worthy to be called your son.'" And rising up, he went to his father. When he was still far away his father saw him and was moved with pity. And running, he embraced him and kissed him. And the son said to him: "Father, I have sinned against heaven and before you. I am no longer worthy to be called your son." But the father said to his servants: "Bring quickly the first robe and clothe him, and give him a ring on his hand, and shoes on his feet. Let us eat and feast. This my son was dead, and he is alive again; he was lost and he is found." And they began to feast.

Now his elder son was in the field. And when he came and drew near to the house he heard music and dancing. And he called one of his servants

117

and asked what these things might be. And the servant said to him: "Your brother has come and your father has killed the fatted calf, because he has received him safe and sound." But he was angry, and he refused to go in. His father then came out and began to entreat him. But answering he said to his father: "See, for so many years I have served you and never have I gone against your command, and never have you given me a young goat that I might feast with my friends. But after this son of yours came, who wasted his property with prostitutes, you killed a fatted calf for him." But the father said to him: "Son, you are always with me, and all that is mine is yours. But it was fitting to feast and to rejoice. Because your brother was dead and is alive again; he was lost, and he is found."'

26. Sabbath before the Third Sunday of Lent, 1

'A certain man had two sons, and the younger of them said to his father: "Father, give me the share of the property that belongs to me."' God, in whose *image and likeness*[1] the human being was created, gave the human the knowledge of good and evil. The one who was more inclined to evil because of his unstable behavior *said* to God: "Allow me to fulfill the taste for work when it touches me in a taste of delight." *'And he divided the property between them.'* Clearly, God bestows glory and honor on the one who clings to good knowledge, but he allows the one who desires to be in evil knowledge to depart in that way.

'And not many days later, having gathered everything, the younger son set out away from home to a distant land, and there he squandered his property by living lustfully.' Since the day of salvation is not there where evil is, he withdrew by himself in order to fulfill all his wants, and he scattered his works into various vices when he fulfilled his every wish shamefully.

'And after he had spent everything a great famine came upon that region and he began to be hungry.' In other words, when he had done

---

[1] Gen 1:26.

many evil things, with the result that he already found them tiresome, he cared not at all for the food of life since he had fulfilled his will by evils. In the excess of vices he lost hope for life.

'*And he went away and joined himself to one of the citizens of that region, and he sent him out to his farm to feed his swine.*' He withdrew from God when he united himself to Malice, which had already made a seat for itself in his mind, and Malice '*sent him*' into the cultivation of vices, in which Malice was residing, in order that he feed his wickedness with vices.

'*And he desired to fill his stomach with the pods that the pigs were eating, and no one gave him anything.*' '*He desired to fill*' his desire from the various changes in his fortune, for which he wanted to blame God. In other words, God would be more at fault for his failings than he would. No creature stood by him, due to the fact that he accused God as the guilty one.

'*And turning inward, he said: "How many hired servants in my father's house have plenty of bread, but I am dying here from hunger."*' Remembering at last his Creator and the evils he had done, because he had no hope in these, '*he said*' pondering: "The ones who by their blood and many labors pay for heavenly things *have* the fullness of righteousness; but I lack the taste for good works." "*I will rise up* from the evil path, *and I will go* along the good path *to my father*, who created me." "*And I will say to him*" with the sighing of a moan: '*Father, I have sinned against heaven,*' "that is, with the heavenly breath that is in the soul," '*and before you,*' "because I have known you as God and even so I have sinned." '*I am no longer worthy to be called your son,*' "on account of the wickedness of my heart."[2] '*Treat me as one of your hired servants,*' "clearly, those who have fulfilled your will with their blood and many labors."[3]

---

[2] Note that in this passage, where the son proclaims in the first person his intent to ask forgiveness, the voices of the scriptural text and of Hildegard's narrative of conversion are merged, from "I will rise up" to "wickedness of my heart."

[3] Here the son utters the words he plans to say to his father, but within a monologue. Single quotation marks mark the son's speech and standard quotation marks signal Hildegard's extension of it.

'*And rising up*' from the vices, '*he went to his father*' at the entrance of good paths. '*When he was still far away*' through bad habits, '*his father*' searching '*saw him and was moved with pity,*' because the son touched him by his love in returning. '*And running*' through mercy, '*he embraced him,*' leaning down with the purpose of justice, '*and kissed him*' with the bond of charity.

'*And the son said to him*' in repentance: "*Father, I have sinned against heaven and before you*, when I did not cease to sin even with knowledge of you." "*I am no longer worthy*, because I am a transgressor, *to be called your son*, that is, that you receive me into my former inheritance." Here, however, he does not speak about the hired servants, but only awaits God's grace.[4] *But the father* through heavenly inspiration *said to his servants,* that is, the virtues, with which humans serve God: "*Bring quickly the first robe,* clearly innocence, which the first human lost in Paradise, *and clothe him* with the righteousness of innocence, *and give him a ring on his hand,* that is, the comprehension of good works, through which he may renounce the devil, *and shoes on his feet,* that he may walk uprightly." "*And bring in the fatted calf and kill it.*" "In other words, call upon the Son of God who brought heavenly abundance;[5] repeat his martyrdom in this." "*Let us eat and feast.*" [This refers to] the taste for good works and rejoicing, because the greenness of the Holy Spirit has blossomed again in him. "*This my son,* whom I created, *was dead,* because he did not have the knowledge of God, *and he is alive again* by returning to me; *he was lost* in the memory of righteousness, because he did not have the fullness of life; *and he is found* on the path of righteousness." '*And they began to feast*' in rejoicing over the lost sheep that was found.[6]

'*Now his elder son was in the field,*' clearly, the one who has good knowledge in the cultivation of heavenly inheritance. '*And when he came and drew near to the house he heard music and dancing.*' When

[4] Hildegard departs from the narrative voice to point out the difference in content (the mention of the hired servants) between the son's inner monologue and the words he speaks to the father.

[5] Latin *pinguedo,* literally fatness.

[6] An allusion to the parable of the lost sheep, Luke 15:3-7.

he considered his paths *'and drew near'* to the dwelling place of virtues through a good alliance, ascending to the heavens *'he heard'* the joy of the heavenly vision,[7] and the comeliness and glory with which God is served. *'And he called one of his servants,'* that is, through meditation he called faith alone; *'and asked'* through searching *'what these things might be'* concerning the grace of God, that might encourage him.

'And the servant said to him: "Your brother has come and your father has killed the fatted calf, because he has received him safe and sound."' Clearly, Faith responded to his pondering that he made an upright journey with the knowledge by which he knows God. "He by whom you were created has repeated the passion of his Son who brought the abundance[8] of life; he has *received him safe* in good report and embraced him."

'But he was angry, and he refused to go in.' Evidently he was astonished that God had made so great a good from so great an evil; he refused to enter and receive his brother because he did not have the repentance necessary for *joy* to be made over him as *over one sinner.*[9]

'His father then came out and began to entreat him.' God sent an admonition to him, that he would remain in the good. *'But answering he said to his father: "See, for so many years I have served you and never have I gone against your command, and never have you given me a young goat that I might feast with my friends."'* In his ponderings he *said* to God: "With measure and moderation *I serve you* through good things, *and never have I gone against your command* by denying it, as my brother did; evidently, it was not allowed that I, by my share of sins,[10] would have so great a report with the virtues about my good actions as this brother of mine about his conversion." *"But after this son of yours came, who wasted his property with prostitutes, you killed a fatted calf for him,"* "in other words, the one who was created by you and by neglecting your

---

[7] Note an example of anagogical interpretation here.

[8] Latin *pinguedo*, literally fatness.

[9] Luke 15:7.

[10] Latin *peccatorum*: either sins or sinners, genitive plural.

commands rejected those works that were necessary for his soul, squandered them with the ravings of his folly, but made an upright journey, and you anointed him with the passion of your son in the abundance of life."

'*But the father said to him: "Son, you are always with me, and all that is mine is yours."*' God admonished: "Good Knowledge, you are always in happiness, and you do not leave me. You have all good things, because I am good.[11] *But it was fitting to feast* in rejoicing over the Holy Spirit's greenness *and to rejoice* that Evil Knowledge had turned itself to the good. For it is necessary that Evil Knowledge return to the good when all good things of the father are praised and magnified in all creation. Similarly, a warrior[12] defeats an enemy, and the enemy, after being conquered, will later be his friend when compelled by necessity, because he will not be able to resist him; therefore, the one conquered should be praised for his service. *Because your brother was dead* in his wickedness *and is alive again* in knowledge of God, mindful of himself in his circumstances; *he was lost* by deceptive judgment, *and he is found* in the true light."

27. The Sabbath before the Third Sunday of Lent, 2

'*A certain man had two sons.*' God '*had*' the angels and the human being. '*And the younger of them said to his father: "Father, give me the share of the property that belongs to me."*' In other words, the human *said to* God: "Father, *give me* the possibility of perfection in work, *which belongs to* me from nature, that I may accomplish that." '*And he divided the property between them,*' so that they could work.

'*And not many days later, having gathered everything, the younger son set out away from home to a distant land, and there he squandered*

---

[11] Earlier in her commentary on this pericope Hildegard refers to the qualities of good and evil knowledge, but they are not personified. Here she speaks directly to a personified Good Knowledge and shortly thereafter she attributes actions to a personified Evil Knowledge.

[12] Isa 42:13.

his inheritance by living lustfully.' Evidently the human was in Paradise for a short time; after following his own will he was expelled from Paradise into the world, *'and there he squandered'* his deeds.

'And after he had spent everything, a great famine occurred in that region, and he began to be hungry.' Clearly, after he had defiled all his works he did not have fullness in the world, where they were not worshiping the true God, *'and he began to be hungry'* for idols. *'And he went away and joined himself to one of the citizens of that region and he sent him out to his farm, so that he would feed his swine.'* He went astray *'and joined himself to'* the devil in the world, and the devil *'sent him'* by temptation into his law, so that he would nourish his inordinate desires with shame and disgrace. *'And he desired to fill his stomach with the pods that the pigs were eating, and no one gave him any.'* He desired to fill the comprehension of his whole spirit with vices, clearly, the inordinate desires for vices, *'and no one gave him any,'* because God does not associate with evil things, nor is the devil able to give any fullness of any good whatsoever with them.

'And turning inward, he said: "How many hired servants in my father's house have plenty of bread?"' Remembering the one by whom he was created, when God gave circumcision to Abraham, *'he said'*: *"How many* who were worshiping God for the sake of a heavenly reward *have* plenty of righteousness, like those who were righteous before circumcision, namely Noah, Enoch, Abel, and others like them? *But I am dying here from hunger*, because I have no fullness of life. *I will rise* up from the worship of idols, *and I will* go through circumcision *to my father, and I will say to him,* worshiping him: *'Father, I have sinned against heaven,'* because I worshiped the sun, the moon, and the stars *'and before you,'* when I abandoned you. *'I am no longer worthy to be called your son,'* just as they who were worshiping you knew.[13] *'Treat me as*

---

[13] Again the son's inner monologue allows Hildegard to merge the voices of the biblical narrative with her own retelling of the story.

one of your hired servants,' clearly, as one like those who deserve eternal life."'[14]

'And rising up, he went to his father.' *'Rising up'* from the worship of demons, *'he went'* to Mount Sinai, receiving the law through Moses. *'When he was still far away'* in the law, because the law cannot lead humankind back to life, *'his father saw him'* when he sent the prophets, speaking about the incarnation of the Son of God, *'and was moved with pity'* when the angel Gabriel announced the Christ to the Virgin Mary. *'And running'* in that very greeting to Mary, *'he embraced him,'* that is, when the heavenly Father sent the word to Jacob and *'embraced'* Israel *'around the neck'*[15] of strength in Judea, and when the Holy Spirit came upon Mary in the conception of Christ, *'and kissed him' with the kiss of his mouth*[16] in the birth of his son.[17]

'And the son,' clearly the human, *'said to him: "Father, I have sinned against heaven,* in the higher creation of the stars, by the worship of idols, *and before you* by denying you. *I am no longer worthy to be called your son,* because I am a sinner."* But the son remains silent about the *hired servants,* because he expects no reward from the work he performed, placing himself in the grace of God alone.[18]

'But the father said to his servants: "Quickly, bring the first robe, and clothe him, and give him a ring on his hand, and shoes on his feet."' *'The father said'* to the apostles, when they were called by Christ: "Don't delay at all, *bring* the garb that Adam lost in Paradise, *and clothe* the new man, *and give him* faith *on his hand,* so that he carries out faith through works, *and shoes on his feet,* namely, mortification of the flesh in preparation for the Gospel. *And bring the fatted calf,* clearly, when the Son of God, who brought the paschal food of life

[14] Again the son utters the words he plans to say to his father, but within a monologue, and I have kept standard quotation marks for the entirety of the son's planned speech and Hildegard's extension of it.

[15] See Gen 29:13; 33:4; Acts 20:37.

[16] Song 1:1.

[17] Note the skillful intertwining of the parable and these major events of salvation history.

[18] Again Hildegard interjects a comment on the son's failure to mention the hired servants when he addresses the father.

to believers, was led before Caiaphas and before Pilate; *and kill it*, clearly, when he was crucified and then excoriated in his passion; *and let us eat and let us feast*, evidently in his resurrection." "*This my Son was dead, and he is alive again; he was lost and he is found.*" Evidently humanity had lost the innocence it had in heaven, "*and is alive again*" in knowledge of God; it "*was lost*" because it did not have the food of life, "*and is found*" in the moaning of penance. '*And they began to feast.*' The apostles were strengthened when the Holy Spirit came over them in fiery tongues.[19]

'*Now his elder son was in the field*': clearly the angels who were created before humankind were in heavenly worship. '*And when he came and drew near to the house he heard music and dancing.*' When, through the heavenly mission, they came down to humankind in greater love than they had done previously they '*heard*' the report of good praise because the apostles were performing wonders and great signs among the people, and the fulfillment of righteousness. '*And he called one of his servants, and asked what these things meant.*' Obviously they '*called*' the oneness of prophecy, seeking the mystical meanings of the prophets, the wonders that he saw. '*And [the servant] said to him: "Your brother has come and your father has killed the fatted calf."*' Through the oracles of the prophets the human '*has come*' to repentance, and God has delivered his Son for his sake, because he has received him safe and sound, set free from the Devil's power.[20]

'*But he was angry and he refused to go in.*' Evidently he was astonished,[21] marveling at how these things could happen, because they are not in want of Christ's suffering or of the joy that results *over one* repentant *sinner.*[22]

'*His father then came out and began to entreat him.*' He showed his will to have mercy when he sent the angels for the people's salvation

[19] See Acts 2:3.

[20] In the first homily on this pericope Hildegard spoke in the voice of Faith, which the servant represents. Here she does not adopt the voice of the servant.

[21] The first part of the commentary (*admiratus est*) keeps the singular (the brother and not the angels), but the second switches to the plural for the angels (*non indigent*).

[22] Luke 15:7.

through the Holy Spirit's admonishing to rebuild the church, that
is, when angels are sent for the needs of humanity. *'But he answered
and said to his father: "See, for so many years I have served you, and never
have you given me a young goat so that I might feast with my friends."'*
In other words, they ruminated over God's examination *'and said'*:
"From the entire time since I was created I have joined myself to
your service, but you did not give me any part of repentance by the
grace with which you redeemed the sins of my brother, with signs
and wonders and virtues of this sort, that I might have new joy in
the new symphony."[23] *"But after this son of yours, who devoured your
property with prostitutes, came, you killed a fatted calf for him."* "After
[the human], who is your creation, used up *your property* by accomplishing his deeds with gluttonous vices, and returned to you in
repentance, you showed him the pouring out of your Son's blood,
the one who brought the abundance of life to believers."

'But the father said to him: "Son, you are always with me."' God
admonished [the angels]: "*You are always with* me in purity and
sanctity, continuously looking upon my face, because a human,
while still in the mortal body, will not be able to see my face. *And
all that is mine is yours.* The miracles I worked in your brother are
yours, because you will always be a messenger between me and
the human. *But to feast*, because humankind was redeemed by
the blood of my Son and strengthened by the pouring forth of the
Holy Spirit, *and to rejoice* in the resurrection of lost humanity *was
fitting, because your brother* the human *was dead* in heavenly things
and in good knowledge, *and is alive again*, in knowledge of God
and in the root of righteousness." "*He was lost*," because in lacking
the food of life before the eyes of God he did not appear bright,
"*and he is found*" in Christ through the moaning of penance, and
redeemed by his blood.[24]

---

[23] The angels speak collectively in the first person singular, mirroring the
elder son.

[24] In commenting on this last sentence Hildegard speaks in the third person, referring to God and Christ and not assuming their voices.

Homilies 28 and 29

The Sunday of the Resurrection

Mark 16:1-7

Mary Magdalene, Mary [the mother] of James, and Salome bought spices so that they might go and anoint Jesus. And very early on the first day of the week they went to the tomb, when the sun had already risen. And they were saying to one another: 'Who will roll back for us the stone from the entrance to the tomb?' And looking up, they saw that the stone was rolled back. It was indeed very large. And entering the tomb they saw a youth sitting on the right side, clothed in a white robe, and they were astonished. He said to them: 'Do not be frightened. You are seeking Jesus of Nazareth, who was crucified. He has risen; he is not here. Behold the place where he was laid. But go, tell his disciples and Peter that he is going before you into Galilee. There you will see him, as he told you.'

28. The Sunday of the Resurrection, 1

Mary Magdalene and Mary [the mother] of James and Salome bought spices. Mary Magdalene [stands for] the Old Testament, which was like a woman sinner in actions but a penitent in symbolic meaning; Mary [the mother] of James [designates] the humanity of the

127

Savior, which established righteousness; Salome [represents] the
Holy Spirit's outbreathing, which made the Gospel known through
the entire world. They *bought spices*; in other words, they desired
various signs and wonders, *so that they might go and anoint Jesus*,
that is, embrace *Jesus* as God and Savior. Clearly, the Old Testament
contains signs like the ram,[1] it prophesies like David, and it sees
like Ezekiel. The Savior's humanity proclaims God's witness and
the Holy Spirit's outbreathing demonstrates great virtues.

*And very early on the first day of the week they went to the tomb
when the sun had already risen.* Clearly, they undertook the good
with one desire, namely, that by good deeds they might see God;
they ran the course of God's mandates[2] so that they might mortify themselves with their vices when the most brilliant deed of
holiness appeared.

*And they were saying to one another: 'Who will roll back the stone
for us from the entrance of the tomb?'* Evidently the Old and New
Testament exhorted each other, *saying*: "'*Who*,' if not God, will
help us '*roll back*' the flesh's weight, because the Old Law pre-
scribes carnal union, but in the New Testament the Holy Spirit's
outbreathing speaks, exhorting us to abstain from these things,
and we are unable to do so except with God's help."[3] At *the entrance* the seed is for sowing; concerning that it is said: *Increase
and multiply and fill the earth*,[4] but clearly *the tomb* itself [repre-
sents] mortification. For neither the Old nor the New Testament
gave commands for virgins, but the Holy Spirit's outbreathing
established that, exhorting as it is written: *I do not have the Lord's
command regarding virgins*.[5]

And looking up they saw that the stone was rolled back; clearly, in
righteous faith they knew that the flesh's weight was removed. *It
was indeed very large*, because the flesh's weight is so heavy that it

---

[1] See Gen 22:13. Hildegard uses the Latin verb *signando* ("signifying")
intransitively.
[2] See Ps 18:6.
[3] Note this instance of Hildegard using the first-person plural, "we."
[4] Gen 1:28.
[5] 1 Cor 7:25.

would be impossible for a human being to throw it off and to cast it away from himself except through God's help. Thus it is said: *Until I place your enemies as the footstool for your feet,*[6] because the devil has confidence *that the Jordan may flow into his mouth.*[7] This very enemy will be conquered in virgins and continent ones, and fornication will be the footstool for their feet.[8]

And entering the tomb, they saw a youth. Clearly, through chastity [they entered into] the flesh's mortification by self-renunciation, when human beings mortify themselves for God. The *youth* [represents] virile fortitude,[9] which is in virginity and in continence, such that a person loses what is in the flesh and approaches in spirit what is not in the flesh, remaining in chastity without blemish and without wrinkle.[10] [He was] *sitting* before God's tribunal, that is, *on the right side* of God's power, as it is said: *Sit at my right hand.*[11] [He was] *clothed in a white robe*, that is, girded with the first garment of innocence, in virginity's radiance. *And they were astonished* at the devil's mockery and the world's clamor.

He said to them: 'Do not be frightened,' that is, he exhorted them not to be afraid, "because the Savior has power in you greater than the frailty of your flesh. In the impossibility and powerlessness of your flesh *'you are seeking Jesus of Nazareth,'* who will be sanctified in your flesh. He *'was crucified,'* and is crucified in you, as it is written: *Truly he bore our weaknesses,*[12] because he suffered for us. *'He is risen'* in your holiness to run the course,[13] and in his coming forth from the highest heaven.[14] *'He is not here'* in such infirmity and instability as you are. *'Behold the place where he was laid,'* that is, [your] judgment was empty when your mind's doubtfulness

---

[6] Ps 109:1; see Matt 23:44; Mark 12:36; Luke 20:42.

[7] Job 40:18.

[8] Ps 109:1; see Matt 23:44; Mark 12:36; Luke 20:42.

[9] Latin *uirilem fortitudinem*, with the initial consonant of *uirilem* echoed in the following word *uirginitate*.

[10] See Eph 5:27.

[11] Ps 109:1; See Matt 23:44; Mark 12:36; Luke 20:42.

[12] Isa 53:4.

[13] See Ps 18:6.

[14] Ps 18:7.

thought that, although he has the power to support[15] you, he was in [a place] of impossibility. *'But go and tell his disciples and Peter,'* that is, on [your] sinful journey, announce [to them] with [his] precepts the ties by which you are bound in the flesh's narrow confine. *'Tell* [them] *that he is going before you into Galilee,'* that is, he comes to meet [you][16] in your shining deeds, when you pass beyond evil and do good. *'There you will see him as he told you,'* that is, he aids, inspires, and reveals good examples, as his incarnation demonstrated to you."

29. The Sunday of the Resurrection, 2

Mary Magdalene and Mary [the mother] of James and Salome bought spices. Mary Magdalene [represents] the knowledge of good and evil because through signification, knowledge of evil is like a sinful woman and knowledge of good is like a penitent. Mary [the mother] of James [designates] rationality, which is holy. Salome [stands for] the quality of the entire carnal appetite. They *bought spices that they might go and anoint Jesus;* evidently they leave behind their own will and do what they do not want, clearly, the sweetest gifts of virtues. They hasten to recognize God in charity.

And very early on the first day of the week they went to the tomb when the sun had already risen. They make haste before the root of evil arises; on the solemnity of faith they search for good desire in rationality before the rising of heat and the fire of carnal desires.

And they were saying to one another: 'Who will roll back for us the stone from the entrance of the tomb?' [In other words] knowledge, rationality, and appetite were conferring, *saying to one another:* "*'Who'* of angels or of human beings will take away from us, who are inclined toward carnal things, the hardness whereby we do not want to do good deeds, at the closing of good desire." *And looking up they saw that the stone was rolled back.* Evidently,

[15] Here Hildegard uses the verb *succurrere*, echoing the uses of *currere* above for running the course.
[16] Hildegard employs the verb *occurrere* here, continuing her play on compounds of *currere*.

with God's grace, hardness was removed so that afterward they would have joy in the good. *It was indeed very large*, because this hardness is so great that a human being is unable to move it away without God's grace.

And entering the tomb, they saw a youth sitting on the right side clothed in a white robe. With a mind resting on good desire *they saw* another life worshiping within the circle of God's power and covered in heavenly desire. *And they were astonished*, on account of the other life they are beginning, since they are human beings.

He said to them, that is, he consoled them with the newness of the other life: "*'Do not be frightened,'* looking back at those things of the flesh that you have renounced. *'You are seeking Jesus of Nazareth, who was crucified,'* that is, seeking him who will make you holy, so that he may be crucified for you in [your] carnal desires, and that through good desires you may be able to do good deeds. *'He has risen; he is not here,'* because now he is not buried within you, as he was before. *'Behold the place where he was laid,'* that is, your mind's disquiet, upon thinking that you were not able to do righteous and holy deeds. *'But go and tell his disciples and Peter that he is going before you into Galilee,'* that is, with good report announce by his footsteps and examples that now you are firm for [doing] our will, and that he is preparing an eternal home for you by crossing over to life. [17]*'There you will see him'* in that invocation: *'Come, blessed ones of my Father,'*[18] *'as he told you'* through the prophets, through himself, and through the Scriptures."

[17] Galilee as a space of crossing over (*transitus*) figures prominently in Cluniac spirituality, as evidenced in Peter the Venerable's introduction of the Feast of the Transfiguration into the Cluniac liturgy, his sermon and liturgical music for the feast, and the architecture of Cluny II with the space designated as Galilee. See Robert Folz, "Pierre le Vénérable et la liturgie," in *Pierre Abélard, Pierre le Vénérable: les courants philosophiques, littéraires et artistiques en Occident au milieu du XIIe siècle*, Abbaye de Cluny, 2–9 July, ed. Jean Châtillon, Jean Jolivet, and René Louis, Colloques internationaux du CNRS 546 (Paris: Éditions du Centre national de la recherche scientifique, 1975), 143–61.

[18] Matt 25:34.

Homilies 30 and 31

The Second Sunday after Easter

John 10:11-16

'I am the good shepherd. The good shepherd lays down his life for his sheep. The hired hand, who is not a shepherd, and whose own the sheep are not, sees a wolf coming, abandons the sheep, and flees. And the wolf snatches and scatters the sheep. But the hired hand flees, because he is a hired hand and has no concern for the sheep. I am the good shepherd, and I know my own and my own know me, just as the Father knows me and I know the Father. And I lay down my life for my sheep. And I have other sheep that are not from this fold; I must bring them also, and they will heed my voice. There will be one flock and one shepherd.'

30. The Second Sunday after Easter, 1

'I am the good shepherd,' "the Word of the Father, the Creator of creatures, because all proceed from me, and I feed them all in fullness."[1] *'The good shepherd lays down his soul for his sheep,'* that is, he

---

[1] This passage is spoken entirely in Jesus' voice, and the punctuation reflects that: italics for the scriptural passage, single quotation marks for Jesus' words throughout, and standard quotation marks for the sections in which Hildegard speaks in the first person, extending Jesus' voice. Hildegard's explanatory comments are not enclosed in quotation marks.

puts his life, by which he raised up all things, in bodily form for the chosen. *'The hired hand, who is not a shepherd, and whose own the sheep are not, sees the wolf coming.'* Clearly *'the hired hand'* [stands for] the devil, who after his ruin joined himself to the sheep in deception. He deceives the sheep because he neither made nor redeemed them. In his astuteness he *'sees'* rationality *'coming'* with temerity. When rationality in evil human beings becomes *'a wolf'* it contradicts the Lord through the knowledge of good and evil. But when God does not want to tolerate this any longer [the hired hand] *'abandons the sheep'* to God, who is stronger, as it is written: *When the strong man, armed, guards his court,*[2] *'and the [hired hand] flees.'* [Clearly the devil] dares nothing more. *'And the wolf,'* that is, rationality, when involved in brothel-like behavior,[3] *'snatches'* good knowledge *'and scatters the sheep,'* routing them with perversity. *'But the hired hand flees because he is a hired hand and has no concern for the sheep.'* [The devil] *'flees'* from truth when he joined himself to holiness guilefully and fraudulently, because he desires no good things.

'I am the good shepherd, and I know my own.' "I, who made all things, *'know'* all the chosen ones who remain in me, and the creatures, since they proceeded from me. *'And my own know me, just as the Father knows me, and I know the Father.'* All look to me, demanding and tasting all the necessary things, *'just as'* divinity *'knows me'* in humanity *'and I know'* divinity. *'And I lay down my life for my sheep'*; in a human body I place the life by which I raised them up.

'And I have other sheep who are not from this fold.' They who stray in their faith with many vices are set aside for repentance, because they have not yet touched me by good works but have opposed me. *'I must bring them also,'* because they are set aside for the life by which I will cry out to them that I made them, *'and they will heed my voice'* because they proceeded from me in true incarnation." *'There will be one flock,'* clearly one congregation in faith, *'and one shepherd,'* namely God blessed in all and above all.

---

[2] Luke 11:21.
[3] Note the play on words in the Latin: *lupanares mores* and *lupus*.

31. The Second Sunday after Easter, 2

'*I am the good shepherd.*' "I, helpful Faith, am the foundation of the virtues." '*The good shepherd lays down his life for his sheep*'; clearly, Faith sends forth a call to the virtues. '*The hired hand, who is not a shepherd, and whose own the sheep are not, sees*' the peril of souls in error, that is, '*the wolf coming,*' namely, unbelief, which is error of various types '*and whose own*' the virtues '*are not,*' because they are not born to unbelief. The '*hired hand . . . abandons the sheep and flees.*' Unbelief casts away the virtues, to which it had joined itself through deception, and withdraws itself from help, because it does not have the potential for helping through what is good. '*And the wolf snatches and scatters the sheep,*' namely, '*snatches*' the fruitfulness of virtues and saddens them. '*But the hired hand flees, because he is a hired hand and has no concern for the sheep.*' Unbelief speaks about good things but does not have good things, because it has falsehood. Good things are not tied to it, and it '*has no concern*' in holiness '*for the*' virtues.

'*I am the good shepherd and I know my own and my own know me, just as the Father knows me and I know the Father.*' "'*I am*' Faith, of great helpfulness, and I know the virtues that were born from me, because they came from me, '*just as*' eternity '*knows me*' by revelation, because I reveal eternity. '*And I lay down my soul for my sheep*'; with gentleness I put forth a sound, because I strike down the enemies who wish to destroy the virtues."

'*And I have other sheep that are not from this fold*'; clearly, "'*I have other*' virtues in oversight, because they are not known among these virtues. '*I must bring them also and they will heed my voice.*' When enemies wish to destroy them I will cry out to them, so that they will come with great aid and through new miracles, '*and they will*' perceive '*my voice,*' admonishing through all things, by many signs." '*And there will be one flock,*' that is, one army in God,[4] '*and one shepherd,*' namely one faith of Jews and of Christians.

---

[4] Latin *militia* designates the army of virtues. Hildegard takes the voice of Faith.

Homilies 32 and 33

The Lord's Ascension

Mark 16:14-20

While the eleven disciples were at table, Jesus appeared to them and upbraided their unbelief and their hardness of heart because they did not believe those who saw that he had risen. And he said to them: 'Go into the entire world and preach the gospel to every creature. The one who has believed and has been baptized will be saved. The one who has not believed will be condemned. And these signs will accompany those who believe: in my name they will cast out demons; they will speak in new tongues; they will pick up serpents; and if they drink any deadly thing it will not hurt them. They will lay their hands upon the sick and they will be well.' And then the Lord Jesus, after he had spoken to them, was taken up into heaven, and he sits at the right hand of God. And they went forth and preached everywhere, with God assisting and confirming their speech by the accompanying signs.

32. The Lord's Ascension, 1

While the eleven disciples were at table, Jesus appeared to them. While the prophets and sages were sleeping, as if in doubt, because they did not yet have the number twelve in the Lord's incarnation, signs *appeared to them* by revelation, as to Abraham through the

135

ram,[1] and as to Jacob through the angel.[2] *And he upbraided their unbelief and hardness of heart*, with scourging in their ignorance and their darkness of knowledge, *because they* saw him in the signs and portents that indicated that he was going to come in human form, but they *did not* fully *believe*.[3]

And he said to them: 'Go into the entire world, and preach the gospel to every creature.' The signs he spoke *said* to the prophets and sages: "Expand yourselves by the Holy Spirit's inspiration into the whole globe; bear fruit as far as the trees extend; reveal God to the one tasting the good in his nature, namely the human being."[4] *'The one who has believed,'* "hearing you with openness of heart," *'and has been baptized,'* "that is, has been immersed in blessings," *'will be saved'* "in salvation." *'The one who has not believed,'* such that he leads himself into the unbelief of faithlessness, *'will be condemned'* by a curse. *'And these signs will attend those who believe.'* "These examples *'will attend'* you, that is, will hold in you." *'In my name they will cast out demons; they will speak in new tongues; they will pick up serpents.'* By their revelation they will put false prophets to flight; in diligent searching they will do things hidden in the prophets and Scriptures; *'they will pick up'* the deceptions of falsehood, as even the deceitful serpent was taken up.[5] *'And if they drink any deadly thing'* of doubt in unbelief, *'it will not hurt them,'* as they will return to repentance.[6] *'They will place their hands'* in word and by deed of truth *'upon the sick,'* namely those who

[1] See Gen 22:13.

[2] See Gen 31.

[3] Note that Hildegard cuts the biblical verse short here, not using "those who saw that he had risen."

[4] Quotation marks in this homily set apart the words Hildegard continues in Christ's voice, using first-person or second-person discourse. Other sentences explain or extend the idea of the Scripture rather than speak directly in Jesus' voice, and those are presented without quotation marks.

[5] Note that Hildegard at first assumes Jesus' voice and then moves to third-person explanation.

[6] Hildegard glosses (*nocebit*, "will harm") with the prepositional phrase *in reuersione ad penitentiam*, which seems to imply simultaneity with the verb in the future.

mingle with idols, *'and they will be well,'* that is, they will speak
and reveal God's righteousness.

*And then the Lord Jesus, after he had spoken to them, was taken up
into heaven, and sits at the right hand of God.* Clearly, when the signs
of miracles were fulfilled in prophecy Christ truly was revealed
in the incarnation, as he had been foretold, *and sits* as God manifested *at the right hand of God,* because he encompasses heaven
and earth in majesty.

*And they went forth and preached everywhere, with God assisting
and confirming their speech by the accompanying signs. And they went
forth* in prophecy and revealed God in the Scriptures, *with God assisting* through Christ's body in his humanity *and confirming* the
Holy Spirit's gifts through the virtues by many miracles.

33. The Lord's Ascension, 2

*While the eleven disciples were at table, Jesus appeared to them and
upbraided their lack of faith and hardness of heart because they did not
believe those who saw that he had risen.* Those who have not yet risen
to perfection were lying in laziness, because they know God but
do not dare to raise themselves up, whence they also lack blessedness. Fear of the Lord *appeared to them* in revelation, inflicting
punishments and fiery hell, *because they* know that God is to be
feared; but upon these demonstrations they *did not* show faith.
And he said to them: 'Go, and preach the gospel to every creature.' Fear
of the Lord *said:* "*Go* from impurity to purity, revealing the goodness of God's justice."[7] *'The one who has believed and been baptized
will be saved.'* Clearly, the one who leaves behind evil things and
begins good things will be called a friend of God.[8] *'The one who
has not believed will be condemned.'* Evidently the one who leads

---

[7] Standard quotation marks in this homily mark the direct words of Fear
of the Lord. A few sentences explain or elaborate on the Scripture rather than
speak directly in Fear of the Lord's voice, and those are presented without
quotation marks.

[8] See Jas 2:23.

himself to evil is God's enemy.[9] *'And these signs will accompany those who believe.'* Praise *'will accompany'* those who love God and who have left behind evil things, establishing good things. *'In my name they will cast out demons, they will speak in new tongues, they will pick up serpents, and if they drink any deadly thing it will not hurt them.'* *'In my name they will'* expel harmful things, and they will be new in their ways of life because they will spurn diabolical arts. If they partake in evil *'it will not hurt them,'* because through penance they will rise up again in the good.[10] *'Upon the sick they will place their hands, and they will be well,'* that is, they will seek strong deeds for the weak and helpless and *'they will be well'* in the reward of the resurrection.

And then the Lord Jesus, after he spoke to them, was taken up into heaven and sits at the right hand of God. Fear of the Lord, when it achieved victory, *was taken up into heaven*, where good desires ascend to God, *and sits at the right hand of God* because it prepares repose among the virtues for the ones who fear God.

And now they went forth and preached everywhere, with God assisting and confirming their speech with the accompanying signs. They who at first had been reclining in laziness *went forth* to good renown and spread abroad the virtues' integrity. Fear of the Lord was helping by [the example of] Christ's martyrdom and giving good examples with holy rewards in eternal life.

---

[9] See Jas 4:4.

[10] The manuscript has a singular verb, *resurget*, but the subject must be those who love God, and therefore I have translated it in the plural. This is the second case in this homily where singular and plural are confusing. Earlier, where praise (*laus*) represents signs (*signa*), Hildegard links *laus* in meaning with the plural verb *sequentur* (these will follow). It is not possible to know whether the *magistra* herself or the copyist failed to keep her allegory grammatically consistent.

Homilies 34, 35, and 36

The Finding of the Holy Cross

John 3:1-15

There was a man of the Pharisees by the name of Nicodemus, a leader of the Jews. He came to Jesus by night and said to him: 'Rabbi, we know that you came from God as a teacher. For no one can perform these signs that you perform unless God is with him.' Jesus answered and said to him: 'Amen, amen, I say to you, unless someone is born anew he cannot see the kingdom of God.' Nicodemus said to him: 'How can a man be born when he is old? Can he enter into his mother's womb a second time and be reborn?'

Jesus answered: 'Amen, amen, I say to you, unless one is reborn from water and the Spirit one cannot enter the kingdom of God. What is born from flesh is flesh, and what is born from spirit is spirit. Do not marvel because I told you to be born anew. The Spirit blows where it wills, and you hear its voice and do not know from whence it comes or where it goes. So it is with everyone who is born of the Spirit.'

Nicodemus replied and said to him: 'How can these things be?' Jesus answered and said to him: 'You are a teacher in Israel and you do not know these things? Amen, amen, I say to you that we say what we know and testify to what we have seen, yet you do not accept our testimony. If I have told you about earthly things and you did not believe, if I tell you about heavenly things, how will you believe? And no one ascends into heaven except he who descends from heaven, the Son of Man who is in heaven. And as Moses lifted up the serpent in the wilderness, so

139

*must the Son of Man be exalted so that everyone who believes in him
will not perish, but will have eternal life.'*

34. The Finding of the Holy Cross, 1

*There was a man of the Pharisees by the name of Nicodemus, a leader
of the Jews,*[1] in other words the false prophets, those coming from
the righteous prophets, clearly incestuous as Balaam was,[2] and
others like him, having indeed the name of wisdom but wanting
to consider God with words and without a deed.

*He came to Jesus by night, and said to him: 'Rabbi, we know that you
came from God as a teacher.'* Indeed, they knew God by nocturnal
knowledge, thinking: "Teacher of all, *'we know'* with our intellect
that you are God."[3] *"For no one can perform these things that you
perform unless God is with him,"* because no one has the capability to do all things except God. For who would be able to make
heaven, the sun, the moon, and other signs, which were arranged
and placed on high, except God, whom no human can see while
remaining in the body?[4]

*Jesus answered and said to him: 'Amen, amen, I say to you, unless
someone is born anew he cannot see the kingdom of God.'* Clearly they
received a response from the Holy Spirit through certain signs
in truth that the heavenly life, which cannot be seen, will be of
greater benefit than this life that can be seen, because in this world
the kingdom of God cannot be seen by human beings.

[1] In this homily Nicodemus represents the false prophets. The Latin verb
forms in the commentary are consistently plural, even though they gloss
Nicodemus.

[2] See Numbers 22–24; 2 Pet 2:15.

[3] Quotation marks in this homily mark the instances where Hildegard
clearly speaks in first- or second-person discourse through the voice of Nicodemus, what he represents (false prophets, nothingness, a sinner) and Jesus.
In other sentences Hildegard explains or elaborates rather than speaking
directly in another voice, and those are presented without quotation marks.

[4] See 1 Tim 6:16.

Nicodemus said to him: 'How can a man be born when he is old?' [In other words] the false prophets said: "What prosperity is there in that invisible life, when this visible life is worth so little?" *'Can he enter into his mother's womb a second time and be reborn?'* "Is it possible that life comes down at the very beginning and becomes the second life, because this visible life comes first, and the heavenly life follows after it?"

Jesus answered their opinion: *'Amen, amen, I say to you, unless someone is reborn from water and the Spirit he cannot enter the kingdom of God.'* By true revelation every creature has a circle in water,[5] such that without water it neither comes into being nor lives, because when *the Spirit of the Lord was borne over the waters*[6] it became evident that the Spirit of the Lord breathed on the water and brought it to life. Thence also the spirit of a human being is revived to life by baptism with water, since the human being alone is in aridity from the first origin because of Adam's disobedience.[7] *'What is born from flesh is flesh,'* because flesh produces flesh, and is human. *'What is born from the Spirit is spirit,'* when it will breathe in water and will see another life. *'Do not marvel because I told you to be born anew,'* "that is, *do not marvel* in disbelief that you may have life, because as disease is brought to the blood,[8] so also the human being will be brought back to the Holy Spirit by water."

'The Spirit blows where it will,' resounding through righteousness, *'and you hear,'* understanding and perceiving, *'its voice,'* that is, its movement. *'And you do not know whence it comes, or where*

---

[5] Note this example of Hildegard's use of a circle, Latin *circuitus.*

[6] Gen 1:2.

[7] Latin *primo ortu* is redundant: "at the first origin." Hildegard associates the water of baptism with that of creation in other texts, probably arguing against the views of the Cathars, who rejected baptism by water in favor of baptism by the Spirit. Indeed, they used this same gospel text, John 3:5, to support their belief. See Kienzle, *Speaking New Mysteries,* 265–67, 278–80.

[8] Latin *tabes* denotes pestilence or disease. Compare *Epistolarium* 1, 55R, 135; *Letters* 1, 55R, 133, where this notion is translated as the blood being tainted. Here Hildegard seems to contrast the process of the blood carrying disease to that of the Spirit bringing the health (of salvation) to the human through water.

it goes' because no human sees it or knows its journeys; it may encompass another life or be able to be seen bodily. *'So it is with everyone who is born of the Spirit,'* clearly the life of every invisible creature whatsoever that moves itself, since whatever lives is first aroused to life invisibly before it moves itself bodily. Hence what is born is called, as it were, aroused by the Spirit.

Nicodemus answered and said to him: 'How can these things be?' Clearly, the false prophets think one should believe in the invisible life more than the visible. *Jesus answered and said to him: 'You are a teacher in Israel, and you do not know these things? Amen, amen, I say to you that we speak what we know and testify to what we have seen, yet you do not accept our testimony.'* Clearly God *answered*: *"'You are'* in the distinguished *persona* of the holy ones, as it were, but you *'do not know'* the truth.[9] I am affirming by the knowledge of speaking and the knowledge of seeing that you do not know the revelation of either attestation." *'If I have told you about earthly things and you did not believe, if I tell you about heavenly things, how will you believe?'* [In other words] *"'if I'* demonstrate the visible things that you are, and you *'do not know'* them, how will you be able to *'know'* the things you cannot see, which I am?" *'And no one ascends into heaven except he who descends from heaven, the Son of Man who is in heaven.'* Evidently no shadowy[10] knowledge makes an ascent into heaven, except what was intincted by that which life established in brilliant form,[11] because humans receive souls from heaven, and they return to heaven through good works because they are also members of the Son of God.[12]

'And as Moses lifted up the serpent in the wilderness,' clearly the Scripture, which was received from the Holy Spirit, showed it

[9] Note that Hildegard extends God's voice for a while here, speaking in first person singular to an audience in second person plural. She then returns to an explanatory mode.

[10] Latin *tenebrosa*.

[11] Latin *intinctum* seems to echo the theme of baptismal water; in other words, no one ascends to heaven without baptism by water.

[12] Hildegard expresses here the theology of procession of souls from God and return of souls to God. She also incorporates the image of the body of Christ, of which one becomes a member by doing good works.

uncovered, that is human wickedness, through the exaltation of salvation from death's ruin.[13] *'So must the Son of Man be exalted'*[14] when the breath of life is sent into human beings for life, so that believers will be saved, when *'every'* soul *'who believes in him'* as a human being *'will not perish'* into nothingness *'but will have eternal life.'* Those who believe in God will be saved; the life seen in the upper realms will be known because the body through which life is known becomes arid, and life abides in God.

35. The Finding of the Holy Cross, 2

There was a man of the Pharisees by the name of Nicodemus. Evil was known from what is upright, because evil is known from the good; Nicodemus means *nothing*, because through it the things which are good and righteous are known and proven.

This man came to Jesus by night, and said to him: 'Rabbi, we know that you came as a teacher from God.' Nothingness *came* in hatred and envy to the highest good *and said*, tempting: "Because you place all things in order, *'we know'* by observing that there is no power except you. *'For no one can do these signs which you perform unless God is with him.'* Clearly, power, victory, and deeds serve no one except you alone, who are God."

Jesus answered, saying to him through revelation: *'Amen, amen, I say to you'* by true demonstration, *'unless one is born anew one cannot see the kingdom of God.'* In other words, "If creation does not carry out its work by that life-giving, which ought not to be empty, and which you do not do because you are nothing, creation does not awaken to the life-giving that fills all things, since any earthly and fallen creature rises again by being reborn at the birth of its beginning."

---

[13] Hildegard employs a masculine accusative participle (*denudatum*), referring to the serpent as the object of "lifted up," at the same time that she glosses the serpent as "human wickedness" (feminine). To render that I have used "it" and "human wickedness" as double objects of the verb "showed" (*ostendit*).

[14] See Num 21:6-9.

Nicodemus said to him: 'How can a man be born when he is old? Can he enter into his mother's womb a second time and be reborn?' The evil that is nothing *said:* "In what way is creation able to exert itself in its work, when it is disobedient to you? *'Can'* it hear again that first *Let there be,*[15] and assume another circle, when you said: *'and they were made?'*"[16]

Jesus answered: 'Amen, amen, I say, to you, unless one is reborn of water and the Spirit one cannot enter the kingdom of God.' The highest good *answered:* "'*I say*' the things you do not want to know; no form of creatures walks or stands or is able to be seen unless it has been created and quickened by the '*water*' of growth '*and*' the life-giving '*Spirit*'. Unless it turns around the wheel that is life, it does not live. When both animals and other creatures are formed in secret they can be said to be born, but when they have touched the air or the growth of greenness or the vigor of fortitude they are said to be reborn." *'What is born,'* that is, brought forth *'from flesh is flesh,'* knowing nothing, because it lacks form—the wheel, namely life; *'and what is born from the Spirit,'* either by air or by growth, *'is spirit,'* because the wheel that is life is complete power. "*'Do not marvel'* that you are alone and do not desire life, *'because I told you that you must be born anew,'* that is, praise life, because I am life, and all creatures live through me."

"'*The spirit blows,*' giving life because the wheel of life that I touch neither stands nor moves nor flies without me, *'where it will,'* when it knows it ought to be so. *'And you hear its voice, and you do not know from whence it comes, or where it goes.'* You perceive its life-giving, giving life to anything whatsoever, or transforming the things given life, because it contains all things invisibly. *'So it is with everyone who is born of the Spirit,'* because such is my power, which you do not know and do not wish to know in life."

Nicodemus said to him: 'How can these things be?' Nothingness introduced doubt: "How *'can'* this *'be,'* because it is not touched and not seen, unless this is a falsehood?" *Jesus answered: 'You are a*

---

[15] Gen 1:1.
[16] Ps 32:9.

teacher in Israel, and you do not know these things?' [In other words],
it countered: *"'You are'* an artisan who polishes all things that must
be polished. What is it that you polish, if not what you *'do not
know'*? However, what *'you do know'*, you do not desire to *'know'*,
and you seek out the things you *'do not know'*, which you will not
be able to know."[17] *'Amen, amen, I say to you, we speak about that
which we know and we testify to what we have seen, yet you do not accept our testimony.'* "Therefore all the things you do not see, I *'know'*
and bring forth to life, revealing in [their] form, because what is
invisible is present to me." *'If I have told you about earthly things
and you did not believe,'* "that is, if you *'do not know'* the earthly
form that is able to be seen," *'how will you believe if I tell you about
heavenly things'* "since you do not understand what is invisible,
that when you wish to go up you do not have a head; when you
wish to sit down you do not have feet. For you *'do not know'* the
face of creation, nor do you *'know'* the journey of the Spirit."

*'No one has ascended into heaven except he who descended from
heaven, the Son of Man who is in heaven.'* "No creature among grow-
ing creatures grows unless its greenness binds it together; *'except
one who descended'* unformed into form, because no form is able
to exist unless it is from me, because creatures first begin to be
formed invisibly, and take life from me, [the life] which I am,
their verdure."[18]

*'And as Moses lifted up the serpent in the wilderness, so must the Son
of Man be exalted, so that everyone who believes in him will not perish
but will have eternal life.'*[19] "As water sends its vapor upwards from
below, because when water's moving vapor goes up the water

[17] Hildegard speaks at length here in the voice of Jesus.

[18] Latin *quae uiror earum sum* ("I [feminine] who am the verdure of those"
[feminine]). Pitra corrected his text to read *quia viror eorum sum*: because I am
the verdure of those (masculine). However, the feminine *earum* understand-
ably refers to creatures (*creaturarum*). The manuscript reads *quae*, and I have
translated it assuming that it refers back to *uita*: Christ, the highest good, is
both the life and the verdure of creatures—clearly a statement against the
Platonic forms. The term verdure echoes the notion of greenness. Below
Hildegard uses the word *vigor*, translated as vigor or strength.

[19] See Num 21:6-9.

that is seen is in a form, so also do vigor and greenness rise up
from me for the strengthening of other creatures, so that every
creature that stands firm in its vigor and greenness will not dis-
solve, because the life from whence creatures live is invisible, and
must be believed to be so because any rottenness whatsoever must
be cast out, and what remains must be held. You are evil alone and
do not desire life but deny life. But whoever praises life is in life."

36. The Finding of the Holy Cross, 3

*There was a man of the Pharisees by the name of Nicodemus, a leader
of the Jews;* in other words, a sinner in many deeds, a transgressor
of those praising his evils. *This man came to Jesus by night,* evidently
to repentance in doubt, *and said to him: 'Rabbi, we know that you are a
teacher who came from God,'* "because you set the measure of repentance, you are from God and not from another." *'For no one can do
these signs which you perform unless God is with him.'* [In other words],
'no one can' bring sinners back to life except through the Holy Spirit.

Jesus answered, saying to him who wants to return to God: *'Amen,
amen, I say to you,'* without doubt, *'unless one is born anew,'* that is,
becomes new by conversion, leaving behind sins, *'one cannot see
the kingdom of God,'* clearly, if one has persevered in evil.

Nicodemus, namely, the sinner, *said to him: 'How can a man be
born,'* that is, become new in holiness, *'when he is old,'* evidently,
decrepit in sins? *'Can he enter into the womb of his mother,'* clearly,
the comprehension of innocence, *'a second time and be reborn,'* that
is, have remorse for his sins and leave sins behind?

Jesus answered: 'Amen, amen, I say to you,' making this known,
'unless one is reborn from water,' casting out *the old man,*[20] repenting
with groans and tears, so that he avoids evil, *'and from the Spirit'*
of compunction for life, so that he does good things, *'one cannot
enter the kingdom of God'* and become a companion of Christ. *'What
is born from flesh,'* in the sordidness of sins, *'is flesh,'*[21] lying in sins

[20] Eph 4:22; Col 3:19.
[21] Hildegard uses alliteration here: *in putredine peccatorum.* I have used
alliteration in English to render that.

without the cleansing of repentance; *'and what is born from spirit,'* stirred to repentance by the Holy Spirit's inspiration, *'is spirit,'* namely, it savors the things that are for life when it repents. *'Do not marvel because I told you: "You must be* reborn; in other words, it is not difficult for you to be restored to life through compunction and repentance."'*

'The spirit,' clearly the Holy Spirit, *'blows where it will'* by the compunction of tears, *'and you hear its voice'* in the confession of a sinner, *'and do not know from whence it comes'* through grace to the sinner's heart admonishing him, *'or where it goes,'* strengthening him so that he perseveres in good things. *'Thus is everyone'* brought back to life *'who is born from the Spirit,'* rising again to life through repentance.

Nicodemus answered and said to him: 'How can these things be?' The transgressor, putting aside hardness,[22] *said to him: 'How can these things be,'* that one who is guilty of many sins becomes innocent from sins? *Jesus answered: 'You are a teacher in Israel, and you do not know these things?'* Repentance *answered*, strengthening and exhorting the sinner: "You will have compunction, sighing upwards with moans, *'and you do not know these things,'* that you will have life by confessing your sins?"[23]

'Amen, amen, I say to you, we speak about that which we know and testify to what we have seen, yet you do not accept our testimony.' "Human beings rise up again to life through confession and obtain much glory at the last; if you wish to persevere in doubt, it will benefit you not at all. *'If I have told you about earthly things,'* so that you leave behind your sins, *'and you did not believe'* that you would rise again to life, *'if I tell you about heavenly things,'* namely, that you will have a great remuneration when you relinquish all that is yours on account of God, *'how will you believe'* that you are going to have a supernal reward?" *'No one has ascended into heaven'* and desired heavenly things *'except he who descended from heaven,'* showing through sighs of the heart what had been hidden and

---

[22] Latin *duriciam*, presumably hardness of heart, but Hildegard does not qualify the noun here.

[23] Sighs and moans reflect the language of the Latin in RB 4.57.

secret in his heart. '*The Son of Man, who is in heaven*' reveals in this through repentance that he is human; moaning begins first in the hidden place of the heart and leads humans at last to contemplation of the invisible, which '*is in heaven*'.

'*And as Moses lifted up the serpent in the wilderness,*'[24] that is, the heart's compunction raised up the heart's aridity away from the vices that are in sins, because compunction draws toward life, '*so must the Son of Man be exalted, so that all who believe in him will not perish but have eternal life.*' He who does not abandon many things raises the sinner from the earthly things in which he lies. He will think he does not need repentance because he does not sin very much. However, as repentant sinners rise up to life, so also those without repentance, whether out of negligence or because of false trust, who think they do not sin, must do penance for this same reason. Together they rise again to life through the grace of God.

[24] See Num 21:6-9.

Homilies 37 and 38

The Octave of Pentecost

Luke 16:19-31

'A certain man was very rich; he wore purple and fine linen and feasted sumptuously every day. And there was a certain beggar, named Lazarus, who was lying at his gate full of sores, longing to be satisfied with the crumbs that fell from the rich man's table, and no one gave him [anything]. But even the dogs came and licked his sores. However, it happened that the beggar died and was carried by the angels to Abraham's bosom.

The rich man also died and was buried in hell. Lifting up his eyes while he was in torment, he saw Abraham far off and Lazarus in his bosom. And calling out, he said: "Father Abraham, have mercy upon me, and send Lazarus to dip the end of his finger in water in order to cool my tongue, because I am suffering in this fire."

And Abraham said to him: "Son, remember that you received good things in your life and Lazarus likewise received evil things. Now he is consoled, but you are suffering. And by all these things, between us and you a great chasm has been fixed, so that those who wish to cross over to you from here are not able, and neither from there [is anyone able] to cross over to this place."

And he said: "Therefore, I beg you, Father, to send him to my father's house. For I have five brothers; let him give testimony to them lest they also come into this place of torments."

But Abraham said to him: "They have Moses and the prophets; let them listen to them." And he said: "No, Father Abraham, but if one

149

from the dead will go to them, they will repent." But *[Abraham] said to him: "If they do not listen to Moses and the prophets, neither will they believe if someone rises from the dead."'*

37. The Octave of Pentecost, 1

'A certain man,' who signifies people living on earth, *'was very rich,'* which designates the wise and prudent,[1] who are extolled in their wisdom but sluggish in both fear and honor of God.[2] They do not look within themselves or recognize themselves as human beings. *'He wore purple and fine linen,'* that is, they are surrounded by the honor people render to them and by the fame in which they rejoice. *'He feasted sumptuously every day';* clearly, without fear of the Lord they demand daily honors as they will.

'And there was a certain beggar named Lazarus lying at his gate full of sores.' Clearly [Lazarus stands for] the uneducated and simple, who moan from their souls' appetite because they would have wisdom and prudence willingly but are unable to rise up to them. By their senses they are humbled at the revealed understanding of wise prelates. They are encompassed everywhere by wretched desires, which *the poor in spirit*[3] have in desire. *'He was longing to be satisfied with the crumbs that fell from the table of the rich man.'* Clearly [the simple were] *'longing'* to be filled by the smallest gifts of wisdom, which exceeded the measure of the gifts, like those scraps that were left over from those who had eaten and *'that fell'* from the understanding a person grasps with his intellect, namely, the height of surpassing prudence. *'And no one gave him [any]';* clearly neither their superfluous will nor their foolish

---

[1] Hildegard uses a verb of signification here: Latin *designat* translated as signifies or represents.

[2] In this homily the rich man represents the wise but proud; Lazarus stands for the simple; Abraham designates the saints in glory. Hildegard expands the voice of each.

[3] Matt 5:3.

inquiry, which are as nothing, *'gave'* the gifts of the wisdom they were uselessly seeking. *'But even the dogs came and licked his sores'*; that is, poor humanity *'came'* into their minds, admonishing their wretched desire, such that no one in their estimation could discuss anything more lofty or more profound than God wills.

'However, it happened that the beggar died.' With God's inspiration the poor, simple, unlearned people humble themselves by that mortification such that all things will suffice for them in the humble knowledge that God has given them. So it is written: *Blessed are the dead who die in the Lord.*[4] *'And he was carried to the bosom of Abraham by the angels,'* that is, exalted by holy virtues in the protection of the holy fathers' holiness.

'The rich man also died'; in other words, those who unjustly extol themselves in their wisdom, as did Origen,[5] *'died'* from all joy and a happy life, so that they rejoice neither with God nor with human beings. *'And he was buried in hell;'* namely, he remained in great weariness, in despair without the assurance of complete hope.

But *'lifting up his eyes while he was in torment, he saw Abraham far off and Lazarus in his bosom.'* Clearly, they looked upon their own knowledge with an afflicted spirit because they are without consolation. Far from hope, they saw in their knowledge the saints' sanctity and glory, and one *poor in spirit*[6] in the grasp and embrace of the joys of the Gospel and the prophets and of those who fulfill them through actions.

'And calling out, he said: "Father Abraham, have mercy upon me."' Bursting into tears, [they] *'said*: "Oh, holiness and glory of the saints, you ought to look after our offspring[7] by helping us. *Send Lazarus to dip the tip of his finger in water and cool my tongue,'* that is, allow poverty of spirit to flow toward us with some consolation. With sweet anointing moisten the smallest work with consolation's wisdom. With the mildest moderation temper the

---

[4] Rev 14:13.

[5] On the legend of Origen's fall, see Kienzle, *Speaking New Mysteries*, 86.

[6] Matt 5:3.

[7] The Pitra edition reads the manuscript as *non gemitus* instead of *nos genitos*.

overflowing speech I uttered.[8] *I am in agony in this fire,* namely, my soul is restrained by burning heat because I do not know what I can do."

'*And Abraham said to him, "Son, remember that you received good things in your life, but Lazarus likewise [received] evil things."*' The saints' glory responded to bright wisdom: "Recall that you, created by God, had good things in abundance in every matter that you undertook, but the poverty of humility, on the contrary," *received* pain and grief. *But now he is consoled*; those who were gentle in God now have joy in faith. *You are truly suffering*; "those who want higher things than they are able to possess are in limitation and doubt."

And by all these things, a great chasm has been fixed between us and you. In the aforesaid matters, the obscurity of God's mysteries stands evident between us, we who followed humility in our knowledge, and you, who had pride in your knowledge. *Those who want to cross over from here to you cannot, and neither from there to cross over to this place.* The ones who are simple on account of God, who attempt *to cross over from* us simple ones *to* your clear minds, without God's dispensation, *cannot* grasp that it is not in their pride; *and neither* can they *cross* from you, the lofty wise ones[9] to us, the unlearned on account of God, such that you would have both fully, namely the exaltation of your mind and your poverty in simplicity, because all things have been appointed justly by God. For the sun does not give its brilliance to the moon, nor the moon its brightness to the sun; neither the sun nor the moon give their brilliance to the stars, nor the stars their brightness to the sun. So the greater do not give their greatness joyously to the lesser; neither do the lesser give their poverty to

[8] The homily mixes singular and plural pronouns here, and perhaps Scripture and interpretation, as Hildegard uses "us" for the voice of the wise and proud, whom the rich man represents, but then reverts to "I" (instead of "we") even though the wise and proud still speak.

[9] Latin *elati sapientes*. I have translated *elati*, often rendered with "proud," as "lofty" because of the numerous references in this homily to height and falling.

the greater; nor do these give their properties to the weak; nor do the weak divide their gifts between those two, as it is written: *Fire kindles in his sight.*"[10]

'*And he said, "Therefore, I beg you, Father, that you send him into the house of my father."*' Evidently the lofty wise ones pleaded: "You, who are the glory of the saints, show poverty, which is heavenly, in the capacity of our bodies, such that such great signs may occur, and you will discern that we believe that God compels us to good. For some say the following: 'Would that we were created such that we would always do good and could despise evil!'"

"*For I have five brothers so that he may warn them, lest they also come into this place of torments,* that is, the five senses *may warn* by signs *lest they also come* through boldness *into* the appointed punishments, and so that they take heed lest they fall in pride, just as we too have fallen."

'*And Abraham said to him: "They have Moses and the prophets."*' The saints' glory *said* to the lofty wise ones: "*They have* the Savior's humanity and the Scriptures. *Let them listen to them* with knowledge and faith."

'*And he said: "No, Father Abraham."*' The lofty wise ones '*said*: "*No,* do not do this, glory of the saints; you who will look after us. *But if anyone,* that is, any human being, *will go from the dead to them, they will repent.* In other words, the unrighteously wise will restrain themselves from evil because of the signs and report from a hidden miracle, that we would be created such that even though we desired to do evil, we were unable to accomplish this, and when we desired good, we were able to do it."[11]

'*But he said to him: "If they do not listen to Moses and the prophets, neither will they believe if anyone resurrects from the dead."*' [In other words, the saints said] to the lofty wise that "*if they do not listen to*" the Savior's humanity and the Scriptures with knowledge and faith, they will understand neither light nor darkness for any

---

[10] Ps 49:3.

[11] See Rom 7:15-23. The thrust of the argument here, presented by the proud, is that humans cannot do evil. Hildegard will refute that through the voice of Abraham, representing the saints.

purpose, [even] if any human being shone forth from unmade signs that have not yet appeared.[12] If human beings were created such that they could do neither evil nor good, they would be like trees. Trees bloom in summer and are dry in winter, and thus were not made in God's image and likeness.[13] Neither would humans have five bodily senses, nor would they know how to praise God, nor would they avoid the devil.[14]

38. The Octave of Pentecost, 2

'*A certain man,*' namely, Pleasure in the human being, '*was very rich,*' in the vicissitudes of the fatness[15] of self will, '*and he wore purple and fine linen,*' that is, he entered into the appetite[16] for sin through pleasures. '*And he feasted sumptuously every day,*' namely, he increased every vice whatsoever before the face of his heart.[17]

'*And there was a certain beggar named Lazarus who was lying at [his] gate covered with sores, longing to be satisfied from the crumbs*

[12] At this point Hildegard stops speaking in the voice of Abraham and the saints and instead reports and explains their words in the third person.

[13] Gen 1:26; see Gen 1:27; 5:3.

[14] Hildegard argues that humans have a rational soul, which differentiates them from other creatures, and enters into twelfth-century debates over the soul. I am grateful for insights on this to Robert Davis, in "Hugh of St.-Victor's *Explanatio* of the Song of Mary on Luke 1:46-55," an unpublished paper presented at the International Congress on Medieval Studies, Kalamazoo, 2009. Hugh rejects the notion of a divided or twofold soul: one sensual, one spiritual, and he makes an analogy from the natural world. He refutes the notion that a soul is necessary for movement and growth, "since we see clearly that bushes and plants are moved and grow without a soul" (*cum manifeste videamus virgulta, et herbas sine anima moveri, et incrementum habere*, PL 175:419C). Hugh further argues that the [human] seed is vivified and receives sense only from a rational soul (*ex hoc ipso verisimilius probetur, semen nonnisi ex anima rationali vivificari, et sensum percipere*, PL 175:419).

[15] Latin *pinguedo.*

[16] Latin *gustum peccati.*

[17] In this homily the rich man designates Pleasure and Lazarus stands for Sighing or Longing for God. These qualities are personified in much but not all of the commentary. Other personified virtues are Heavenly Desire, Hope, and Fear of the Lord.

that fell from the table of the rich man.' Clearly, Sighing for God was moaning, remaining at rest before the obvious vices of its pleasure, *'covered with'* foolishness, such that it understands neither good nor evil completely, due to love of the flesh. [It was] *'longing'* that the least blame be allowed it, so that it would be permitted to commit even the slightest sin without danger—the sins left over from the expanse of pleasure, such that Pleasure did not pay attention to them. *'And no one gave him [any].'* At its beginning it did not find that this was permitted, and neither through pleasure could it have this to full satisfaction. *'But the dogs came and licked his sores,'* that is, forgetfulness of God—the fact that the human being forgets God[18]—*'came'* shaking and poured on the foolishness that does not understand God due to love of the flesh but softens the human being's mind and makes it doubtful.

'However, it happened that the beggar died.' With God's help Sighing, which was in doubt, failed, such that every doubt receded from it. *'And he was carried by the angels to the bosom of Abraham,'* that is, Sighing was carried by Heavenly Desire into the appetite[19] for Hope. *'The rich man also died and was buried in hell.'* Pleasure expired, suffocated by Fear of the Lord, since Fear of the Lord is a sort of hell for Pleasure.

'But lifting up his eyes while he was in torment, he saw Abraham far off and Lazarus in the bosom of [Abraham]', that is, raising its knowledge upward in its limitation, Pleasure saw Hope as something foreign and sighed in its heart for God with the appetite for Hope.

'And calling out, he said: "Father Abraham, have mercy [upon me],"' that is, wailing, it prayed: "O paternal Hope, spare me." *Send Lazarus to dip the end of his finger in water in order to cool my tongue,* [in other words]: Grant Moaning for God the smallest taste of this[20] matter with sweet allurement, so that I may have some happiness for the deeds I have carried out with my tongue. *Because I*

---

[18] Hildegard clarifies this construction (*obliuio Dei*) as an objective genitive: the human forgets God, not God the human.

[19] Latin *gustus*.

[20] Latin *causae suae*; the antecedent is somewhat ambiguous, and so the vague translation "this" is chosen.

am in agony in this fire, that is, I am pressed down by that weight, because I fear God."

'*And Abraham said to him: "Son, remember that you received good things in your life, but Lazarus likewise received evil things."*' Hope responded to Pleasure: "One born in the flesh, looking back, you have an abundance of sweetness in the deeds of your will. In contrast, the one wailing '*received*' every pain on account of his love for God. *But now he is consoled, but you are truly suffering.* Clearly, at this time he has the clarity of faithfulness, but you are shaken with terror.

And in all these things shaken by struggles, *a great chasm,* namely a tempest of vices *has been fixed* that is, arranged, *between us,* in other words, *between* those who belong to me, Hope, *and you,* who look to sensual pleasure.[21] *Those who want to cross over,* clearly, those who moan to God to descend, looking back toward consent, just as the soul sometimes consents to the body from the hope which they have for God, *to you,* who are in the throes and terrors of your flesh, *would not be able* because of righteousness, for virtues do not communicate to vices. *And neither from there,* from those sufferings, in which you suffer from vices, *to cross over to this place,* to those who rejoice in hope for God, for vices do not mingle with virtues."

Pleasure *said* trembling to Hope: "*I beg, you Father,*" who represents Hope, "*that you,* sparing us, *send him,* Sighing for God, *to the house of my father,* in other words, to the dwelling of cupidity, so that terrified with great fear, it may recover from its inordinate desires. *For I have five brothers; let him give testimony to them lest they also come into this place of torments*: in other words, associations, clearly the body's five senses that are associated with me. Let it show them some terror to frighten them, so that they will recover from the burning of inordinate desires. For if any human would rise '*from the dead*', people would be frightened; also in this way my companions, the body's five senses, will be shaken in the

---

[21] The glosses here are quite difficult to render in translation and are clearer in the form of running commentary than when separated from the scriptural text.

terror of enduring those sufferings, when we suffer greatly from fear of the Lord, since we are not allowed to do what we would do willingly."

'*And Abraham said to him: "They have Moses and the prophets,"'* "namely baptism's cleansing and the gifts of the Holy Spirit." "*Let them listen to them*, by carrying out divine precepts." '*And he said: "No, Father Abraham, but if one from the dead will go to them, they will do penance."'* Clearly Pleasure '*said*: "Do not confine them in this way. If any one of the virtues, from the unheard-of and hidden miracle, like the thunder of a sudden sign in a sigh,[22] will go with the motion of terrifying shaking to the associations of the five senses, in headlong weeping, they will abstain from evil, such that they will not carry it out."' It is as if [Pleasure] were to say: "Since I am unable to carry out as I wish those deeds that I would willingly do, therefore, let the five senses that are in my body at least be frightened and restrained by some unexpected happening, so that it will not please them to sin."

'*But he said to him: "If they do not listen to Moses and the prophets, neither will they believe if someone resurrects from the dead."'* [In other words] Hope said to Pleasure that if the senses do not consent to righteousness and holiness through baptism's cleansing and the gifts of the Holy Spirit, it would be of no benefit if one of the virtues wanted to shake them by some unheard-of signs, or by weeping and lamentation. Just as the ropes did not bind Samson, but were broken,[23] so neither would those terrors of sighing shake them to repentance, but they would vanish into emptiness.[24]

[22] Latin *tonitruo repentini signi in suspirio*, uses alliteration.

[23] See Judg 16:8-9.

[24] Here, as in the first homily on this pericope, Hildegard does not take the voice of Abraham—in this case, Hope—at the conclusion. She seems to be using the third person to wrap up the homily.

Homilies 39 and 40

The Third Sunday after Pentecost

Luke 14:16-24

'A certain man gave a great banquet and invited many. And he sent his servant, at the hour of the banquet, to tell the ones who had been invited to come, since everything was ready then.

And they all began at once to excuse themselves. The first said: "I have purchased a farm and I must go out to see it. I pray you, have me excused." And another said: "I have purchased five yoke of oxen and I am going to inspect them. I pray you, have me excused." And another said: "I have married a wife and therefore I cannot come."

And after returning, the servant reported these things to his master. Then the householder became angry and said to his servant: "Go out quickly to the squares and streets of the city and bring in the poor and weak, the blind and lame." And the servant said: "Sir, it has been done as you commanded, and there is still room." And the master said to the servant: "Go out to the highways and compel them to come in so that my house may be filled. For I tell you that none of those men who were invited will taste my banquet."'

39. The Third Sunday after Pentecost, 1

'A certain man gave a great banquet and invited many.' Clearly, Adam gained this fallen world which will end at some point, and

which the banquet signifies;¹ *'many'* are those who were going to be born from Adam. *'And he sent his servant at the hour of the banquet to tell the ones who had been invited to come, since everything was ready then.'* Adam admonished creation, which had been subjected to him in servitude at the time of the world, to show humankind, which had been *'invited'* for the cultivation of the world, that they would *'come'* and display zeal, desire, and will, just as he himself worked, planted, and tended. All things manifested obedience to Adam with the greenness and benefit of their fruits, because he was the first one, to whom God had subjugated them: "The things that are necessary for you, you find in us, and therefore be obedient with us, just as we also obey our Creator."²

'And they all began at once to excuse themselves.' At the outset of their action human beings *'excused themselves'* from obedience, with the result that they did not obey God in the condition in which they were created, as did other creatures that remain in their own condition.

'The first said to him: "I have purchased a farm and I must go to see it. I pray you, have me excused."' Those who first did contrary acts knowingly said to creation: "I have acquired power, I have taken hold of it by the sweat of labor, and I cannot refrain. I am working, so that I can consider what I may do." Although they sigh with a sigh and a moan, nonetheless, they do wrong, because the rest of creation shows obedience to God.³

'And another said: "I have purchased five yoke of oxen, and I am going to test them. I pray you, have me excused."' Next those who established secular discipline said in their knowledge: "I acquired the rituals of sacrifices with the five senses," with which they began these things out of pride, as if they and not God established all

¹ Latin *designat* provides an example of Hildegard using a verb of signifying.
² Creation, replying to Adam's admonishment above, seems to be admonishing humans, who then begin to offer excuses.
³ The singular pronoun in the Latin, *ei*, apparently refers to God, although one might expect *ipsi*. Sighing and moaning are normally signs of repentance, but Hildegard makes it clear here that they are not in this case.

these things themselves. [They spoke] suppliantly, fearful but yet resistant.

'And another said: "I have a wife, and therefore I cannot come."' Those who want to live freely said: "Having excess freedom, I was drawn through carnal desires to beget children. This suffices for us. I am not able to do such small things and to cultivate, as the elements and other creatures do and cultivate, but let creation serve us as it wishes." And these do not ask to be excused, because they are seen as augmenting creation.[4]

'And returning, the servant reported these things to his master.' On the contrary, creation did with all humans differently than Adam did. Adam sinned in foolishness, but his descendants in cleverness. They showed that the human being refused to keep his own condition. Whence it is written: *'Will all the tribes lament over themselves?'*[5]

'The angry householder said to his servant: "Go out quickly in the squares and streets of the town and bring in the poor and weak, the blind and lame."' Adam, frightened and trembling because he foresaw these future things in the spirit and even saw that the world would not thus make progress and flourish among his descendants, as with himself, *'said'* to creation: "Plant and bloom in the earth's circle, in the woods of great forests, in deserted, arid, uninhabitable, and abandoned places *'and bring'* them into the circle for the sight and use of human beings, so that all people may come and see what is useful to them in these things, such that they may still be worthy for something."

'And the servant said: "Master, it has been done as you commanded, and there is still room."' Creation *'said'* in obedience: "I must serve you; it has been arranged, as they edify your desire. The earth *'still'* possesses the power it brought forth, when it will be hardened and struck by work, bringing forth wine, because the earth before the flood was fragile and delicate, but after the flood became hard and firm."

[4] Here Hildegard comments on the apparent discrepancy in the text: the third invitee does not offer an excuse.
[5] Rev 1:7; see Rev 18:9; see Matt 24:30.

'And the master said to the servant: "Go out to the highways and streets and compel them to come in, so that my house may be filled."' Adam *'said'* to creation: *"Go out* in servitude into every circle and ambit of human deeds and into the bending of plants.[6] Bind the earth fast so that it opens itself and may sprout everywhere with greenness and fruit, and even with the vigor of the most vigorous sap, namely wine. For the vine is more a plant than a tree, and like a plant it is both planted in the earth and nourished, so that the womb of complete comprehension may be full, which I comprehend in the world."[7] *"For I tell you that none of those men who were called will taste my banquet."'* "I assert to all creatures *'that none'* of the virile vigor[8] that dwells with creatures will touch the world, with the sense of touch in a way such that creation would obey them as it has obeyed me and will bring them such easy fruit as it did for me. For I transgressed in foolishness, but they in rebellion."

40. The Third Sunday after Pentecost, 2

'A certain man gave a great banquet and he invited many.' He who is full of the desire for pleasures made great delights at the end of time, at which he cannot be secure because he is either separated by God's power or about to die bodily. He gave orders to more and more through Vanity.[9] *'And he sent his servant at the hour of the banquet to tell the ones invited to come, since everything was ready then.'* And *'he sent'* Vanity, calling out at the time of the delights of pleasure and admonishing those who were like himself to hasten, that they would find complete fullness of their desires. *'And they all began at the same time to make excuses.'* Shaken, *'they all began at*

---

[6] With the phrase *in inflexionem herbarum* Hildegard seems to mean the training of vines, because she speaks of wine shortly thereafter.

[7] Here Hildegard uses alliteration for emphasis (Latin *comprehensionis, comprehendo*) as below (*uirilium uirium; gustabit, gustu*).

[8] Latin is plural: *uirilium uirium.*

[9] This is one of the few *expositiones* in which Hildegard focuses not on a virtue but on a vice: Vanity.

the same time to make excuses' anxiously, when a human is anxious in heart, pondering what he should do.

'The first said: "I have purchased a field and I must go out to see it."' The outset, when a human aims toward something, *'said'* wisely to that one, to Vanity: "I searched diligently for a beginning, since it must be done this way, investigating, scrutinizing what purpose it may have, how I may be able to carry out this matter. With entreaties, *I pray you*, who suggest vain things to me, *have me excused* in secret, lest you hand me over, because I want to restrain myself from vain things."

'And another said: "I have purchased five yoke of oxen, and I am going to inspect them."' *'Another,'* performing deeds, *'said*: "I have drawn to me *five* bonds of those sweating in toil, clearly seeing, hearing, going around everywhere, here and there displaying understanding and will, *and I am going to inspect* whether my deed is good or evil. *I pray you* humbly, *excuse me* as one who resists my own self in dread."'

'Another said: "I have married a wife."' Carrying out deeds to completion, he *'said'* in his knowledge: "I sent the fire of concupiscence into my flesh, so that I could perceive the concupiscence within me. *'And therefore I cannot come'* with my salvation to the pleasure of delights, but I must flee these things lest I perish." And he does not ask to be excused, because he wants to cast these things out from himself publicly.[10]

'And returning, the servant reported these things to his master.' Vanity, *'returning'* in bitterness of trouble, told the *'master,'* who was full of the desire for pleasures. *'Then the angry householder said to his servant*: "Go out quickly to the squares and streets of the city, and bring in the poor and weak, the blind and lame."'* In terror, the sweet desire for pleasure *'said'* to Vanity: "*Go out* on the spot to the common people and to the powerful of the more than powerful: armed soldiers, and the soldiers' attendants, and the poor, and

---

[10] Hildegard again explains the inconsistency of the text, namely that the third invitee does not ask to be excused, but she does it in another way.

the poorer, and lead them to me, because I find someone among them consenting to me."

'*And the servant said: "Master, it has been done as you commanded."*' Vanity '*said*': "I serve you in moderation, *and there is still room* for your will, because the wise and knowledgeable have not yet come to you." '*And the master said to the servant: "Go out to the highways and roads and compel them to come in, so that my house will be filled."*' The desire for pleasure '*said*' to Vanity: "Extend yourself to the wise and to those who have been embraced by holiness; admonish and constrain them forcefully *to come in* to me, so that they will consent to me, that is, so that my desire will be full." "*For I tell you that no one of those men who were invited will taste my banquet.*" "I announce to you who serve with me, that is, those who disdained my calling and refused to consent to me, that no might will touch my delights in any sweetness and pleasantness of my inordinate desires, but in bitterness and sorrow I will test them until the end."

Homilies 41 and 42

The Nativity of Saint John the Baptist

Luke 1:57-68

The time came for Elizabeth to give birth, and she bore a son. And her neighbors and relatives heard that the Lord had magnified his great mercy for her, and they rejoiced with her. And it happened on the eighth day that they came to circumcise the boy, and they were going to name him after his father Zechariah. But his mother, responding, said: 'By no means; he shall be called John.' And they said to her: 'There is no one among your relatives who is called by this name.' Then they made signs to his father, [inquiring] what he would want him to be called. And asking for a writing tablet, he wrote down: 'His name is John.' And they all marveled.

Then instantly his mouth was opened and his tongue loosed, and he spoke, blessing God. And fear came upon all their neighbors. And through all the hill country of Judea all these words were divulged. And all who heard them consigned them within their hearts, saying: 'Who do you suppose this child will be?' For the hand of the Lord was with him.

Then his father Zechariah was filled with the Holy Spirit, and prophesied, saying: 'Blessed be the Lord God of Israel, for he has visited and redeemed his people.'

41. The Nativity of Saint John the Baptist, 1

The time came for Elizabeth to give birth, and she bore a son. The desire to do good deeds *came* to completion for Abel, Noah, and

Enoch, and the other righteous ones who existed before the law, and it produced circumcision, the first sign of holiness.

And her neighbors and relatives heard that the Lord had magnified his great mercy for her, and they rejoiced with her. Those who were not her kin, but were nonetheless close together in the good,[1] as well as those bound by the same family *heard* that God in this newness praised the sign of holiness among earlier holy ones; *and they rejoiced* in the righteousness that was given to them in circumcision.

And it happened on the eighth day that they came to circumcise the boy, and they called him after his father Zechariah. A great sacrament arose from circumcision by means of the Lord's incarnation; those who were in the law wanted to confer the Old Law on him by the circumcision of the Old Law, because they wanted him to have it, as did any man[2] born from man and woman.

But his mother, responding, said: 'By no means; he shall be called John.' The old righteousness, which existed before the law, exhorted: *'By no means'* will he be called circumcised; *'he shall be called'* "the gift of a giving God."[3] *And they said to her: 'There is no one among your relatives who is called by this name.'* And *they* in the ancient law *said* to those who existed before the law: "We find no one in the holiness by which you were sanctified and by which we were sanctified *'who is called by this name'* of new grace."

Then they made signs to his father, inquiring what he would want him to be called. They searched the prophecy that was in the Old Law for what the cause of the Lord's incarnation would be. *And asking for a writing tablet, he wrote down: 'His name is John.' And they all marveled.* Seeking all the intricacies of the Scriptures, they discovered that *'his name'* would be the gift of humankind's salvation. In amazement, every creature became amazed by these

[1] Hildegard uses the Latin adjectives *alieni* and *propinqui* here to describe the neighbors.

[2] Hildegard intends *homo* here to be male, since she is referring to the literal sense of the Scripture and circumcision.

[3] In this homily Hildegard gives a voice to the Old Law, designated by Elizabeth, and later to the prophecy in the Old Law, represented by Zechariah.

things.[4] *Then instantly his mouth was opened and his tongue was loosed, and he spoke, blessing God.* The manifestation of prophecy was unlocked, and the righteousness of the church, *and he spoke,* praising God in human form.

And fear came over all their neighbors, and through all the hill country of Judea all these words were divulged. All born from human beings were amazed and trembled; over the height of the old institution *all these words were* led around like a wheel, as far as they could understand them. *And all who heard about them consigned them in their hearts, saying: 'Who do you suppose this child will be?'* And all who heard with good intention *consigned* the new perceptions and understandings in the new law *in their hearts* with good desires, *saying: 'Who do you suppose this child will be'* "in the new law, since he is not from the world?" *For the hand of the Lord was with him. For* God's power and work *was with him* in miracles.

Then his father Zechariah was filled with the Holy Spirit and prophesied, saying: 'Blessed be the Lord God of Israel, for he has visited and redeemed his people.' The prophecy that had been in the Old Law *was filled with the Holy Spirit,* like a balsam tree producing sap in truth, [and it said] in true revelation: *'Blessed be the Lord God'* "in the holiness of true circumcision," *'for he has visited and redeemed'* "the church with his body in refreshment and fullness."

42. The Nativity of Saint John the Baptist, 2

The time came for Elizabeth to give birth, and she bore a son; in other words, Humility of Mind came to be humbled so that deeds would proceed from her, and she brought forth holy deeds. *And her neighbors and relatives heard that the Lord had magnified his great mercy for her, and they rejoiced with her.* The angels and other saints heard that the Lord had magnified his great mercy by the increase

---

[4] This word play, *in stupore* and *obstupuit*, appears in other *expositiones* and is rendered with some sort of repetition in English.

and inspiration of the virtues, *and they rejoiced with her* that she accomplished good fruit.[5]

And it happened on the eighth day that they came to circumcise the boy, and they were going to name him after his father. At the deed's end, or at the death of human beings, the angels and saints *came* to remove the putridity of the ash[6] by sanctifying good deeds; *and they were going to name* them holy, after God from whom they went forth. *And his mother, responding, said: 'He shall be called John.'* Humility of Mind, *responding, said: 'By no means'* "are my deeds to be praised from my own merits, but from the grace of God."[7] *And they said to her: 'There is no one among your relatives who is called by this name.' And they said* to Humility of Mind: "There is nothing other found among your holy deeds, except that you be called a holy soul."

Then they made signs to his father, inquiring what he would want him to be called, in other words, submitting to God's judgment what merit he would want to give.[8] *And asking for a writing tablet, he wrote down saying: 'His name is John.' And* revealing in the knowledge of good and evil that Humility of Mind made a righteous journey, [he said] in right judgment: "Through the grace of God, a soul may be holy by good deeds." *And they all marveled.* The entire assembly of saints *marveled* at that one's[9] merits. *Then instantly his mouth was opened, and his tongue, and he spoke, blessing God.* Praise of the Father was manifested, and rationality, and they greatly esteemed God.

And fear came over all their neighbors, and throughout the hill country of Judea all these words were divulged. Fear from astonishment at the new harmoniousness—because a person first is astonished at

[5] Hildegard glosses with the verb *perfecit* (accomplished, performed) in contrast to *peperit* (gave birth) in the Scripture.

[6] Latin *cineris.* Hildegard seems to use metonymy: ash to symbolize the flesh. Pitra in his edition altered it to read *carnis.*

[7] Here Hildegard gives a speaking role to Humility of Mind, which Elizabeth represents, then to the neighbors and relatives. Zechariah's voice is likened to the voice of God.

[8] The Latin here is *illi,* which seems to refer to Humility of Mind.

[9] Latin *illius* probably refers to Humility of Mind, as does *illi* above.

that which is unknown[10]—*came over* the angels and over all the holiness of those who saw, and all holy deeds *were divulged. And all who heard about them consigned them in their hearts, saying: 'Who do you suppose this child will be?'* Understanding these matters signifies[11] joy and sighing on account of divine grace. Thinking about holiness, [they said]: "Oh, how joyful and how holy is that soul in its deeds!" *For the hand of the Lord was with him,* that is, divine help was in shining light and deed. *Then his father Zechariah was filled by the Holy Spirit, and prophesied, saying: 'Blessed be the Lord God of Israel, for he has visited and redeemed his people.'* God *was filled* by the praise of his holiness, *and prophesied* in holiness, *for he has visited* that soul by inbreathing *and* accomplished its rescue from sin magnificently, on account of the good with which it has always contemplated him.

[10] Another play on words with Latin *stuporis* and *stupet*.

[11] Latin *notando*. This is one of the few instances in the homilies where Hildegard uses a verb that expresses signification.

Homilies 43, 44, and 45

The Fourth Sunday after Pentecost

Luke 5:1-11

While the crowds rushed toward Jesus to hear the word of God he was standing by the lake of Gennesaret. And he saw two boats resting by the lake, but the fishermen had gotten down from them and were washing their nets. Then getting up into one of the boats, which belonged to Simon, he asked him to put out a little from the land. And he sat down and taught the crowds from the little boat. When he had finished speaking, he said to Simon: 'Put out into the deep and let down your nets for a catch.' And Simon answered him: 'Master, toiling all through the night we caught nothing. But at your word I will let down the nets.' And when they had done this, they gathered a great abundance of fish. But their nets were breaking, and they signaled to their companions who were in the other boat to come and help them. And they came and filled both boats, so that they nearly sank. When Simon Peter saw that, he fell down at Jesus' knees, saying: 'Depart from me, for I am a sinful man, Lord.' For astonishment had overwhelmed him, and all who were with him, at the catch of fish they had taken; so also James and John, sons of Zebedee, who were companions of Simon. And Jesus said to Simon: 'Do not be afraid; henceforth you will be catching human beings.' And when they had brought their boats to land, they left everything behind and followed him.

43. The Fourth Sunday after Pentecost, 1

While the crowds rushed toward Jesus to hear the word of God he was standing by the lake of Gennesaret. In other words, the substance of creatures hastened toward God *to hear* that sound, when God said, *'Let there be.'*[1] God *was standing*, as if ready for work, when *the Spirit of the Lord was borne over the waters.*[2]

And he saw two boats; evidently *he saw* the elements and other creatures *resting by the lake*, because they, like flying things, were tempered from water. *But the fishermen had gotten down from them and were washing their nets.* Clearly, the ranks of created beings were obeying and carrying out their deeds.

Then getting up into one of the boats, which belonged to Simon, he asked him to put out a little from the land. In his providence, for the creation[3] of the human being, he showed that the human would be placed in dignity before others, that is, from other creatures. *And he sat down and taught the crowds from the little boat.* In majesty he established order with the rationality he had given to the human.

When he had finished speaking, he said to Simon: 'Put out into the deep and let down your nets for a catch.' When God had created the creatures, *he said* to the human: "Be superior among creatures, and perform deeds of benefit."[4] *And replying, Simon answered: 'Master, toiling all through the night we caught nothing.'* Clearly, the human *answered him*: "Creator, I remained in ignorance, such that I was useless." *'But at your word I will let down the nets.'* "In honor of the knowledge of good and evil I want to work, so that I may know evil, because it is not enough for me to know good."

And when they had done these things they enclosed a great abundance of fish. The human transgressed the divine command in Paradise, taking hold of *a great abundance* of vices and sorrows. *But their nets were breaking, and they signaled to their companions who were*

[1] Gen 1:3, 6.

[2] Gen 1:2.

[3] Latin *in creaturam* seems to express purpose here.

[4] Hildegard extends the speech of God, whom Jesus represents, and the human, whom Peter designates.

in the other boat, to come and help them. The law God had given to humanity was broken. For the purpose of service and assistance humans yoked to themselves creatures that are in another form and nature than the human is, in service and by necessity. *And they came and filled both boats so that they nearly sank.* They *came* and *filled* themselves with great perils and sorrows, so that they barely withstood the resulting evils.

When Simon Peter saw that, he fell down at Jesus' knees, saying: 'Depart from me, for I am a sinful man, Lord.' The human, thrown into many hardships, perceived that he would return to God's remembrance because he was created by Him, *saying* with sighs and moans: "It is just that you withdraw from me, because I have traveled away[5] from you." *'I am a sinful man, Lord,'* "such that no longer" *'am I worthy to be called your son.'*[6] *For astonishment had overwhelmed him and all who were with him at the catch of fish they had taken.* Sadness had taken hold of him and all the elements and creatures; the sorrows and miseries in which they were enveloped took hold.

So also James and John, the sons of Zebedee, who were the companions of Simon, clearly the patriarchs and the prophets, who were the sons of edification in the law, evidently in the knowledge of Adam. *And Jesus said to Simon: 'Do not be afraid; henceforth you will be catching human beings.'* God, through the prophets and the law, *said* to the human: "*'Do not be afraid'*; you will not be cast down on account of the injustice and sadness in which you lie. On account of the good deeds you are going to perform you will be turned toward the comprehension of the heavenly Jerusalem."

And when they had brought their boats to land, they left everything behind and followed him. The family and race of humankind[7] with the elements and the other creatures dwelled among earthly things until they saw God in a human body; *they left everything behind,* that is, the Old Law and heresy and self-interest in sins, *and followed him* in faith and in the gospel of peace.

---

[5] Hildegard uses the word *peregrinus* here, most often meaning "pilgrim."
[6] Luke 15:19, 21.
[7] Latin *genus et genus humanum.*

44. The Fourth Sunday after Pentecost, 2

While the crowds rushed toward Jesus to hear the word of God he was standing by the lake of Gennasaret. The Scriptures were revealing God eagerly; they knew and revealed that he was to be incarnated; all the works of God were and are confirmed by the Holy Spirit.[8] *And he saw two boats resting by the lake. He saw two,* namely in his predestination, because although he was God, he would become a man for humankind's sake, with the fortitude of the Holy Spirit. *But the fishermen had gotten down from them and were washing their nets,* that is, through circumcision divinity came *down* and was revealing the law.

Then getting up into one of the boats, which belonged to Simon, he asked him to put out a little from the land. When the fullness of time came,[9] the Word of the Father assumed a human body, when the Father had sent his Son to admonish humankind by his teaching so that they would remove themselves from earthly things more than they had before. *And he sat down and taught the crowds from the boat,* that is, he admonished *the crowds* when he revealed the Scriptures to them in a human body.

When he had finished speaking, he said to Simon: 'Put out into the deep and let down your nets for a catch.' When the Father handed over the Son to suffering, he said to the Son who had assumed a human body: *'Put out into'* "the depth of the gospel" *'and let down'* "the law of the gospel to convert the peoples."[10]

And Simon answered him: 'Master, toiling all through the night we caught nothing. But at your word I will let down the net.' The Son of God *answered him*: "Father, you sent me into the world, which was sweating in the shadowy[11] knowledge of the Old Law; I accom-

---

[8] This and the other two sentences in the paragraph reveal a threefold structure, mirroring the role of each person of the Trinity.

[9] Gal 4:4; see Eph 1:10.

[10] In this homily Hildegard extends the speech of God the Father, whom Jesus represents, and the Son of God, whom Peter designates.

[11] I have translated the Latin: *tenebrosa* ("dark") with English "shadowy," which seems to convey the nuance of the *umbra*, or shadow, of the old meaning better than "dark" would.

plished nothing because of their unbelief. But at your command I will accomplish the gospel precepts among the nations."[12]

And when he had done this, they gathered a great abundance of fish. When he had converted his disciples to the gospel *they enclosed a great abundance* of heavenly desires. *But their net was breaking;* clearly they lost certain things, so that they could not fulfill everything. *And they signaled to their companions, who were in the other boat, to come and help them.* [In other words], they called out to God the Father, because he was God, to assist and succor them. *And they came and filled both boats*: evidently, when humans believed that Christ was true God and true man, *so that they nearly sank* to that level where it would be dangerous to think any more about God.

When Simon Peter saw that, he fell down at Jesus' knees, saying: 'Depart from me, for I am a sinful man, Lord.' Evidently the incarnated Son humbled himself and gave thanks to the Father, before the Father's majesty, when he said: *'The Father is greater than I,'*[13] and when he said, *'Into your hands I commend my spirit.'*[14]

For astonishment had overwhelmed them, and all who were with him, at the catch of fish they had taken. Clearly, obedience *had overwhelmed* him when he was obedient to the Father, and all the others who desired heaven. *So also James and John, the sons of Zebedee, who were companions of Simon,* that is, those who cultivated good deeds *and* those also who achieved their perfection, the sons of the kingdom, *who were companions* of the humanity of God's Son.

And Jesus said to Simon: 'Do not be afraid; henceforth you will be catching human beings.' The Father *said* to the Son: *'Do not be afraid,'* "because you will accomplish everything, gathering them in through faith, as it is written: *'The Lord said to my Lord, sit at my right hand, until I place your enemies as a footstool for your feet.'*"[15] *And when they had brought their boats to land, they left everything behind and followed him.* When the believers put aside all earthly things,

---

[12] Hildegard uses the noun *preceptum* twice here: *in precepto tuo* and *precepta*. I translate the first as "command" and the second as "precepts."

[13] John 14:28.

[14] Ps 30:6; Luke 23:46.

[15] Ps 109:1.

because they relinquished their will and their very selves, they were subject to God's commands.

45. The Fourth Sunday after Pentecost, 3

While the crowds rushed toward Jesus to hear the word of God he was standing by the lake of Gennesaret. The virtues hastened to Fortitude in order that they would be taught by her and that they would be edified in those things,[16] because she remained in the fire of the Holy Spirit. *And he saw two boats resting by the lake*: clearly conversion and salvation *resting* in the stability of the Holy Spirit. *But the fishermen had gotten down from them and were washing their nets.* The searchers, inquirers for good things, left themselves behind and put aside their own wills.

Then getting up into one of the boats, which belonged to Simon, he asked him to put out a little from the land. Fortitude, for the conversion of the righteous, showed how they would put aside the will of the flesh and cease from sins. *And he sat down and taught the crowds from the boat*, that is, Fortitude exhorted the virtues on conversion.

When he had finished speaking, he said to Simon: 'Put out into the deep and let down your nets for a catch.' When Fortitude *had finished* admonishing, such that they took delight in her, she *said* to the righteous ones: "Ascend *from virtue to virtue*[17] into Charity's embrace."[18]

And Simon answered him: 'Master, toiling all through the night we caught nothing.' The righteous *answered* in anguish: "'*Master*', to whom obedience is owed, '*toiling through*' the devil's nocturnal plots, we cannot overcome him." '*But at your word I will let down the net,*' "that is, with your grace, we will go to the virtues."

---

[16] Latin reads first *ab ipsa*, clearly "by her" (Fortitude), and *edificarent in ea*. The pronoun shift from *ipsa* to *ea* indicates an antecedent different from Fortitude. The verb *edificarent* seems to be taken as a middle or passive voice here. The virtues are instructed by Fortitude. There is no indication that they in turn go out and teach the things learned from Fortitude.

[17] Ps 83:8.

[18] Here the crowds designate the virtues; Jesus stands for Fortitude; Simon Peter represents the righteous. Hildegard extends the voices of Fortitude and the righteous.

And when they had done these things they enclosed a great abundance of fish. When they began *these things they gathered a great abundance* of good deeds. *But their net was breaking* when they desired more than they were able to contain in their minds and wills.

And they signaled to their companions who were in the other boat to come and help them. To their coworkers, *who were in* salvation because they had been *in* the battle of victory and were saved, they moaned to *come and help them,* so that with their aid they too would stand in victory. *And they came and filled both boats, so that they nearly sank.* Evidently they will be so victorious in faith and deed from their conversion that they will look upon salvation, but yet occasionally they may be wearied by the devil.

When Simon Peter saw that, he fell down at Jesus' knees, saying: 'Depart from me, for I am a sinful man, Lord.' The righteous prostrate themselves before God, *saying:* "We are not worthy to be with God, because we are in such great contamination." *For astonishment had overwhelmed him and all who were with him at the catch of fish they had taken.* [In other words] fear and trembling *had overwhelmed* them and the companions of that same conversion, in fright at the teaching about their conversion and how they would accomplish it. *So also James and John, the sons of Zebedee, who were companions of Simon*: evidently rationality and knowledge, which are from God,[19] *had overwhelmed* them with the thought that they would be in the custom of the righteous. *And Jesus said to Simon: 'Do not be afraid,'* "trembling from this weariness and suffering," *'henceforth you will be catching humans'* "when you will be a pillar of cloud[20] and an example to humanity." *And when they had brought their boats to land, they left everything behind and followed him.* They hold conversion and salvation in all deeds of earthly circumstances because they cast away doubt and sadness and turn those into joy as they persevere with God in Fortitude.

---

[19] The Latin reads *qui* and not *quae,* apparently confusing the sons, the antecedent in the scriptural text, with the gloss, two feminine nouns.

[20] Exod 13:21-22; 14:19; 33:9-10; Num 12:5; Deut 31:15; 2 Esdr 9:12, 19; Ps 98:7; Sir 24:7.

Homilies 46, 47, and 48

The Ninth Sunday after Pentecost

Luke 19:41-47

When Jesus drew near to Jerusalem and saw the city he wept over it, saying: 'If only you knew on this your day the things that bring you peace. But now they are hidden from your eyes. Indeed, the days will come upon you, and surround you, and hem you in on all sides, and cast you to the ground, and your children who are within you. And they will not leave a stone upon a stone, because you have not known the time of your visitation.' And after entering the temple he began to drive out the ones who were selling in it and the buyers, saying to them: 'It is written that "my house is a house of prayer," but you have made it a den of robbers.' And he was teaching daily in the temple.

46. The Ninth Sunday after Pentecost, 1

When Jesus drew near to Jerusalem and saw the city he wept over it. When God *drew near* to the creation, intending to create creatures,[1] *he saw* the human being when out of deep love he

[1] Hildegard offers three interpretations for this pericope and thus presents the clearest example of her trinitarian theology, namely that the three persons of the Trinity are working throughout history. In the first of these homilies Jesus represents God the Creator; in the second he remains himself as the

made the human being *in his own image and likeness.*[2] And he said: *'If only you knew on this your day the things that bring you peace.'* Clearly, he said: *'If only you knew'* "the things that I know, you would guard against your death, for if you seek anything other than me you will perish." And he said: *From every tree of Paradise you may eat, but do not eat from the tree of the knowledge of good and evil.*[3] The *'things that bring you peace on this your day,'* "when you have the knowledge of good, are yours in great honors; but they" *'are now hidden from your eyes'* "because you do not know that if you have disobeyed my command" *you will surely die.*[4]

'Indeed, the days will come upon you,' "which you reckon as your days, but they are night for you, when you have perceived that" *you will surely die.*[5] *'And they will surround you'* "with hardships, like a forceful wind,"[6] *'and [they will] hem you in on all sides'* "in exile, such that you will be alienated from God." *'They will cast you to the ground and your children who are in you,'* "that is, they will lead you from Paradise to earth, and those born from you, who are in your womb." *'And they will not leave a stone upon a stone,'* "that is, any knowledge upon any perception," *'because you have not known the time of your visitation,'* "evidently the first day of your honor. Hence you will always stray from vice into vice."

And after entering the temple he began to drive out the ones who were selling in it and the buyers. When all these sorrows were accomplished in the human being, God was made human, and made the human being his temple, so as to remove unbelief and illicit desires from the human. [He was] *saying to them* and showing: *'It is written'* by true revelation *that "my house,"* that is, the human

---

Son of God incarnate; in the third he stands for the Holy Spirit. The second homily of the set contains the only specific mention of doctors of the church by name. On Hildegard's trinitarian exegesis of this pericope, see Kienzle, *Speaking New Mysteries*, 163–69.

[2] Gen 1:26-27.

[3] Gen 2:16-17.

[4] Gen 2:16-17.

[5] Gen 2:16-17.

[6] An example of alliteration here: *ualidus uentus.*

being, *"is a house of prayer,"*[7] because chastity and holiness ought
to reside in the human. *'But you,'* "who are perverse," *'have made
it a den of robbers'* "because fraud and falsehood are made by the
devil." *And he was teaching daily in the temple,* that righteous judgments of wisdom and honor ought to reside in the human being.

47. The Ninth Sunday after Pentecost, 2

When Jesus, the Son of God, *drew near to Jerusalem,* clearly, when
the fullness of time[8] came, in which God sent his Son so that human
beings would see him incarnate, he *saw the city,* every edifice of
the Old Law from Abel all the way to himself, and *he wept over
it,* so that he might draw forth the fountain of wisdom over all
its writings and institutions. [He was] *saying: 'If only you knew on
this your day the things that bring you peace':* "in other words, the
things I know. You are under the devil's shadowy influence; you
do not recognize me because you have never seen me. Now you
have the law in the fullness of your will, as it pleases you." *'But
now the things that bring you peace are hidden from your eyes,'* "that
is, they are concealed from your knowledge."

*'Indeed, the days will come upon you, and surround you, and hem
you in on all sides, and cast you to the ground, and your children who
are within you.'* "Clearly others" *'will come'* "in transformation
and clarity, the doctors of the New Testament with their teaching: Gregory, Ambrose, Augustine, Jerome, and others like them.
They will return to the spiritual meaning and will cleanse from
pride your worship with the sacrifice of rams and bulls and cast
it down toward humility; by spiritual understanding they will
lead carnal institutions toward humility." *'And they will not leave
a stone upon a stone,'* "that is, they will leave no letter—not one
iota, and no worship of yours, unless it is changed." *'Because you
have not known the time of your visitation,'* "that is, because you
have refused to know the first day on which all creatures will be
resplendent, so that another light would shine on your children."

---

[7] See Isa 56:7; Jer 7:11; Matt 21:13; Mark 11:17.
[8] Gal 4:4; Eph 1:10.

And after entering the temple he began to drive out the ones selling in it, and the buyers, that is, the Gospel entered by the Word of God and drove out avarice and idols and other filthy things that humans were holding in place of God. He was *saying to them: 'It is written that "my house is a house of prayer."'*[9] In his teaching through spiritual transformation and interpretation [he was saying] that "the edifice of revelation is the house of truth, since neither heaven nor earth reveal any God other than me, but my edifice, where you will find me, reveals the truth to you." *'But you have made it a den of robbers,'* "that is, by your unbelief you, not believing in my incarnation, [*have made it*] your own will and the devil's filth by thefts." *And he was teaching daily in the temple,* that in this vision of the new edifice and interpretation of the Old Law the Son of God himself proceeds to spiritual understanding in the church up until the end.

48. The Ninth Sunday after Pentecost, 3

When Jesus drew near to Jerusalem, that is, the Holy Spirit's admonition leaned down to the human being, full of vices and filth, *he saw the city,* namely the edifice of salvation, [and *saw*] that the human being would be converted from sins to righteousness. *And he wept over it, saying: 'If only you knew on this your day the things that bring you peace.'* In other words [the Spirit], moved by deep love, admonished: *'If only you knew'* "as I do, the dangers you were in because of your distress, you would crush yourself like a winepress,[10] and like a mill you would turn yourself here and there."[11]

---

[9] See Isa 56:7; Jer 7:11; Matt 21:13; Mark 11:17.

[10] See Isa 5:2; 63:3; et al. The comparison of the world to a winepress appears in Augustine and other writers. See *Sancti Aurelii Augustini sermones de uetere testamento,* ed. Cyril Lambot, CCSL 41 (Turnhout: Brepols, 1961), 19, 6, p. 258, ll. 222-23: *mundus est torcular; abundant pressurae eius;* and Hildegard, *Epistolarium* I, 77R, p. 179, ll. 77-79; *Sciuias* 1, 3, 31, p. 59, ll. 626-29; *Sciuias* 1, 4, 1, p. 62, ll. 99-100; *Sciuias* 3, 8, 15, p. 497, ll. 674-76. For other examples see *Expos. euang.* 314.

[11] The image of the world as a mill also appears in Augustine and other sources: Augustine, *Enarrationes in Psalmos,* ed. Eligius Dekkers and Johannes Fraipont, CCSL 38–40 (Turnhout: Brepols, 1956), ps. 36, s. 1, 2, pp. 338–39, ll.

'On this your day,' "which you consider your day since you are full of vices and filth, you mistake the fights of the devil for peace, and wounds for joys, and even impurity for purity." *'But now they are hidden from your eyes,'* "that is, from your heart's knowledge."

'Indeed, the days will come upon you' "when a reddening light will descend upon you, [12] which is penitence," *'and surround you and hem you in on all sides'* "with the tears of weeping and with sighs." *'And [they will] cast you to the ground, and your children who are within you'*: "clearly, they will throw you to the ground as you say, 'I am a sinner,' such that they will reduce to nothing even all the iniquities that are born from you." *'And they will not leave a stone upon a stone.'* "Penitence will so permeate you that it will not leave aside any vice or any filth; indeed, it will cleanse you from all those" *'because you have not known the time of your visitation,'* "that is, because you forgot that you were a sacred soul."

And after entering the temple he began to drive out the ones who were selling in it, and the buyers. The Holy Spirit's admonition *entered* the human's heart and from it chased pride and those who bought[13] lust for themselves with whores. [He was] saying to them: *'It is written that "my house is a house of prayer," but you have made it a den of robbers.'*[14] Clearly the human heart was strengthened, and the worship of angels and the example of the saints will take place there. "By your iniquity and the devil's temptation it was formerly a brothel." *And he was teaching daily in the temple,* so that the praise of the angels and the joy of the peoples could take place openly in the human being.

25-26: *et molendinum puto dictum mundum istum; quia rota quadam temporum uoluitur, et amatores suos conterit.* Hildegard, *Epist.* 25R, I, p. 72, ll. 46-48. For other examples see *Expos. euang.* 314.

[12] Latin *rutilans lux*, an image used by Ambrose and Jerome for the light of repentance. Ambrose of Milan, *De Noe*, ed. Karl Schenkl, CSEL, 32/1 (Vienna: F. Tempsky, 1897) 27, 103 (p. 484, l. 11: *diuersi tamquam radiorum solis nunc rutilantium*); Jerome, *Commentarii in Ezechielem libri xiv*, ed. Franciscus Glorie, CCSL 75 (Turnhout: Brepols, 1964), 1, 1 (p. 13, l. 266: *scintillas rutilantes*). See also Hildegard, *Sciuias* 2, 1, 11; 2, 2; 2, 3, p. 118, ll. 285-86; p. 124, ll. 13-20; p. 135, ll. 79-82.

[13] Latin *adtraxerunt*: literally, brought or attracted to themselves.

[14] See Isa 56:7; Jer 7:11; Matt 21:13; Mark 11:17.

Homilies 49 and 50

The Eleventh Sunday after Pentecost

Mark 7:31-37

Going out from the region of Tyre, Jesus went through Sidon to the Sea of Galilee, through the region of the Decapolis. And they brought to him a deaf man, who was also mute, and they begged him to lay his hand upon him. Taking him away from the crowd privately, he put his fingers into his ears, and he spat and touched his tongue. Then, looking up to heaven, he sighed and said to him: 'Eph'phatha,' that is, 'Be opened.' And immediately his ears were opened, and the bond on his tongue was released, and he spoke rightly. Then he ordered them to tell no one; but the more he ordered them, the more zealously they proclaimed it. They were greatly astonished, saying: 'He has done all things well; he has even made the deaf to hear and the mute to speak.'

49. The Eleventh Sunday after Pentecost, 1

Going out from the region of Tyre, Jesus went through Sidon to the Sea of Galilee, through the region of the Decapolis. Born from the Jewish people, *Jesus went through* the prophets *to* crowds of peoples who were tossed this way and that by many things, *through the region* of angels and humans, specifically the nine orders of angels

181

and the tenth of humankind.[1] *And they brought to him a deaf man:*—
in other words, prophecy *brought* the Old Testament, which did
not hear him—*who was also mute,* since it did not speak of spiritual
matters, *and they begged him to lay his hand upon him,* that is, to place
the work of truth over it by his revelations.

*Taking him away from the crowd privately, he put his fingers into his
ears, and he spat and touched his tongue.* By his incarnation, *taking*
the Old Testament *away from* the sacrifices of rams and bulls[2] by
the mystical meaning[3] of the Holy Spirit and the gospels, *he put*
the Holy Spirit's gifts *into* its *ears,* so that it could obtain a sense
of hearing different from what it had had before. With his breath,
admonishing, *he touched his tongue* when he revealed to the law
the words for recognizing and proclaiming the Father and the Son
and the Holy Spirit. *Then, looking up to heaven, he sighed and said to
him: 'Eph'phatha,' that is, 'Be opened.'* When sacred humanity shone
forth in heaven, rationality turned the law into spiritual matters.
He said admonishing, "Open your heart completely to the truth
of the Gospel."

And immediately his ears were opened for hearing faith. *The bond
on his tongue was released;* the binding that had made the law *mute,*
because it lacked mercy, was released by the words of the Gospel.
And he spoke rightly, preaching faith and that it may be restored
by repentance.

Then he ordered them to tell no one: evidently the pride and fame
were removed from the law, which they first had while they
wanted to seem more righteous than they were.[4] *But the more he*

[1] Pseudo-Dionysius specifies nine orders of angels in *The Celestial Hierarchy* (Pseudo-Dionysius, *The Complete Works* [New York and Mahwah, NJ: Paulist Press, 1987], 143–91, at 160–61.

[2] See Dan 3:40.

[3] Latin *mistica.*

[4] Hildegard moves her focus to the crowd, using plural verbs, and then returns to the individual human being, using singular forms. She links the healed man with an individual human being as representative of humankind. I have kept the masculine singular pronouns and adjectives for the most part, in order to indicate this gliding back and forth from the healed man to the human being.

ordered them, clearly the more they humbled themselves, following God's commands, *the more zealously they preached it*: in other words, when great joy came upon them, since the human being had help everywhere from God, so that when he was righteous he humbled himself, and when he fell he sought repentance. *They were greatly astonished* at the new miracles that had appeared, *saying: 'He has done all things well'* by changing the Old Law into the spiritual understanding. *'He has even made the deaf to hear'* when the obscure and secret prophecy was revealed for a new sense of hearing, *'and the mute to speak,'* by knowing, seeing, and preaching that Christ is God and man, the righteous one in righteousness.

50. The Eleventh Sunday after Pentecost, 2

Going out from the region of Tyre, Jesus went through Sidon to the Sea of Galilee, through the region of the Decapolis. God [went out] from the sins of human beings because when the human turns toward sin, God leaves him. Through the Spirit's admonition God *went through* to the disturbances of temptations, which the human being must traverse in order to leave sins behind and cross through them, so that advancing rightly he may reach the tenth choir and become the hundredth sheep.[5]

And they brought to him a deaf man, who was also mute, and they begged him to lay his hand upon him. Through confession and sighs the priests *brought* God the human, who does not hear the commands of God but transgresses, *and* who does not speak righteousness but deceit. Through prayers and sighs *they begged* God to help and introduce his work to him. *Taking him away from the crowd privately, he put his fingers into his ears, and he spat and touched his tongue.* Drawing the human in, the grasp of God's love lifted him up from the habit of sins. Through the Holy Spirit's gifts the ears of his heart opened, and God gave him the sweetest taste through the rationality of the soul. *Then, looking up to heaven, he*

---

[5] An echo of the ranks of angels above and a reference to the parable of the lost sheep, Luke 15:3-7.

sighed and said to him: 'Eph'phatha,' that is, 'Be opened.' And immedi-
ately his ears were opened, and the bond on his tongue was released, and
he spoke rightly. Through his cry God revealed himself incarnated,
saying in this way that *'sins are dismissed from you'*:[6] [in other
words] "you cry out to me and recognize me." All the filth of his
soul was cleansed because he heard God, and the implication of
evil habit was taken away from him, such that he became a new
man,[7] speaking God's justice.

Then he ordered them to tell no one; God does not want the human
to give the devil any response that could come through pride
concerning what happened to him, as if one might say, "Now I
am holy." *But the more he ordered them* to humble themselves, *the*
more zealously they preached it, not in pride but in humility, the joy
of the soul from praise to praise, from joy to joy. *They were greatly*
astonished, since the house of God was prepared in him, always
performing miracles, *saying: 'He has done all things well,'* turning
the righteous from the unrighteous, and that one from evil to
good. *'He has even made the deaf to hear and the mute to speak,'* because God has made him a new man,[8] with a life in him different
from what he had had before.

---

[6] Matt 9:2.
[7] See Eph 4:24; Col 3:10.
[8] See Eph 4:24; Col 3:10.

Homilies 51 and 52

The Tenth Sunday after Pentecost

Luke 18:10-14

'Two men went up into the temple to pray, one a Pharisee and the other a tax collector. The Pharisee, standing by himself, was praying: "God, I give you thanks that I am not like other people: robbers, the unjust, adulterers, and like this tax collector. I fast twice on the Sabbath; I give a tenth of everything I own." The tax collector, standing far off, did not want to raise his eyes to heaven, but was beating his breast and saying: "God, be merciful to me, a sinner!" Amen, I say to you, the latter, not the former, became righteous and went down into his house, away from the other. For everyone who exalts himself will be humbled, and he who humbles himself will be exalted.'

51. The Tenth Sunday after Pentecost, 1

'*Two men*' are the two generations from Adam until the last day, for the first are from the birth of the world, like Samson, the second from the birth of excess in carnal fatness,[1] like Goliath.[2]

---

[1] This is one of the many times Hildegard uses the Latin *pinguedo*, which has the connotation of fullness or excess, as with expensive oil.

[2] The parable is spoken in Jesus' voice, but the Pharisee and tax collector also speak, and Hildegard assumes their voices in certain instances. Therefore there

Their thoughts went upwards, flying up *'into the temple,'* that is,
into God's sight, *'to pray,'* clearly to praise God. *'One a Pharisee'*
designates[3] those who are from the birth of the world; they are not
in fatness of the flesh. They are often harsh and cruel and think
they are good, but they are not, because they have not drunk that
continence from the *living water,*[4] but from their birth. *'The other,'*
in another vicissitude, *'a tax collector'* [designates the ones who
are] in carnal fatness; with their deeds they satisfy the taste for
sin, which they have had in their inordinate desire.

'The Pharisee, standing by himself, was praying.' Vices do not constrain them to humility; he prayed all alone because he boasts
about his innocence, as if he worshiped it, and does not look to
another or need the help of another who would console him. *"God,
I give you thanks that I am not like other people."* [In other words]:
"You, who made all things, I bless you, because I do not need to
lament or weep, since I do not have the taste for sin as others do
who are in the fatness of the flesh." *"Robbers"* through desire for
others' possessions, *"unjust"* in unclean thoughts, *"adulterers"*
when they carry out sins against another, *"and like this tax collector,"* who can never be satisfied in the fatness of his nature. *"I fast
twice on the Sabbath"*: "I remove myself from sin, so that I do not
pollute another during my life." *"I give a tenth of everything I own"*:
"I practice chastity in all my bodily senses."

*'The tax collector, standing far off, did not want to raise his eyes to
heaven.'* Those who sin in fatness of the flesh [stand] in the faraway
land of sinners, unoccupied by good deeds; in anxiety over fear of
the Lord [they do not want] to raise their knowledge up to holiness. *'But he was beating his breast and saying: "God, be merciful to me,*

are three levels of voice and three primary levels of quotation: italics for the
scriptural passage, single quotation marks for Jesus' words throughout, and
standard quotation marks for the sections where the Pharisee speaks, or the
tax collector, or Hildegard, when she assumes their voices in the first person.

[3] Hildegard employs a verb of signification here: *designat.*

[4] See Jer 2:13; 17:13; Zech 14:8; John 4:10, 11; 7:38; Rev 7:17.

a sinner!"[5] Constricting[6] his heart, he confessed: "You who created all things, who possess both grace and power for this, make me stop sinning, as it is written: Do not recall the crimes of my youth and ignorance,[7] because I am unable to restrain myself from sin."

'Amen, I say to you, the latter, not the former, became righteous and went down into his house, away from the other.' When the human being humbles himself he says these things from God and recognizes himself as a sinner and leaves his sins behind. He praises his Lord and considers his sins a slave and not a master; in his body he makes his paths straight in the confession of faith, that they have God's grace from divine vision.[8] *'For everyone who exalts himself will be humbled.'* The one who out of pride calls himself holy is a liar. That one does not seek God and therefore is abandoned often by God and other human beings. The one who rejoices in the harvest is deceived greatly, since when a person does not toil he receives no compensation, but is deceived by his own estimation. *'He who humbles himself will be exalted'*: evidently one who scrutinizes his sins, searching for [the places] where he has wounded his soul, and who prostrates himself with a sigh, crying out to God, and calls upon all creatures to assist him. They lift him up and bear him to God, as it is said: *'I live,'* says the Lord; *'I do not wish the death of a sinner.'*[9]

52. The Tenth Sunday after Pentecost, 2

'Two men went up into the temple to pray.' They signify two honors, namely the knowledge of good and of evil; they [*went up*] like fire and smoke—because there is neither fire without smoke nor smoke without fire—into the figure of the human body, in which God's work lies hidden, so that they would praise God

[5] See Ps 77:38.
[6] Latin *in constrictione* seems to indicate a physiological process Hildegard associates with a spiritual change of heart.
[7] Ps 24:7.
[8] The subject of the plural verb *habent* is not clear.
[9] Ezek 33:11.

together. The good sometimes overwhelms the evil, and the evil the good,[10] and yet they praise one God. *'One a Pharisee,'* that is, good knowledge, *'and the other a tax collector,'* namely, evil knowledge.[11]

'The Pharisee, standing by himself, was praying.' Without scoffing, not wanting to communicate with evil, aware of itself, good knowledge was praising God. *"God, I give you thanks that I am not like other people. God* of all, *I give you* praises and tell you *that I am not* in investigation or in dissimulative duplicity *like* the other vices. *Robbers* because I do not reject but praise your gifts, *unjust* since I do not condemn your judgments but embrace them, *adulterers* because I do not overstep your institutions, but I learn them willingly, *and also this tax collector,* that is, just as the hypocrites do.

I fast twice on the Sabbath: I cut off the two-tongued speech from your sanctuary. *I give a tenth of everything I own:* in the Ten Commandments I offer you praise, who are the one God, from every sphere of my intellect, by which I know you."

'The tax collector, standing far off, did not want to raise his eyes to heaven, but was beating his breast.' Building with faithfulness in exile, *'he did not want'* to elevate what he knows to the protection of divine assistance, but [he was] crushing the vigor of his intellect, *'saying':* "God, *be merciful to me, a sinner!"*[12]—in other words, "Creator of all, you know me and therefore, if you wish, you can convert me away from my contrariness toward you."[13]

'Amen, I say to you, the latter, not the former, became righteous and went down into his own house away from the other.' Knowledge of God [went down] by confessing; knowledge of evil [became righteous] in that God is higher than what knowledge of evil itself can accomplish. Good knowledge returned to itself and praised God from its body. *'For everyone who exalts himself will be humbled':* they who ascend in knowledge more than they are able will be

[10] See Isa 5:20.

[11] This paragraph illustrates well how Hildegard uses the phrases *scientia boni* and *bona scientia, scientia mali* and *mala scientia* synonymously.

[12] See Ps 77:38.

[13] See Matt 8:2; Mark 1:40; Luke 5:12.

weak and impoverished. *'He who humbles himself will be exalted'*: heaven and earth receive and honor the one who has subjected himself to God.[14]

---

[14] Hildegard uses parataxis here: literally "the one who has subjected himself to God, heaven and earth receive and honor him."

Homilies 53, 54, 55, and 56

The First Sunday of Advent

Luke 21:25-33

'There will be signs in the sun and the moon and the stars, and upon the earth distress of nations from perplexity at the sound of the sea and of the waves, humans fainting from fear and foreboding of the things that are coming upon the entire world. For the powers of heaven will be shaken. And then they will see the Son of Man coming in a cloud with great power and majesty. When these things begin to take place, look up and lift up your heads, because your redemption is drawing near.' And he told them a parable: 'Look at the fig tree and all the trees. When they produce their fruit, you know that summer is near. So too, when you see these things happening, know that the Kingdom of God is near. Amen, I say to you, this generation will not pass away until all [these] things have taken place. Heaven and earth will pass away, but my words will not pass away.'

53. The First Sunday of Advent, 1[1]

'There will be signs in the sun and the moon and the stars,' that is, many portents will give unusual '*signs*', different from the way

---

[1] A note, added in a later hand, Wiesbaden Handschrift 2, f. 459va, reads *Littera.*

in which they were appointed and from those that would be familiar to humankind. *'And upon the earth distress of nations'*: what is higher will be turned into another mode, as also will be what is lower. The happiness of humans will be turned into anguish, and increase into loss, *'from perplexity at the sound of the sea and of the waves.'* For water sustains greenness[2] and the life of creatures, because water is above the earth and beneath the earth. For the *spirit of the Lord was borne over the water*[3] and brought it to life, so to speak. Therefore when human beings perform evil deeds the air and the water are struck and the water extends those evil deeds to the sun, the moon, and the stars, since these reflect from the water. And so those heavenly bodies shake humans violently with unaccustomed terrors, in accordance with their deeds, *'from perplexity'* because the waters have been poured out by the Holy Spirit, *'and the sound of the sea and of the waves'* because these emit a sound, wailing on account of the perverse deeds of humankind. *'Humans fainting'* because human happiness will be changed into aridity and into sadness *'from fear'* of those portents, *'and foreboding,'* since they believe greater things are to come: *'the things that are coming upon the entire world'* because humankind will then lack faith, hope, and consolation. *'For the powers of heaven will be shaken,'* namely, the angels [*will be shaken*] toward judgment and into wrath, since humans already will have cast the Lord behind. Therefore, the angels will become angry with them, just as they did before the incarnation of the Lord.[4]

'And then they will see the Son of Man coming' in judgment: Christ *'in a'* splendid and terrifying *'cloud, with great power'* of humanity *'and majesty'* of divinity. *'When these'* signs that were foretold *'begin to take place,'* clearly when they emerge at that time, *'look up'* to God

---

[2] *Viriditas*, a key Hildegardian term. See Kienzle, *Speaking New Mysteries*, 100, 210–11; Peter Dronke, "Tradition and Innovation in Medieval Western Colour-Imagery," *Eranos Jahrbuch* 41 (1972): 51–107, at 82, 84.

[3] Gen 1:2.

[4] The theme of the angels' anger perhaps reflects the influence of Origen's exegesis. See Kienzle, *Speaking New Mysteries*, 88–89; *Expo. Euang.* 27.

and *'lift up your heads'* without shame, fearing nothing, *'because your redemption'* "from the hardships you suffer" *'is drawing near.'*

And he told them a parable by way of comparison: *'Look at the fig tree,'* because fig trees abound on earth, *'and all the trees.'* *'When they produce their fruit,'* namely when first they send forth flowers, *'you know'* from what is usual *'that summer is near'* by the change in the air. *'So too, when you see these things happening,'* clearly the *'signs'* and the portents that were predicted, *'know that the Kingdom of God is near'* for the reward of the righteous. *'Amen, I say to you,'* to all humankind, *'This generation'* of people *'will not pass away,'* that is, be consumed. Evidently human beings will not be lacking over the earth *'until all these things have taken place,'* that is, are fulfilled. *'Heaven,'* clouds and highest things that humans see, *'and earth,'* on which humanity dwells, *'will pass away'* after being transformed from instability into a better and more stable condition. *'But my words,'* "the things I have said to you on all these things," *'will not pass away.'* They will be changed into a state other than that which they have been called, because all things will be fulfilled for certain.

54. The First Sunday of Advent, 2[5]

'There will be signs in the sun and the moon and the stars,' that is, portents in Christ so that those in error will oppose the humanity of the Savior, and in the church when heretics will attempt to attack the church, and among priests, teachers, and the spiritual people when they will turn away from the truth toward falsehood. *'And upon the earth,'* namely, among worldly people, [there will be] *'distress of nations,'* clearly of different nations, so that the errors of one people and province will contaminate another people and province and will turn [them] to faithlessness. *'From the perplexity'* that *'the sound of the sea,'* resounding shamelessly, and *'of the waves'* will emit, Antichrist will summon many storms

---

[5] A note, added in a later hand, Wiesbaden Handschrift 2, f. 459vb, reads *Allegoria.*

of errors, *'and'* Antichrist's own heretical ministers will run to and fro throughout the entire world with their falsehoods and deceptions.[6] *'Humans [will be] fainting'* in sorrow and doubt *'from fear and foreboding'* when they doubt and fear which faith will save them; when doubting, they await the command and judgment of God. These *'are coming upon the entire world,'* that is, pressing down upon all creation. *'For the powers of heaven,'* namely, the bishops and the leaders in the church, who like columns ought to uphold strongly all the institutions and mysteries of the church that belong to heaven, *'will be shaken'* in fear and doubt, so that they withdraw, not daring to defend or to speak openly about righteousness and the things that look up at God.

'And then,' clearly, in all these things, *'they will see,'* with both sight and intellect, *'the Son of Man coming in a cloud'*: Christ [coming] in the minds of the faithful, who will endure in martyrdom much suffering and tribulation for the sake of Christ and of the truth; [coming] *'with great power'* of the holy incarnation *'and majesty'* of divinity. The faithful will deny the Antichrist and will know Christ himself as true God and true human.[7] *'When these things,'* clearly sufferings, *'begin to take place, look up and lift up your heads, because your redemption is drawing near.'*

And he told them a parable by way of comparison. *'Look at the fig tree,'* evidently the prelates who should both gently reproach and mildly rebuke those in their charge,[8] in the same manner as the *'fig tree'* produces *'fruit'* both sweet and bitter, *'and [look at] the other trees,'* namely, other persons. *'When they produce their fruit'* of righteousness *'you know that summer is near'*: clearly, *summer* [designates] heat from the ardor and gifts of the Holy Spirit. *'So too, when you see these things happening,'* plainly, the martyrdom and the tribulations of the saints and the fruit of good works, *'know that the*

---

[6] The Latin contains two relative clauses here; they have been removed for a more fluent reading in English.

[7] The Latin contains two purpose clauses here, in which the verb in the subjunctive is closely equivalent to the future. The future is used instead of the purpose construction to achieve a more fluent reading in English.

[8] Compare RB 2:23-40; 64:12-13.

Kingdom of God is near,' that is, the reward of eternal blessedness. *'Amen, I say to you,'* with certainty, *'this generation'* of humans *'will not pass away until all [these] things have taken place'*: the portents, and the *'signs'*, and the sufferings of the saints. *'Heaven and earth,'* things that are hidden and revealed in all these aforesaid cases, which humankind can know and see temporally, *'will pass away,'* so that they may be led to the end. *'But my words,'* "clearly, all the things I say to you for your salvation,"[9] *'will not pass away.'* They will be led to the end, as if they did not exist,[10] but they will remain forever, leading faithful humanity to eternal glory.

55. First Sunday of Advent, 3

'There will be signs,' that is, portents *'in the sun,'* namely, those human beings who by their virtues demonstrate that there is nothing before or after or beyond God. They are so godlike that they surpass human measure, and they glow with the love of God so much that they are more excellent in this than other human beings, as Samson was.[11] *'And the moon,'* evidently the virgins and the chaste,[12] who demonstrate that the humanity of the Savior is sinless and spotless, *'and the stars,'* clearly the good lay people, who demonstrate that the grace of God is heavenly. Through it they are found in almsgiving and the most holy work. *'And upon the earth,'* namely, in the human senses, which bow to fallen and worldly things, *'distress,'* evidently error and madness, which neither know God nor consider the world with integrity. *'Of nations,'* clearly different peoples, *'from perplexity at the sound of the sea and of the waves,'* that is, the contradiction of the most evil

---

[9] Note that Hildegard keeps the first person of the biblical text here, asserting her own voice as teacher to her community. While she occasionally speaks through the biblical voices in her commentary in this set of homilies, for the most part she simply explains the words spoken by adding material to them.

[10] The Latin contains a result clause here, which has been removed for a more fluent reading in English.

[11] See Judg 13:24–16:31.

[12] See Phil 2:15-16.

noise of the princes in this world and the lesser ones: the weak and the poor. *'Humans fainting'* because they have neither virtues nor the joy of life, *'from fear,'* such that they also not know death, *'and foreboding'* of deceitful valuations, *'the things that are coming'* unexpectedly *'upon the entire world.'* Among the human beings living in the world, some will allot life to themselves and others death, in accordance with the valuation of their own mockeries. *'For the virtues,'* namely, faith, justice, and salvation, *'of heaven,'* because they always point toward what is heavenly, *'will be shaken'* in sorrow, because then they will find no place or repose with humankind.

'And then they will see the Son of Man coming in a cloud,' through prophecy and miracles, Christ *'coming'* into the world through report, that is, in the minds of humans and in the foreshadowing[13] of prophecy, *'with great power'* of miracles and mysteries *'and majesty'* of one touched by divinity.

'When these things begin to take place,' clearly, in the evils that will exist among the faithless through schisms and false beliefs[14] and also in the signs of God's miracles that will happen then among the faithful, *'look up'* by knowing and *'lift up your heads'* toward God by fortitude, namely by faith. *'Because your redemption is drawing near'* "in salvation, such that you will see the sun of righteousness[15] when in your martyrdom you resist evil and thus reach God."

And he told them a parable by way of comparison: *'Look at the fig tree'*—that is, with keen attention *'look at'* the bitterness of martyrdom and of anxieties, because *'these things'* will later console the suffering, just as the *'fig tree'* bears *'fruit'* that is displeasing at

---

[13] *Umbra* is an exegetical term here. Hildegard may have borrowed it from Augustine, *De Genesi ad litteram libri duodecimo*, ed. Joseph Zycha, CSEL 28/1 (Vienna: F. Tempsky, 1894), 4.11, et al., but she could have heard or read it in the many writers he inspired.

[14] *Incredulitates* can and probably does refer to the erroneous beliefs of heretics. Schism may refer to the 1159–1177 schism. See Kienzle, *Speaking New Mysteries*, 252–53.

[15] See Mal 4:2.

first and later sweet—'*and all the trees,*' namely the other virtues
that follow with '*signs*' and portents. '*When they produce their fruit,*'
"that is, they reveal martyrdom and then signs," '*you know*' "in
your hearts" '*that summer is near.*' Clearly, the heat of the Holy
Spirit and fullness of sanctity in soul and body [are] '*near.*' '*So
too, when you see*' by sure revelation '*these things happening,*' these
bitter things oppose the virtues, and the virtues [oppose them],
with the result nonetheless that the virtues attain the victory, as it
is written in another gospel passage: *The kingdom of heaven endures
force.*[16] '*Know that*' it '*is near,*' because schisms and other evils will
no longer endure for a long time, but at that time will be finished
quickly, because the ones who persevere in the good will attain
it. '*Amen, I say to you*' all, '*this generation,*' namely humankind,
'*will not pass away*' from darkness to light, from the fallen to the
eternal, '*until all [these] things,*' the battles among virtues and vices
that he foretold, '*have taken place,*' that is, until all the vices have
been so sifted out and thoroughly scrutinized by the virtues that
they will no longer be able to raise themselves up, and even the
devil will be so overcome by the virtues that he will no longer be
able to rage. '*Heaven,*' evidently those longings that reach only
toward heaven, so that humankind on account of God abandons
earthly things, '*and earth,*' clearly inordinate earthly desires when
humankind trespasses in worldly matters, '*will pass away.*' Those
longings and these inordinate desires will cease to have a temporal existence on that very last day, because eternal things will
be present then. '*But my words,*' namely human beings who were
created by the word of the Father, '*will not pass away,*' because they
will exist forever, such that rewards will be owed to the good and
punishments to the evil.

56. The First Sunday of Advent, 4

'*There will be signs in the sun and the moon and the stars,*' clearly
'*there will be*' miracles in faith and human knowledge and human

---

[16] Matt 11:12.

understanding. *'And upon the earth,'* evidently in earthly circumstances, *'there will be distress of nations from perplexity at the sound
of the sea and of the waves,'* that is, troubles from carnal desires,
from the appetite of the flesh: the inordinate desires of worldly
pleasure and licentiousness. *'Humans fainting'* in doubt *'from fear
and foreboding,'* that is, dread such that they know how to discern
neither God nor the devil [and] investigation *'of the things that are
coming,'* namely falling *'upon the entire world,'* over the circle of the
soul and of the body, where all sensuality is contained. *'For the
virtues of heaven'*—namely rationality, faith, hope, charity, and the
soul's other strengths, because they are heavenly—*'will be shaken'*
before the tempests that are in the sphere of the body, coming and
going, like the wheels that Ezekiel saw.[17]

'And then they will see' with a true sign *'the Son of Man,'* namely
the virtues already born in the human being, *'coming in a cloud,'*
clearly in the pupil of the eye of knowledge, *'with great power'*
overcoming all the darkness, *'and majesty'* when the good con-
quers evil. *'When these things,'* licit and illicit, good and evil, *'begin
to take place'* such that they complete their course, *'look up'* gazing
'and' with joy *'lift up your heads,'* that is, celestial harmony, *'because
your redemption is drawing near,'* "in proximity so that you may
flee from evil doings."

And he told them a parable by way of comparison: *'Look at the fig
tree.'* "Through it you know good through evil, because when you
have been scandalized by evil you turn toward the good"; *'and all
the trees,'* that is, all licentiousness, which sows itself in different
places. *'When they produce their fruit, you know'* by sensing, *'that
summer is near'*. Clearly, when first they were soiled they reveal
their consciences, repenting with groaning and weeping sounds,
because they were evil. The heat of the Holy Spirit produces the
flowers of the virtues. *'So too, when you see'* with certainty *'these
things happening,'* "that is, when you who wish to understand
me, so that you hold *'these things'* in your understanding," *'know
that the Kingdom of God is near,'* "namely [that] the reward of

[17] See Ezek 10:9.

heaven touches you." *'Amen, I say to you,'* to believers, *'this gen-eration,'* clearly of virtues and vices, *'will not pass away until all [these] things have taken place.'* It will not cease to exist before the virtues and vices have completed all their battles, such that the virtues vanquish and the vices succumb. *'Heaven,'* namely, the heavenly causes that are sluggish in human beings, *'and earth,'* clearly earthly cures,[18] which are indeed foolish, *'will pass away.'* Evidently they will be lacking in the erring minds of human be-ings, who are so impeded that they accomplish neither effectively. *'But my words will not pass away.'* Clearly the battles waged with integrity that vanquish evil will not be ridiculed by vanity, but they will have a heavenly reward, as it is written: *The righteous will shine like the sun.*[19]

[18] *Caelestes causae* and *terrenae curae.* Hildegard's medical work is entitled *Causae et curae.*
[19] Matt 13:43.

Homilies 57 and 58

The Dedication of a Church

Luke 19:1-10

Jesus entered and was passing through Jericho. A man was there named Zacchaeus; he was the chief of the tax collectors and was rich. He was trying to see who Jesus was, and was not able on account of the crowd, since he was small of stature. Running on ahead, he climbed a sycamore tree so that he would see him, since he was going to pass that way. When he had come to that place and looked up, Jesus saw him and said to him: 'Zacchaeus, make haste and come down, for today it is necessary for me to stay at your house.' So he made haste and came down, and received him rejoicing. When everyone saw [that], they murmured, saying that he had lodged with a man who is a sinner. However, Zacchaeus, standing, said to the Lord: 'Behold, half of my goods, Lord, I give to the poor; and if I have defrauded anyone of anything, I restore it fourfold.' Then Jesus said to him: 'Today salvation has come about for this house, since he is a son of Abraham. For the Son of Man came to seek out and to save what was lost.'

57. The Dedication of a Church, 1

Jesus entered and was passing through Jericho. In other words, God, when all things were created through his Word, was arranging and settling the creatures of the fallen world in accord with his vision. *A man was there named Zacchaeus; he was the chief of the tax collectors and was rich.* Virtue and righteousness were still in that man; he was first good in righteousness, but he kept that righteousness down with tares;[1] again he was reestablished through Christ in uprightness. *He was the chief of the tax collectors,* that is, the head of injustice because he began it, *and was rich,* because in his power there was good and evil.

He was trying to see who Jesus was, and was not able on account of the crowd, since he was small of stature. He was inquiring with his knowledge *who* God *was*; with his capacity he wanted to know good and evil, to comprehend the good completely, as one walled in by the devil's plots. He *was small of stature,* clearly in the measure of humanity with respect to God. *Running on ahead,* more than he should in his capacity and beyond his perception, *he climbed* a *sycamore tree so that he would see him, since he was going to pass that way.* Out of pride he deceived himself in this, such that his kin also later worshiped creation instead of God. The sycamore tree [denotes] boldness, when Adam in his foolish behavior withdrew from Zion because he wanted to be like God in the knowledge of good and evil, since the power of God judges both, namely good and evil, because there is a passage.[2]

When he had come to the place and looked up, Jesus saw him; clearly God had *come* in *the fullness of time*[3] to what was predestined: that he willed his Son to be incarnated in human form. *And Jesus said to him,* that is, the Savior, the Son of God, once clothed in flesh, called the human when he wanted to save him and free him from the devil's power, and said: *'Zacchaeus,'* "you ought to be made righteous, because I have been incarnated; therefore" *'make haste'* "to repent" *'and come down'* "from pride." *'For today it is necessary for me to stay at your house';* "when by my father's will I have been

---

[1] Hildegard, in another example of metonymy, uses the biblical image of tares or a weed, Latin *zizania,* to describe sin.

[2] Latin *transitus* refers to the passage from this world to the next. See Homily 29, p. 131.

[3] See Gal 4:4.

incarnated in the world, that is, in the flesh I received from the Virgin, who was born a human being just as you, from a carnal union," *'it is necessary for me'* "to remain for now in incarnation." *So he made haste,* in the repentance of the absolution for sins, *and came down* from pride, putting aside his own will, and his carnal pleasure, and the idols he worshiped, *and received* Christ with the revelation of the *new man,*[4] *who was created according to God, rejoicing* in happiness because of the remission of sins.

When everyone saw that, they murmured, saying that he had lodged with a man who was a sinner; in other words, those who were wasting away because of the Old Law and who were hypocrites *saw* in their evil will; *they murmured* in their hearts that he, in love and grace and because he so loves *'sinners'*, would rather be born from a human sinner, although he was without sin.

However, Zacchaeus, standing, said to the Lord: 'Behold, half of my goods.' Removed from the course of his sins, the one who has already been found in righteousness begins to do good deeds; in repentance against his carnal will, he *said:*[5] *'Behold, half of my'*[6] "will, which I considered unjustly in place of good things, out of evil habit and carnal pleasure, and idols." *'Lord, I give to the poor.'* "Savior, he said, I abandon them, as if I offered them to you, following your footsteps, so that I may become blessed, with those who are *poor in spirit,*[7] fulfilling the gospel. However," *'I give half'* "in this way, because in the remaining part I may still perceive that I am a human being and ash;[8] remaining in the body, I am not able to be heavenly in all respects." *'And if'* "in any matter" *'I have defrauded anyone of anything,'* "by magical and diabolic arts" *'I restore it.'* "I will replace those things, punishing myself" *'fourfold,'* "clearly by good knowledge, wisdom, humility, and charity."

---

[4] See Eph 4:24; Col 3:10.

[5] Hildegard extends the voice of Zacchaeus at length here.

[6] In both homilies Hildegard uses a synonym, *medietatem,* for *dimidium* in the scriptural text.

[7] Matt 5:3.

[8] Another example of metonymy with the word ash (*cinis*).

Then Jesus said to the one who thus forsakes his sins: *'Today salvation has come about for this house.'* In this time when the Son of God was born for the salvation of humanity, new redemption *'has come about'* for human beings who live in physical bodies as in their houses.[9] It *'has come about'* in the form of the holy incarnation, when *the Word* of the Father *was made flesh.*[10] One who obtains salvation and the remission of his sins *is a son of Abraham*, namely, an heir of the heavenly kingdom with the Son of God. *'For the Son of Man came to seek and to save what was lost.'* Christ *'came'* in his humanity *'to save'* by his blood and holiness *'what'* through the devil *'was lost'*: clearly the human being, in order that the human, redeemed by the Son of God, would know his Creator.

58. The Dedication of a Church, 2

Jesus entered and was passing through Jericho. The Son of God comes through the Holy Spirit's admonition; his grace permeates those who are lacking in good deeds. *A man was there named Zacchaeus*: clearly one who makes himself strong in wickedness by invoking the transgression of God's commands. Nevertheless, one will be made righteous afterward through God's grace. *He was the chief of all the tax collectors and was rich himself*; in excess of carnal pleasure, which has no shame, he was frequently eager for vices.

He was trying to see who Jesus was. Striving to contradict, the human being discussed inwardly what would hinder or harm God if he should live carnally. *But he was not able on account of the crowd, since in stature he was small. On account of* the iniquity of these thoughts *he was not able*, because such perverse contradictions do not prevail against God, but will be reduced to nothing in his opinion. *Running ahead, he climbed a sycamore tree to see him, since he was going to pass that way.* Hastening in this will of his, he elevated himself to the height of a fall through the sweetness of his pleasure; through evil temptation he turned himself away

[9] Hildegard expands the voice of Jesus and his teaching but does not adopt first or second person speech here as she does in the next homily.
[10] John 1:14.

from heavenly things. Nevertheless, he does not want God to forsake him for excesses like these, because God well knows that the human being was created from fragile material.

When he had come to the place and looked up, Jesus saw him. Although the Son of God had seen that this human's way of life was evil, by his grace and through his mercy Christ did not want to forsake him. *He said to him, 'Zacchaeus, make haste and come down.'* Calling him, *he said*: "You, who were first a transgressor, now will be made righteous by repenting; be humble, so that you are absolved from your sins." *'For today it is necessary for me to stay at your house.'* "When I am seeking you in your heart, if you desire to be saved I will be glorified in you as a holy dwelling." *So he made haste,* repenting, *and came down,* since through humility the human being begins to leave behind his sins, *and received him* in his sighing, *rejoicing* in the tears of salvation.

When everyone saw that, they murmured, saying that he had lodged with a man who was a sinner. The crowd of his evils rushed in upon him, *saying* indignantly within themselves that it would be neither just nor appropriate for God to receive the *'sinner'*, because he had perpetrated many evils.

However, Zacchaeus, *standing, said to the Lord: 'Behold, half of my goods.'* Stable in victory, made righteous out of transgression, repenting and confessing his sins, he *said: 'Behold, half of my'* "life, since I cannot be fully perfect while I live in the frailty of the flesh." *'Lord, I give to the poor, and if I have defrauded anyone of anything, I restore [it] fourfold.'* "God, I make myself poor and weak, trusting that you will receive me in repentance," *'and if* "by some vice, I have led anyone and even my own self to evil, I will conquer my own self against my will and leave behind my evil habit, and afterward perform a good deed, and thus persevere in it until the end."[11]

Then Jesus said to him: 'Today salvation has come about for this house, since he is a son of Abraham.' By the Holy Spirit's admonition,

[11] Hildegard at first lengthens the introduction to Zacchaeus's words, using third person discourse, but she then switches to the first person to adopt and extend the voice of Zacchaeus, the sinner, as she did for Jesus.

Jesus received him in repentance when he did penance,[12] and *said to him: 'Salvation has come about'* "for your heart and soul by the suffering of redemption for all, because the conqueror of the devil exists."[13] The one who was thus saved through redemption *'is a son'* of the eternal kingdom in the dove's simplicity.[14] *'For the Son of Man came to seek out and to save what was lost.'* The *'Son of Man,'* who is *a priest according to the order of Melchizedeck,*[15] was born into the world to receive the living sacrifices among tax collectors and sinners *'and to save'* those who are converted to life through repentance, *'lost'* in the stains of their sins before they were cleansed.

[12] Hildegard uses the Latin *penitentia* twice here. The first instance is translated by repentance; the second refers to the act of doing penance.

[13] Here Hildegard adopts second person speech as she takes on and expands the voice of Jesus.

[14] See Matt 10:16.

[15] See Ps 109:4; Heb 5:6, 10; 6:20; 7:11, 17.

Bibliography

For the works of Hildegard of Bingen see the Abbreviations list.

Primary Sources

Ambrose of Milan. *De Noe*. Edited by Karl Schenkl, 413–97. CSEL 32/1. Vienna: F. Tempsky, 1897.

Anselm of Canterbury. *Memorials of St. Anselm*. Edited by Richard William Southern and Franciscus Salesius Schmitt. Auctores Britannici Medii Aevi I. London: Oxford University Press for the British Academy, 1969.

Augustine of Hippo. *De doctrina christiana*. Edited by Josef Martin. CCSL 32. Turnhout: Brepols, 1962.

———. *De Genesi ad litteram libri duodecim*. Edited by Joseph Zycha. CSEL 28/1. Vienna: F. Tempsky, 1894.

———. *Enarrationes in Psalmos*. Edited by Eligius Dekkers and Johannes Fraipont. CCSL 38–40. Turnhout: Brepols, 1956.

———. *In Iohannis euangelium tractatus CXXIV*. Edited by Radbodus Willems. CCSL 36. Turnhout: Brepols, 1954.

Bede the Venerable. *Homeliarum euangelii libri II*. Edited by David Hurst. CCSL 122. Turnhout: Brepols, 1955.

Bernard of Clairvaux. *The Parables and The Sentences*. Edited by Maureen O'Brien. *The Parables*. Translated with an introduction by Michael Casey; *The Sentences*. Translated by Francis R. Swietek, Introduction by John R. Sommerfeldt. Cistercian Fathers 55. Kalamazoo, MI: Cistercian Publications, 2000.

————. *Sancti Bernardi Opera*. 8 vols. Edited by Jean Leclercq and Henri Rochais. 8 vols. Rome: Editiones cistercienses, 1957–77.

Bernard of Cluny. *In parabolam de uillico iniquitatis sermo*. PL 184:1021–32. Paris: Garnier, 1854.

Biblia Latina cum Glossa Ordinaria. Facsimile reprint of the Editio Princeps, Adolph Rusch of Strassburg 1480/81. 4 vols. Introduction by Karlfried Froehlich and Margaret T. Gibson. Turnhout: Brepols, 1992.

Gregory the Great. *Homiliae in euangelia*. Edited by Raymond Étaix. CCSL 141. Turnhout: Brepols, 1999.

————. *Moralia in Iob*. Edited by Marcus Adriaen. CCSL 143-143B. Turnhout: Brepols, 1979–85.

Guibert of Gembloux. *Epistolae quae in codice B. R. Brux. 5527–5534 inueniuntur*. Edited by Albert Derolez, Eligius Dekkers, and Roland Demeulenaere. CCCM 66, 66A. Turnhout: Brepols, 1988–89.

Haymo of Auxerre. *Homiliae de tempore*. PL 118:11–746. Paris: Garnier, 1852.

Heiric of Auxerre. *Heirici Autissiodorensis Homiliae per circulum anni*. Edited by Richard Quadri. CCCM 116, 116A, 116B. Turnhout: Brepols, 1992–94.

Jerome. *Commentarii in Ezechielem libri XIV*. Edited by Franciscus Glorie. CCSL 75. Turnhout: Brepols, 1964.

John Scotus. *Homélie sur le prologue de Jean*. Edited by Edouard Jeauneau. SCh 151. Paris: Cerf, 1969.

Odo of Cambrai. *Homilia de uillico iniquitatis*. PL 160:1131–50. Paris: Garnier, 1854.

The Rule of St. Benedict in Latin and English with Notes. Edited by Timothy Fry. Collegeville, MN: Liturgical Press, 1980.

Rupert of Deutz. *De glorificatione Trinitatis et processione Spiritus Sancti*. PL 169:13–202. Paris: Garnier, 1854.

Speculum uirginum. Edited by Jutta Seyfarth. CCCM 5. Turnhout: Brepols, 1990.

Trithemius, Johannes. *Johannes Trithemii Opera Historica*. Vol. 2. Edited by Marquand Freher. Frankfurt, 1601; repr. Frankfurt: Minerva, 1966.

Vita domnae Juttae inclusae. Edited by Franz Staab in "Reform und Reformgruppen im Erzbistum Mainz. Vom 'Libellus de Willigisi consuetudinibus' zur 'Vita domnae Juttae inclusae.'" Appendix II, 119–87, at 172–87. In *Reformidee und Reformpolitik im Spätsalisch-Frühstaufischen Reich. Vorträge der Tagung der Gesellschaft für Mittelrheinische Kirchengeschichte vom 11. bis 13. September 1991 in Trier.* Edited by Stefan Weinfurter. Quellen und Abhandlungen zur Mittelrheinische Geschichte 68. Mainz: Selbstverlag der Gesellschaft für Mittelrheinische Kirchengeschichte, 1992.

Secondary Literature

Augustine and the Bible. Edited and translated by Pamela Bright. Notre Dame, IN: University of Notre Dame Press, 1999.

Brémond, Claude, Jacques Le Goff, and Jean-Claude Schmitt. *L'exemplum.* Typologie des sources du moyen âge occidental, fasc. 40. Turnhout: Brepols, 1982.

Bruun, Mette. *Parables: Bernard of Clairvaux's Mapping of Spiritual Topography.* Brill Studies in Intellectual History 148. Leiden: Brill, 2007.

Burnett, Charles, and Peter Dronke, eds. *Hildegard of Bingen: The Context of Her Thought and Art.* London: Warburg Institute, 1998.

Carlevaris, Angela. "Ildegarda e la patristica," 65–80 in *Hildegard of Bingen, The Context of Her Thought and Art.* Edited by Charles Burnett and Peter Dronke. London: Warburg Institute, 1998.

Casey, Michael. "An Introduction to Ælred's Chapter Discourses." *Cistercian Studies Quarterly* 45/3 (2010): 279–314.

Caviness, Madeline. "Artist: 'To See, Hear, and Know All at Once,'" 110–24 in *Voice of the Living Light: Hildegard of Bingen and Her World.* Edited by Barbara J. Newman. Berkeley and Los Angeles: University of California Press, 1998.

———. "Hildegard as Designer of the Illustrations to Her Works," 29–62 in *Hildegard of Bingen: The Context of Her Thought and Art.* Edited by Charles Burnett and Peter Dronke. London: Warburg Institute, 1998.

Cross, James E. "Vernacular Sermons in Old English," 561–96 in *The Sermon*. Typologie des sources du moyen âge occidental, fasc. 81–83. Directed by Beverly Mayne Kienzle. Turnhout: Brepols, 2000.

Daim, Falko, and Antje Kluge-Pinsker, eds. *Als Hildegard noch nicht in Bingen war: Der Disibodenberg—Archäologie und Geschichte*. Regensburg and Mainz: Schell und Steiner/Verlag des Römisch-Germanischen Zentralmuseums, 2009.

Dronke, Peter. "Tradition and Innovation in Medieval Western Colour-Imagery." *Eranos Jahrbuch* 41 (1972): 51–107.

Flanagan, Sabina. *Hildegard of Bingen, 1098–1179. A Visionary Life*. 2d ed. London and New York: Routledge, 1998.

Folz, Robert. "Pierre le Vénérable et la liturgie," 143–61 in *Pierre Abélard, Pierre le Vénérable: les courants philosophiques, littéraires et artistiques en occident au milieu du XIIe siècle, Abbaye de Cluny, 2–9 juillet*. Edited by Jean Châtillon, Jean Jolivet, and René Louis. Colloques internationaux du CNRS 546. Paris: Éditions du Centre national de la recherche scientifique, 1975.

Gibson, Margaret. *The Bible in the Latin West*. Notre Dame, IN, and London: University of Notre Dame Press, 1993.

Holdsworth, Christopher. "Were the Sermons of St Bernard on the Song of Songs ever Preached?" 295–318 in *Medieval Monastic Preaching*. Edited by Carolyn A. Muessig. Leiden: Brill, 1998.

Jutta and Hildegard: The Biographical Sources. Translated and annotated by Anna Silvas. University Park: Pennsylvania State University Press, 1999.

Kienzle, Beverly Mayne. *Cistercians, Heresy and Crusade 1145–1229: Preaching in the Lord's Vineyard*. Woodbridge, UK: Boydell and Brewer, 2001.

———. *Hildegard of Bingen and Her Gospel Homilies: Speaking New Mysteries*. Medieval Women: Texts and Contexts 12. Turnhout: Brepols, 2009.

———. "Performing the Gospel Stories: Hildegard of Bingen's Dramatic Exegesis in the *Expositiones euangeliorum*," 121–40 in *Visualizing Medieval Performance: Perspectives, Histories, Contexts*. Edited by Elina Gertsman. Aldershot, UK: Ashgate, 2009.

————, director. *The Sermon*. Typologie des sources du moyen âge occidental, fasc. 81–83. Turnhout: Brepols, 2000.

————. *"Verbum Dei et Verba Bernardi*: The Function of Language in Bernard's Second Sermon for Peter and Paul," 149–59 in *Bernardus Magister: Papers Celebrating the Nonacentenary of the Birth of Bernard of Clairvaux*. Edited by John R. Sommerfeldt. CS 135. Kalamazoo, MI: Cistercian Publications, 1992.

Leclercq, Jean. *The Love of Learning and the Desire for God*. Translated by Catharine Misrahi. 3rd ed. New York: Fordham University Press, 1982.

————. "Recherches sur d'anciens sermons monastiques." *Revue Mabillon* 36 (1946): 11–14.

————. *Women and St. Bernard*. CS 104. Kalamazoo, MI: Cistercian Publications, 1989.

McGinn, Bernard. "Hildegard of Bingen as Visionary and Exegete," 321–50 in *Hildegard von Bingen in ihrem historischen Umfeld*. Edited by Alfred Haverkamp. Mainz: von Zabern, 2000.

————. "The Originality of Eriugena's Spiritual Exegesis," 55–80 in *Iohannes Scottus Eriugena: The Bible and Hermeneutics. Proceedings of the Ninth International Colloquium of the Society for the Promotion of Eriugenian Studies.* Leuven and Louvain-la-Neuve, June 7–10, 1995. Edited by Gerd Van Riel, Carlos Steel, and James McEvoy. Leuven: Leuven University Press, 1996.

————. "The Spiritual Heritage of Origen in the West," 263–89 in *Origene maestro di vita spirituale. Milano, 13–15 settembre 1999*. Edited by Luigi F. Pizzolato and Marco Rizzi. Milan: Vita e Pensiero, 2001.

Muessig, Carolyn A., ed. *Medieval Monastic Preaching*. Leiden: Brill, 1998.

Newman, Barbara J., ed. *Voice of the Living Light: Hildegard of Bingen and Her World*. Berkeley and Los Angeles: University of California Press, 1998.

Nikitsch, Eberhard J. "Wo lebte die heilige Hildegard wirklich? Neue Überlegungen zum ehemaligen Standort der Frauenklause auf dem Disibodenberg," 147–56 in *"Im Angesicht Gottes suche der Mensch sich selbst": Hildegard von Bingen 1098–1179*. Edited by Rainer Berndt. Berlin: Akademie Verlag, 2001.

Schmitt, Wolfgang Felix. "Charisma gegen Recht? Der Konflikt der Hildegard von Bingen mit dem Mainzer Domkapitel 1178/79 in kirchenrechtsgeschichtlicher Perspektive." *Hildegard von Bingen 1098–1998, Binger Geschichtsblätter* 20 (1998): 124–59.

Silvas, Anna, trans. and annot. *Jutta and Hildegard: The Biographical Sources.* University Park, PA: Pennsylvania State University Press, 1999.

Van Engen, John. "Abbess: 'Mother and Teacher.'" 30–51 in *Voice of the Living Light*, ed. Barbara Newman.

———. "Letters and the Public Persona of Hildegard," 379–89 in *Hildegard von Bingen in ihrem historischen Umfeld*. Edited by Alfred Haverkamp. Mainz: von Zabern, 2000.

Vogüé, Adalbert de. *The Rule of Saint Benedict: A Doctrinal and Spiritual Commentary.* Cistercian Studies 54. Kalamazoo, MI: Cistercian Publications, 1983.

Waddell, Chrysogonus. "The Liturgical Dimension of Twelfth-Century Cistercian Preaching," 335–49 in *Medieval Monastic Preaching*. Edited by Carolyn Muessig. Leiden: Brill, 1998.

Liturgical Index

The homilies are listed here in the order of the liturgical year and not of the critical edition of the manuscript. The designations of the feasts for the homilies vary in the manuscript tradition. Specific details can be found in the *apparatus criticus* of the *Expositiones euangeliorum*. Hildegard's monasteries followed the model of Cluny, which did not impose a uniform liturgy on its houses as Cîteaux did. References comparing the feasts in the Riesenkodex with the Cluny readings established by Raymond Étaix, "Le lectionnaire de l'office à Cluny," *Recherches augustiniennes* 11 (1976): 91–159, are given in brackets when there is a corresponding entry.

The Last Sunday before Advent, Homilies 3 and 4 (John 6:1-4)
    [Étaix, 101, 71: The Fourth Sunday in Lent]
The First Sunday of Advent, Homilies 53, 54, 55, and 56 (Luke 21:25-33)
    [Étaix, 95, 5: Second Sunday of Advent]
The Eve of the Lord's Birth, Homilies 5 and 6 (Matthew 1:18-21)
    [Étaix, 96, 14: The Eve of the Lord's Birth, when on a Sunday]
The Lord's Birth, Homilies 7 and 8 (Luke 2:1-14)
    [Étaix, 97, 22: The Lord's Birth]
The Lord's Birth, Homily 9 (John 1:1-14)
    [Étaix, 97, 21: The Lord's Birth]
The Eve of the Epiphany, Homilies 10 and 11 (Matthew 2:13-18)
    [Étaix, 98, 31: The Fourth Day after the Feast of the Innocents]
The Feast of the Epiphany, Homilies 12 and 13 (Matthew 2:1-2)
    [Étaix, 99, 41: The Feast of the Epiphany]

The Sunday in the Octave of the Epiphany, Homilies 14 and 15 (Luke 2:42-52)
  [Étaix, 100, 52: The Second Sunday after the Lord's Birth]
The Second Sunday after the Epiphany, Homilies 16 and 17 (John 2:1-11)
  [Étaix, 100, 53: The Third Sunday after the Lord's Birth]
The Third Sunday after the Epiphany, Homilies 18 and 19 (Matthew 8:1-13)
  [Étaix, 100, 54: The Fourth Sunday after the Lord's Birth]
The Feast of the Purification of the Blessed Virgin Mary, Homilies 20 and 21 (Luke 2:22-32)
  [Étaix, 114, 29: The Purification of Saint Mary]
Septuagesima Sunday, Homilies 22 and 23 (Matthew 20:1-16)
  [Étaix, 100, 59: Septuagesima]
The First Sunday in Lent, Homilies 24 and 25 (Matthew 4:1-11)
  [Étaix, 101, 64: The First Sunday in Lent]
Sabbath before the Third Sunday in Lent, Homilies 26 and 27 (Luke 15:11-32)
The Sunday of the Resurrection, Homilies 28 and 29 (Mark 16:1-7)
  [Étaix, 103, 87: Holy Easter]
The Second Sunday after Easter, Homilies 30 and 31 (John 10:11-16)
  [Étaix, 104, 97: the Sunday after the Octave of Easter]
The Lord's Ascension, Homilies 32 and 33 (Mark 16:14-20)
  [Étaix, 104, 104b: The Lord's Ascension]
The Finding of the Holy Cross, Homilies 34, 35, and 36 (John 3:1-15)
  [Étaix, 106, 121: The Octave of Pentecost; Étaix, 116, 51: On the Holy Cross]
The Octave of Pentecost, 1, Homilies 37 and 38 (Luke 16:19-31)
  [Étaix, 108, 146: The First Sunday after the Octave of Pentecost]
The Third Sunday after Pentecost, Homilies 39 and 40 (Luke 14:16-24)
  [Étaix, 108, 147: The Second Sunday after the Octave of Pentecost]
The Nativity of Saint John the Baptist, Homilies 41 and 42 (Luke 1:57-58)
  [Étaix, 119, 79: In the Octave of Saint John]
The Fourth Sunday after Pentecost, Homilies 43, 44, and 45 (Luke 5:1-11)
  [Étaix, 108, 147: The Fifth Sunday after the Octave of Pentecost]
The Eighth Sunday after Pentecost, Homilies 1 and 2 (Luke 16:1-9)
  [cf. Étaix, 109, 153: Matthew 7:15]
The Ninth Sunday after Pentecost, Homilies 46, 47, and 48 (Luke 19:41-47)
  [Étaix, 109, 155: The Tenth Sunday after the Octave of Pentecost]
The Tenth Sunday after Pentecost, Homilies 51 and 52 (Luke 18:10-14)
  [Étaix, 108, 156: The Eleventh Sunday after the Octave of Pentecost]

The Eleventh Sunday after Pentecost, Homilies 49 and 50 (Mark 7:31-37)
    [Étaix, 108, 157: The Twelfth Sunday after the Octave of Pentecost]
The Dedication of a Church, Homilies 57 and 58 (Luke 19:1-10)
    [cf. Étaix, 134, 33: Luke 6:43]

Scripture Index

Additional Scriptural references indicated in the footnotes as cf. are not included in the index.

Topical Index

Terms within the twenty-seven gospel pericopes are generally not included as separate entries. Consult instead the Scripture Index.